Politics and the People

Politics and the People
Scotland, 1945–1979

Malcolm R. Petrie

EDINBURGH
University Press

Edinburgh University Press is one of the leading university presses in the UK. We publish academic books and journals in our selected subject areas across the humanities and social sciences, combining cutting-edge scholarship with high editorial and production values to produce academic works of lasting importance. For more information visit our website: edinburghuniversitypress.com

Edinburgh University Press Ltd
The Tun – Holyrood Road
12 (2f) Jackson's Entry
Edinburgh EH8 8PJ

First published in hardback by Edinburgh University Press 2022

Typeset in 10.5/13pt Sabon by
Manila Typesetting Company, and
printed and bound by CPI Group (UK) Ltd,
Croydon, CR0 4YY

A CIP record for this book is available from the British Library

ISBN 978 1 4744 5698 2 (hardback)
ISBN 978 1 4744 5699 9 (paperback)
ISBN 978 1 4744 5700 2 (webready PDF)
ISBN 978 1 4744 5701 9 (epub)

Contents

Tables

Abbreviations

CPA	Conservative Party Archive
CSA	Campaign for a Scottish Assembly
EDC	Eastern Divisional Council
EEC	European Economic Community
FCA	Falkirk Council Archives
ILP	Independent Labour Party
MCA	Middle Class Alliance
NEC	National Executive Committee
NLS	National Library of Scotland
NUM	National Union of Mineworkers
ORC	Opinion Research Centre
PKCA	Perth and Kinross Council Archives
PLDF	People's League for the Defence of Freedom
SEC	Scottish Executive Committee
SNP	Scottish National Party
STUC	Scottish Trades Union Congress
SUA	Scottish Unionist Association
SUMC	Scottish Unionist Members' Committee
TUC	Trades Union Congress
UAA	University of Aberdeen Archives
UCS	Upper Clyde Shipbuilders
UDA	University of Dundee Archives
WDC	Western Divisional Council

Acknowledgements

The research for this book started with the award of an Early Career Fellowship by the Leverhulme Trust (ECF-2015-391). That Fellowship began in 2015 at the University of Edinburgh before I moved to the University of St Andrews a year later. Both institutions offered a supportive research environment; in addition, the School of History at St Andrews provided funding and leave that enabled the completion of this book. My understanding of post-war Scottish politics has benefited from talking to – and reading the work of – numerous scholars, who I won't list in full here. Nevertheless, I am particularly grateful to Ewen Cameron and Colin Kidd, who have been a welcome source of support and advice throughout the duration this project. Further, the participants at the seminars in modern Scottish and British history at the universities of Cambridge, Edinburgh, Glasgow, Oxford, and St Andrews offered valuable feedback on aspects of the subsequent analysis. Any errors that remain in this study are, naturally, my own.

Discussions with the students I am fortunate enough to teach at St Andrews played an important role in helping me clarify the arguments that follow. Special thanks are due to the final-year undergraduates who made teaching a module about radical politics in twentieth-century Scotland such an enjoyable experience despite the challenges posed by a global pandemic. Similar debts are owed to Sarah Leith, Daniel Leaver, and Amber Ward, whose doctoral projects I have had the privilege of supervising, and who have taught me so much about twentieth-century Scotland.

This project was aided by the archivists and librarians at the National Library of Scotland, the Conservative Party Archive at the Bodleian Library, the Labour History Archive and Study Centre at the People's History Museum in Manchester, Glasgow's Mitchell Library, the university libraries in Aberdeen, Dundee, Edinburgh, St Andrews and Stirling, and the public libraries and archives in Aberdeen, Dundee, Falkirk, and Perth. The Conservative Party kindly granted permission to consult material at both the National Library of Scotland and the Bodleian Library. I would also like to acknowledge the patience and understanding of the editorial team at Edinburgh University Press.

My son, Arthur, was born during the early stages of the research for this study: if this book has taken longer to complete than I had initially planned, it is because he and I had more important things to do. In any case, this book – or, as he would describe it, my 'boring computer work' – is for him, and for my wife, Fiona, without whose support and love nothing would have been possible.

Introduction
Democracy, Sovereignty and the
Constitution: Scotland, 1945–1979

THIS STUDY IS CONCERNED with the course of politics in Scotland in the years between 1945 and 1979. This was a period bookended by two general elections that, in their different ways, seemed, both to contemporaries and to subsequent observers, to mark significant shifts in the political and economic priorities of the United Kingdom government. At the same time, Scottish politics underwent a profound, and complicated, realignment, as the fortunes of the Unionists – as the Conservatives continued to be known in Scotland until 1965 – declined, the Scottish National Party (SNP) began to gain previously unseen levels of popular support, and, ultimately, Scotland came to be viewed as an electoral stronghold of the Labour Party. The post-war era produced, as a result, two significant political shifts in Scotland. The first was an explicit decoupling of Scottish electoral politics from broader British trends. There had, of course, been certain features unique to the Scottish political landscape in the 1940s and 1950s, not least the relative strength of the Unionist Party; still, in the immediate post-war years Scottish politics was, in its essentials, shaped firmly by the two-party contest that defined politics at Westminster. Yet by the 1970s this was no longer true, as the rise of the SNP and the waning of Scottish Conservatism, as well as the halting return of independent Liberalism, created a more unpredictable four-party political contest in Scotland. The second development was a corollary of the first, as, from the late 1960s onwards, the electoral successes enjoyed by the SNP prompted a debate over the constitution and proposals for a devolved assembly that would come to dominate Scottish, and, at certain moments, British, politics in the decade that followed.

Together, these changes point towards the fundamental questions that motivate *Politics and the People*. Why did Conservative support in

Scotland fall so sharply from the 1960s onwards? Why was it the SNP, rather than the Liberals, that appeared to benefit from the fading of the two-party politics of the mid-twentieth century? And what was the impact and legacy of the turn towards constitutional reform that took place in the aftermath of these electoral shifts? These are questions that have, to be sure, received detailed consideration from historians and political scientists. Nonetheless, by bringing changing understandings of the relationship between government and the people into the fore-ground alongside an examination of the language that contemporaries used to discuss issues of democracy, representation and sovereignty, the intention is that this study will offer a different – and, it is hoped, worth-while – vantage point from which to view post-war Scottish politics.

Of particular importance to the analysis that follows is an assess-ment of the persistence and evolution of a forceful anti-statist rhetoric within Scottish politics. Although this appeal to individual freedom was, in some senses, merely an outgrowth of the anti-socialism of the 1920s, which had been crucial to the inter-war electoral victories achieved by the Unionists and their Conservative allies in England and Wales, it was revised after 1945 to take account of the social and economic reforms implemented by the post-war Labour government.[1] This renewed cri-tique of overbearing centralised bureaucracies propelled Unionism's striking electoral recovery in the decade after 1945, not least because it allowed the party's representatives to assume the role of defenders of individual liberty while also criticising the extent to which nationalisa-tion and the welfare state had encroached upon the autonomy tradition-ally afforded to Scotland's legal, commercial and political institutions.[2] But, as will be seen, anti-statism would prove to be a malleable language, one that could, in subsequent decades, be adapted in such a way as to be directed against remote government from Westminster in general rather than remaining a narrow critique of Labour's policies alone.

The growing centrality of the constitution to Scottish politics is reflected in this book's second area of focus. The change that took place in the anti-statist rhetoric of the mid-twentieth century was accompanied by a newer emphasis upon matters of sovereignty and representation. Observed from one angle, the Scottish experience was, in this respect, hardly exceptional. The relatively abrupt decision of successive govern-ments in the 1970s to adopt the referendum as a means of resolving constitutional tensions that could not be addressed by existing political mechanisms presented a challenge to the established doctrine of parlia-mentary sovereignty across the UK, even if only temporarily.[3] The asso-ciated issue of UK membership of the European Economic Community

(EEC), which was confirmed by the result of the June 1975 referendum, raised similar questions. Indeed, the debates over representation and the demands for direct democracy that began to be articulated in Scotland during the late 1960s and early 1970s might also be treated as individual instances of a much wider international movement. But there were still aspects of the way that these disputes unfolded in a Scottish context that were unique, and which merit attention. Long before the establishment of the SNP, it had been commonplace, even among declared supporters of the Union, to assert that Scotland remained a distinct nation, and that the Union settlement of 1707 had seen the creation of a partnership between Scotland and England, not the mere absorption of the former by the latter.[4] The question of sovereignty was, however, more complex. Most often, though, Scotland's post-1707 sovereignty was held to be located, in an abstract sense, alongside England's in the Crown-in-Parliament; what exercised those in favour of Scottish independence was the question of how Scotland's measure of Parliament's sovereignty could be extricated from Westminster. The advent of the referendum as a constitutional mechanism, however, upended such understandings by giving new weight to the notion of popular sovereignty. Versions of this idea, which made use of certain aspects of Scottish history, were not unknown within Scottish nationalism earlier in the century. Nevertheless, it would take the arguments that surrounded the European and devolution referendums of the 1970s, and the realisation that such polls could be construed as determining the collective view of the Scottish people on constitutional matters, to grant popular sovereignty more immediate political significance.

This purpose of this study is, then, to present an account of post-war Scottish politics that prioritises the way in which people, mostly but not always politicians, thought, or at least spoke or wrote, about political and constitutional issues. It is, though, avowedly not an exercise in intellectual history: while ideas and ideologies do feature, it is, with a handful of exceptions, in the context of discussions of popular or electoral politics. As will become apparent, this book also seeks to situate this exploration of events in Scotland within a broader British setting. This is, it should be stressed, not to make any contemporary political point, but to suggest that the political realignment that occurred in Scotland during the 1960s and 1970s might be understood better, or at least differently, when placed into conversation with developments elsewhere in Britain. The growing support for the SNP evident from the 1960s onwards was, to state a truism, a result of shifts in popular political opinion in Scotland. But such changes can be interpreted too as one manifestation of a more general sense of disenchantment with established political parties and institutions that was visible across Britain.

EXPLAINING POLITICAL CHANGE: HISTORIES OF POST-WAR SCOTLAND

The post-war realignment of Scottish politics has generated a considerable academic literature.[5] This has, historically, tended to focus on the fortunes of individual political parties, with many of the most influential contributions often coming, unsurprisingly given the relative proximity of the period, from political scientists.[6] The sustained electoral decline endured by the Scottish Conservatives, which began at the end of the 1950s when the party still wore the Unionist label and continued almost without respite for the remainder for the twentieth century, has produced arguably the richest strand of analysis.[7] Initial accounts of the relatively weak Conservative performance in Scotland appeared in the 1980s and early 1990s, as the majority of Scottish voters appeared to be largely resistant to the appeal of the Conservative governments that had dominated politics at Westminster since 1979. These early assessments tended to emphasise the political impact of social and economic structures. Scotland, with its proportionately larger working class, higher rate of local authority tenancies, and a middle class that was more likely to be employed in the public sector, was, in this reading, almost certainly going to prove to be a less welcoming environment for the Conservatives. Instead, what needed to be explained was the remarkable performance of the party prior to the 1960s, when Unionists had been able to overcome these material hurdles.[8] Explanatory power was, in this regard, granted to Unionist identity and ideology. In the case of the former, Unionism drew, it was argued, on deep-rooted aspects of Scottish culture and society, including the Protestantism that was the dominant religious identity among working- and middle-class electors, as well as the affinity that many individual Scots felt with Britain's overseas Empire. Further, mid-century Unionists seemed to be more willing to craft a distinctive Scottish appeal than their Conservative successors.[9] On the latter question of ideology, Unionism was believed to have demonstrated a degree of flexibility absent from subsequent forms of Conservatism, practical in its economic outlook and, recognising that Scotland was an overwhelmingly working-class society, willing to see the state play a significant economic role and to endorse the welfare state.[10] This pragmatism, it has been proposed, enabled the party to build a cross-party appeal that could reach former Liberal voters and elements of the skilled working class.

The growth in support for the SNP has often been viewed as an outcome of the same influences put forward to explain the weakening of Scottish Conservatism. If Conservatism relied upon a widely shared Protestantism and a sense of Britishness that hinged upon the Empire, then the SNP was, it seemed, the beneficiary of the processes of secularisation and decolonisation that unfolded during the 1960s, which, alongside a wider decline in class allegiance and deference, undercut established political identities.[11] Equally, the economic benefits of the Union were no longer self-evident once economic planning was widely held to have failed in the 1960s, and the UK entered a period of perceived economic decline, epitomised by the Labour government's devaluation of sterling in November 1967.[12] The impact of these developments was recognised in early surveys of the SNP, which began to appear in the years after the party's pivotal by-election victory at Hamilton in 1967.[13] Critical here was the contention, echoed subsequently, that the interventionist economic policies pursued by consecutive UK governments, whether Conservative or Labour, had, by expanding the remit of the Scottish Office, contributed to a growing sense of Scotland as a distinct economic unit while also raising economic expectations, only for these to then be frustrated in the second half of the 1960s.[14] The new-found ability of the SNP to attract support from disillusioned Scottish voters has also been attributed to organisational improvements within the party, and to the discovery of North Sea oil, which strengthened the economic case for independence.[15]

Of course, the most significant short-term consequence of the SNP's victory at Hamilton was the response it provoked from the major UK political parties. While the Conservatives flirted with the notion of supporting a devolved Scottish assembly as a way of fending off the challenge posed by the SNP, it nevertheless fell largely to Labour, in government until 1970 and then again between 1974 and 1979, to attempt to answer the constitutional question in Scotland.[16] Yet, perhaps curiously given the dominant electoral position enjoyed by Labour in Scotland from the 1960s until the close of the twentieth century, the party has, notwithstanding the publication during the 1970s of some intriguing explorations of Labour attitudes towards devolution, received less attention in subsequent years.[17] In part, this is an understandable result of the preference among historians for change rather than continuity, a weakness that, as will become evident, this study shares. As Conservative fortunes slipped and support for the SNP rose sharply before once more waning by the end of the 1970s, Labour's performance in Scotland remained blandly reliable in comparison: although the fluctuations in the party's vote share were slightly more pronounced, at the six general elections held between 1964 and 1979 Labour MPs were returned consistently in between forty to forty-six of Scotland's seventy-one constituencies. As one of the few recent histories of the Labour Party in Scotland has noted, this encouraged the 'myth' that Scotland was a nation that was, for exactly the same socio-economic reasons believed to have acted as a natural limit on Conservative support, inherently inclined towards the Labour Party.[18] This was despite Labour never managing to match the Unionists' achievement of gaining an outright majority of the popular vote in Scotland, although the party did come close at the 1966 general election.

If there has been a common thread in histories of Scottish politics after 1945, then, it has been the priority accorded to the social and economic landscape in which politics took place. This legacy can be observed in the impressive range of recent work on deindustrialisation in the post-1945 period, which has made an often compelling case for the importance of long-term economic changes, and especially the falling levels of employment in traditional industries such as mining and shipbuilding, in accounting for the growing backing for constitutional reform evident within the Scottish labour movement in the late 1960s and 1970s, with devolution coming to be considered as a chance to tackle the specific economic challenges facing Scotland. Here, popular support for a devolved assembly is depicted as a way of meeting the 'moral economy' expectations of communities that depended upon the employment provided by the nationalised industries, and who felt increasingly let down by central government.[19]

This book adopts a different perspective, affording a more central role to politics, and, in particular, to the ways in which political parties framed their appeals to the Scottish electorate after 1945. In doing so, it reflects, to an extent, the impact of recent historiographical contributions, which have paid greater attention to the intellectual and cultural aspects of twentieth-century Scottish politics. Initially, this was a response to the institution of the devolved Scottish Parliament in 1999, which stimulated reflections on the nature and durability of the 1707 Union, and on the ideas that had sustained it until the early twenty-first century.[20] The subsequent elections of minority and then majority SNP administrations in Edinburgh in 2007 and 2011, and the 2014 referendum on Scottish independence that resulted, further encouraged examinations of the ideology and political thought of Scottish nationalism, both in the post-war era and across the twentieth century more broadly. Nationalism has, in such studies, often been interpreted more flexibly than in the past, encompassing advocates of devolution as well as those committed to Scottish independence.[21]

Politics and the People complements these studies by focusing on how these ideas operated within the context of electoral politics, and on how political parties in Scotland sought to communicate with the public. Equally, though, there are important differences. The constitutional question, for example, while clearly central to any narrative of Scottish politics in this period, features here rather more obliquely, as a way of thinking about how popular understandings of representation and sovereignty might have evolved and the political impact of such changes. Furthermore, this book examines Scottish politics in the light of interventions in the historiography of post-war Britain. The debates over responses to the creation of the welfare state, and the limits of any purported post-war consensus, provide one productive area of engagement, allowing a reconsideration of the nature of post-war Unionism's attraction for Scottish voters.[22] Similarly, recent literature on the politics of the late 1960s and early 1970s, and especially that concerned with the career and influence of Enoch Powell, have encouraged a willingness to see the SNP's breakthrough as one consequence of a broader loss of faith in government that assumed different forms across the UK.[23] This was, as these studies have noted, a political moment in which the traditions and conventions that had previously reinforced popular support for Britain's institutions of representative government began to dissolve. If, in Scotland, this was a development that seemed to benefit the SNP, an awareness of the wider context remains vital.

STRUCTURE AND METHODOLOGY

The exploration of Scottish politics between 1945 and 1979 offered here is concerned primarily with how political identities are constructed and maintained, the rhetoric and language that politicians use in their efforts to secure the support of the public, and how such appeals to the public change over time. The analysis concentrates upon the political campaigns undertaken by the major political parties in this period, making use of a range of source material, including internal party records and opinion surveys, contemporary newspapers and journals, election literature, and diaries and memoirs. Priority is given, it should be stated, to evidence from those regions where the SNP would experience the greatest electoral success during the 1970s: Perthshire, Stirlingshire, and the rural north-east and south-west of Scotland. Such an approach carries with it the danger of focusing excessively on political change at the expense of overlooking what remained the same. Still, the attention this study affords to how political languages could be adopted and adapted by different political parties necessitates that more consideration be granted to those areas where the transformation of Scottish politics was most dramatic, as constituencies that had been Unionist strongholds since the 1920s seemed to suddenly transfer their loyalties to the SNP.

The book is structured in four chapters; the first three run in broadly chronological order, spanning the 1940s to the 1970s, while the fourth is more thematic and self-contained. Chapter One examines the foundations of Unionist support in Scotland between the general elections of 1945 and 1959. This period has been portrayed as one in which Scottish politics was relatively tranquil, with electoral results mirroring British patterns and the Unionist acceptance of Labour's post-war reforms softening the edges of political debate. This chapter challenges such a narrative; it reveals instead the centrality to post-war Unionism of an appeal couched in terms of a liberal individualism. This rhetoric, animated by fears of totalitarianism, enabled the creation of an anti-socialist coalition that could attract many erstwhile Liberals, as well as voters with nationalist sympathies. The gradual crumbling of that coalition in the second half of the 1950s is then traced, as the anxieties caused by rising inflation and discontent with the levels of taxation required to fund the welfare state led to a sense of frustration among Unionist supporters, creating the opportunity for the partial re-emergence of independent Liberalism. Chapter Two continues this narrative into the 1960s, beginning with a consideration of the sharp decline in Unionist fortunes that occurred in the first half of the decade, which encouraged the party to shed its distinctive Scottish identity by adopting the Conservative label, and to discard the traditional Unionist defence of individual liberty in favour of a commitment to modernisation and even to economic planning, a model that Unionists had criticised when espoused by the Labour Party. The chapter then places Unionist decline within a broader context, as the critique of socialism and state bureaucracy that had been essential to political debate during the 1940s and 1950s curdled into a deeper mistrust of central government that damaged the Conservatives as much as Labour. This phenomenon was apparent throughout the UK; in Scotland, however, it will be demonstrated that such views appeared to encourage support for the SNP.

Chapter Three extends the analysis offered in the preceding chapters by examining the upsurge in support for the SNP during the late 1960s and early 1970s, which culminated in the party's dramatic performance at the two general elections of 1974. Rather than echoing accounts that emphasise the importance of the debates surrounding a possible devolved Scottish assembly, or the political impact of North Sea oil, this chapter recovers two equally significant, but often overlooked, factors that together demonstrated how the individualist rhetoric of the post-war era could, with an appropriate change in emphasis, be embraced by supporters of constitutional change. Attention is given first to the concerns that arose in Scotland at the prospect of the United Kingdom joining the EEC. The emphasis shifts thereafter to the reform of Scottish local government; canvassed during the 1960s and undertaken in the early 1970s, this entailed the abolition of the ancient royal burghs and the creation of a new tier of larger regional authorities. Both Europe and local government reform heightened fears that the institutions of government were becoming increasingly bureaucratic and remote from the people. There was, moreover, a consensus among the leadership of the major UK political parties in favour of both the new local government structure and Common Market membership; this enabled the SNP to position itself as the sole representative of Scottish interests, and as the only electoral vehicle available to those opposed to these measures.

If the first three chapters are interested in the varied ways in which politicians sought to exploit an individualist and anti-bureaucratic language that had deep roots in Scottish politics, and often adopt a constituency-level perspective, then Chapter Four concentrates on the constitutional implications of such appeals. In consequence, the chapter is more engaged with national political debates and events at Westminster; equally, while the earlier chapters foreground Unionist, Liberal and SNP perspectives, it is here that the position of the Labour Party is given greater attention. The chapter opens with an exploration of understandings of sovereignty in the 1940s and 1950s via an examination of the activities of the Scottish Plebiscite Society and the Covenant movement, concluding that, although these organisations aimed to use extra-parliamentary methods such as local ballots and mass petitions to stimulate public support for devolution, neither group made the case that sovereignty in Scotland was popular rather than parliamentary. Likewise, at this stage the SNP still maintained that securing a majority of Scotland's parliamentary representation was the only legitimate route to independence. The chapter then considers the popularisation of ideas of popular sovereignty in Scottish and British politics during the 1960s and 1970s, with an emphasis on the impact of the introduction of the referendum into UK politics. The resort to direct democracy, often

regarded as simply a matter of political convenience, was in truth suggestive of a more profound loss of faith in parliamentary democracy, of
a growing suspicion that MPs were no longer functioning as representatives of the people but were, increasingly, a class apart. At a UK level, the
advent of the referendum heralded a new willingness to question parliament's claim to represent the people. In Scotland, this chapter shows,
the impact was even more intense: the European and devolution referendums of 1975 and 1979 did more than test Scottish opinion on Europe
and devolution; they also fostered a belief that Scotland was a distinct
constitutional entity, capable of expressing its collective political will
through popular, rather than parliamentary, means. What was an issue
of representation for the UK as a whole became in Scotland a question
of constitutional legitimacy, and, in turn, of national identity.

The conclusion underlines the central argument of the book: that an
anti-bureaucratic, individualist rhetoric, deployed by competing political parties at different times and to different ends, played a crucial role
in the reshaping of post-war Scottish politics. As well as being vital to
explaining the decline of Unionism and the rise in support for the SNP,
the change in the focus of this rhetoric from the economy to the constitution had important implications for popular understandings of the
relationship between Parliament and the people. Mistrust of central government, and a sense that politicians had become disconnected from the
electorate, weakened the authority of the Westminster Parliament, and
encouraged a search for other avenues for the expression of political
opinion; in Scotland there arose a belief that there existed a distinctive
tradition of popular sovereignty. The conclusion ends by discussing the
longer-term impact of this shift, and the ways in which it shaped the
campaigns in favour of devolution that took place during the 1980s and
1990s, and especially the positions adopted by the Labour Party.

NOTES

1. On the inter-war period, see: McKibbin, 'Class and Conventional Wisdom';
   Jarvis, 'British Conservatism and Class Politics in the 1920s' and 'The
   Shaping of Conservative Electoral Hegemony, 1918–39'; Hutchison,
   'Scottish Unionism between the two world wars'; Williamson, *Stanley
   Baldwin*; Smyth, 'Resisting Labour'.
2. Cragoe, 'We like local patriotism'.
3. The 1973 'border poll' in Northern Ireland was agreed by the Conservative
   government. The 1975 referendum on EEC membership was pursued by
   the subsequent Labour government.
4. Morton, *Unionist-Nationalism*; Kidd, *Union and Unionisms*.

5. For excellent broader surveys of Scotland in the twentieth century, see: Harvie, *Scotland and Nationalism* and *No Gods and Precious Few Heroes*; Hutchison, *Scottish Politics in the Twentieth Century*; MacDonald, *Whaur Extremes Meet*; Cameron, *Impaled upon a Thistle*.

6. See, for example: Miller, *The End of British Politics?*

7. This has, for reasons that will become evident in Chapter One, tended to incorporate an assessment of the fortunes of Scottish Liberalism.

8. Kendrick and McCrone, 'Politics in a Cold Climate'; Kellas, 'The Party in Scotland'.

9. Mitchell, *Conservatives and the Union*; Seawright and Curtice, 'The Decline of the Scottish Conservative and Unionist Party: Religion, Ideology or Economics?'; Seawright, *An Important Matter of Principle*; Dyer, 'The Evolution of the Centre-Right and the State of Scottish Conservatism'; Keating, 'The Strange Death of Unionist Scotland'.

10. Finlay, 'Unionism and the Dependency Culture' and 'Patriotism, Paternalism and Pragmatism: Scottish Toryism, Union and Empire, 1912–65'.

11. For differing interpretations of the significance of Empire in this period, see: Devine, 'The Break-up of Britain? Scotland and the End of Empire'; Nielsen and Ward, '"Cramped and Restricted at Home"? Scottish Separatism at Empire's End'.

12. The question of whether this decline was real or merely alleged remains controversial. See: Tomlinson, 'Thrice Denied'.

13. Hanham, *Scottish Nationalism*; Brand, *The National Movement in Scotland*.

14. Mitchell, *The Scottish Question*, Chapter 7.

15. Lynch, *SNP*.

16. On the Conservative response, see: Pentland, 'Edward Heath, the Declaration of Perth and the Scottish Conservative and Unionist Party'.

17. Brown (ed.), *The Red Paper on Scotland*; Keating and Bleiman, *Labour and Scottish Nationalism*. Although see the relevant chapters in: Donnachie, Harvie and Wood (eds), *Forward! Labour Politics in Scotland, 1888–1988*. Also still valuable is: Marr, *The Battle for Scotland*, Chapters 3 and 4.

18. Hassan and Shaw, *The Strange Death of Labour Scotland*, especially Chapter 1.

19. Phillips, *The Industrial Politics of Devolution*, 'Deindustrialization and the Moral Economy of the Scottish Coalfields, 1947 to 1991', and 'The Closure of Michael Colliery in 1967 and the Politics of Deindustrialization in Scotland'; Tomlinson, 'Deindustrialization not Decline'; Gibbs, 'The Moral Economy of the Scottish Coalfields'; Phillips, Wright and Tomlinson, 'Deindustrialization, the Linwood Car Plant and Scotland's Political Divergence from England in the 1960s and 1970s'; Gibbs, *Coal Country*.

20. Devine, *The Scottish Nation*; Devine (ed.), *Scotland and the United Kingdom, 1707–2007*; Kidd, *Union and Unionisms*; Jackson, *The Two Unions: Ireland, Scotland and the Survival of the United Kingdom, 1707–2007*.

21. Jackson, 'The Political Thought of Scottish Nationalism'; Mitchell, *The Scottish Question*; Gibbs and Scothorne, '"Origins of the Present Crisis": The Emergence of "Left-Wing" Scottish Nationalism, 1956–1979'; Craig, *The Wealth of the Nation*; Hames, *The Literary Politics of Scottish Devolution*; Jackson, *The Case for Scottish Independence*.
22. Greenleaf, *The British Political Tradition II: The Ideological Heritage*, pp. 263–346; Jones and Kandiah (eds), *The Myth of Consensus*; Green, 'The Conservative Party, the State and the Electorate, 1945–1964' and *The Ideologies of Conservatism*.
23. Schwarz, *The White Mans's World*; Schofield, *Enoch Powell and the Making of Postcolonial Britain*.

1

Unionism, Liberalism and Anti-Socialism: Politics in Scotland After 1945*

THE MIDDLE DECADES OF the twentieth century have often been over-looked in accounts of modern Scottish politics. While there has been some consideration of the political impact of the Second World War, and, in particular, of Thomas Johnston's tenure as Secretary of State for Scotland in the wartime coalition government, broader assessments of the period remain rare.[1] This relative neglect is, perhaps, understand-able: by the 1940s the distinctive radical tradition that had shaped the Scottish political left in the early twentieth century had faded, assimi-lated within a Labour movement now increasingly British in outlook; equally, with the partial exception of the Covenant campaign of the late 1940s, there were as yet few signs of the vociferous debate over Scotland's constitutional status that would become so characteristic of Scottish politics after the late 1960s. From a parliamentary perspective, as Ewen Cameron has suggested, mid-century Scottish politics can pres-ent an 'uninteresting landscape', with few Scottish MPs enjoying promi-nence at Westminster and election results seeming to largely echo wider British trends.[2] It was not until the 1959 general election, when Unionist support slipped despite the Conservatives enjoying a third successive electoral victory at a UK level, that Scottish politics began to follow a visibly divergent path.

The outward 'Britishness' of Scottish politics in the immediate post-war period is, on one level, to be expected. The extension of the franchise after 1918 had, alongside the continued growth of a national media, helped to foster a more uniform British political culture centred upon

---

* This chapter expands upon research first published in: Petrie, 'Anti-Socialism, Liberalism and Individualism'.

events at Westminster.[3] Similarly, the increase in state intervention in the economy during the Second World War, and the subsequent nationalisation of key industries and establishment of the welfare state by the Labour government returned to power at the 1945 general election, can plausibly be viewed as having encouraged Scots to consider themselves as participants in a national, 'British', economy.[4] Nonetheless, discrete Scottish patterns could still, at times, be glimpsed beneath this relatively harmonious surface. Most notably, the economic settlement that emerged after 1945 provoked sustained opposition. While such hostility was visible across Britain, what in England was understood as a question of competing economic philosophies was in Scotland imbued with an additional constitutional significance. For some in Scotland, the Labour government's programme of nationalisation represented a challenge to the institutional autonomy felt to have been guaranteed by the Treaty of Union, and, indeed, even to Scottish identity. As historians and political scientists have recognised, after 1945 Unionists embraced these complaints, and posed as the protectors of Scottish distinctiveness, critical of Labour's alleged efforts to impose socialist homogeneity.[5]

But the Unionist adoption of a defence of Scottish identity, and the extent to which this complemented time-honoured Conservative critiques of socialism as a threat to individual liberty, was not merely a feature of the party's time in opposition, jettisoned once the party returned to office in 1951. Rather, as this chapter will demonstrate, the idiom through which this appeal was expressed, which blended individualism with constitutional concerns, continued to mould Unionist rhetoric into the 1950s, with implications for Scottish politics more broadly, since it was echoed – with appropriate adjustments in emphasis – by the Liberals and the SNP. Fundamentally anti-socialist, this language shared some roots with the 'libertarian strand' in British political thought identified by W. H. Greenleaf.[6] It must be stressed that libertarian should not, in this context, be interpreted in a literal sense, or as suggesting an early embrace of neoliberal ideas; rather, it denotes an inclination towards individual freedom, a preference for markets over centralised economic planning, and a scepticism towards state-run bureaucracies. If this disposition existed principally at the level of rhetoric, and could often lack intellectual coherence, it nevertheless retained a certain political potency.[7] There were, then, limits to the so-called post-war consensus in a Scottish setting, as the policies pursued by the Labour government after 1945 drew criticism, principally from Unionists, but also from Liberals and nationalists.

This chapter explores the ways in which such criticism shaped the temper of Scottish politics in the often neglected period between the

Second World War and the 1959 general election. It highlights the centrality to Scottish political debate of a claim to defend individual liberty and to oppose an increase in the authority of central government that could, at times, encompass an appeal to Scottish national identity. Attention is paid chiefly to the Unionists, although consideration is also given to the positions adopted by the Liberals and the SNP. The analysis commences with an account of Unionist concerns regarding the potential consequences of economic policies introduced during the Second World War, and how these wartime anxieties conditioned reactions to the reforms implemented by the post-war Labour government. Crucial is a consideration of the rhetoric employed by Unionists as they sought to return to power, a goal achieved in 1951. The focus then moves to the broader bases of the Unionist appeal, and an examination of the degree to which Unionists were able to build a coalition of all those opposed to socialism, including erstwhile Liberals and even, at times, nationalists. The chapter concludes with an assessment of the gradual weakening of this anti-socialist coalition after 1955, as frustration appeared to grow among Unionist supporters.

The emphasis placed on rhetoric necessitates a focus on what politicians said and wrote, or, at least, were willing to put their names to; as such, it relies upon speeches, election literature and other printed material. This is, of course, not to suggest that this is the only way in which political history can be approached; neither does it mean that we should treat politicians' words as an accurate reflection of their true beliefs. It is, nonetheless, to take seriously the attempts of political representatives and activists to secure popular support, and to convince electors to view issues in a certain way. Political ideologies are, as scholars of rhetoric have reminded us, composed of more than sets of policy positions: they are, in the words of Alan Finlayson and James Martin, at least as much a matter of creating 'a "mood", an emotional register and a style of presentation.'[8] The immediate intention here is to recover, as far as possible, the mood that the political right sought to cultivate amongst voters in post-war Scotland.

DEFENDING INDIVIDUAL FREEDOM: THE RHETORIC OF POST-WAR UNIONISM

In February 1942, senior Unionist officials and parliamentarians gathered in Edinburgh to discuss the domestic impact of the war effort. The meeting was almost certainly prompted by the coalition government's decision the previous year to establish a committee to investigate proposals for post-war reconstruction; this committee would, in November 1942, publish what would come to be known as the Beveridge Report, which outlined the basis for the post-war welfare state. Many of those in attendance in Edinburgh expressed their fears for the future, and their concerns that restrictions introduced during the conflict, such as rationing and government direction of industry, would prove difficult to unwind in peacetime. Frank Watt, the Unionist MP for Edinburgh Central, cautioned that, while certain controls might be necessary in the context of the war, they had to ensure that any interference with 'individual liberty' was only temporary, otherwise society would be reduced permanently to the status of 'a state-controlled machine'.[9] Watt's fears were echoed by several of his colleagues. Walter Elliot, MP for Glasgow Kelvingrove and a former Secretary of State for Scotland, usually identified with a more conciliatory strand of Unionism, agreed that the economic regulations introduced since 1939 must be removed as soon as the war ended.[10] Urging the need to 'avoid' the growth of 'bureaucracy', Elliot warned of 'a danger of following two divergent lines of policy simultaneously. We were fighting for liberty but tended to use tyranny'. Elliot's counterpart in Edinburgh North, Alexander Erskine-Hill, spoke in similarly anxious tones while adding a note of conspiracy, complaining that 'sweeping and ill-considered changes' were being instituted 'under cover of wartime necessity'; he warned that it may prove 'impossible' to return to 'the principles of private ownership and individual enterprise on which reconstruction after the war should properly be based.'[11]

These statements were clearly inspired by partisan concerns, at least in part; nevertheless, they should encourage a certain scepticism towards suggestions that the experience of war fostered a more sympathetic stance among Unionists on questions of economic intervention and welfare provision. In the inter-war period Unionists had, of course, been willing to countenance a greater role for the state, especially after the advent of the National Government in 1931.[12] But this partial embrace of corporatism was motivated principally by a desire to protect the existing economic order and to limit the appeal of more radical alternatives. Such measures, moreover, were combined with still-pungent denunciations of the dangers of socialism and collectivism, dismissed uncomplicatedly as close relatives of Bolshevism. There was for Unionists an obvious difference between their measured reforms and the creeping socialism they perceived as having arrived with the Labour Party's entry into the wartime coalition government in 1940. Unionists duly surveyed subsequent developments with a certain foreboding: a resolution passed unanimously at the party's 1942 conference pronounced that those present were 'apprehensive of the growth of Bureaucracy' and were convinced that only a swift return to pre-war principles of 'private enterprise' would bring about a revival in 'industrial and commercial prosperity.'[13]

Unionist anxieties in the early 1940s functioned on two levels. The first was a conviction that the war had benefited the Labour Party politically. Although the major parties had agreed an electoral truce in 1940, there persisted a belief among Unionist members that, at a local level, Labour activists were failing to honour this agreement and were instead continuing their propaganda efforts.[14] Further, Unionists were certain that their supporters were more likely to be engaged in military service than Labour members who, it was believed, were to be found disproportionately in the protected industrial occupations and had therefore been able to maintain their political organisation. The second was a deeper, more ideological fear that, if Labour was able to form a government after the war then the economic controls introduced in wartime would become permanent, thereby providing the foundations for the establishment of a socialist regime. Speaking before an audience of Unionist constituency party chairmen in March 1944, Arthur Young, MP for Glasgow Partick and the Unionist whip in the House of Commons, demonstrated how these concerns reinforced each other. Young alleged that Labour members were agitating for an early end to the coalition government, and predicted, correctly, that a general election would be held as soon as victory in Europe had been secured. He called on those present to ensure that they were prepared for any such contest. Setting such pragmatic issues to one side, Young then addressed more profound questions, warning his audience that 'it would be a tragedy if, after all the sacrifices made to preserve our freedom and the British way of life, we find ourselves regimented in a Socialist state differing little from Totalitarianism.'[15]

It is, then, unsurprising that, when a general election eventually arrived in July 1945, Scottish Unionists, like their Conservative colleagues in England and Wales, foregrounded their commitment to individual liberty and demanded the lifting of wartime economic restrictions. Notoriously, the campaign saw Winston Churchill, the outgoing Prime Minister, deliver a radio broadcast warning that a Labour victory, and the introduction of socialism, would trigger an inexorable descent into tyranny.[16] There remains some uncertainty as to whether Churchill was inspired directly by Friedrich von Hayek's *Road to Serfdom*, published a year earlier, or if he merely inadvertently echoed the lurid warnings found in that book.[17] In any case, Churchill's intervention proved ill-judged and was widely believed to have backfired; the scale of the subsequent Labour victory suggested that few voters had been swayed by his words. Yet the speech should not be dismissed as simply a blunder from a leader struggling to adopt the right tone as the war moved towards a close. Assertions that socialism represented a threat to individual freedom, and would inevitably end in some form of dictatorship, were central to the Conservative campaign in 1945, and built upon a tradition established in the 1920s, when party propaganda had routinely accused the Labour Party of being sympathetic towards communism.[18] Notes issued to Conservative activists during the 1945 campaign stated that the 'British people' valued 'individual liberty above everything'; Conservatives, it was asserted, shared this outlook, and were 'resolutely opposed to the conception of the all-powerful State which regulates every form of national activity by means of a monstrously inflated bureaucracy'.[19] Similar views were espoused by Unionist candidates in Scotland. In Kinross and West Perthshire, the Unionist candidate William McNair Snadden announced that he believed in 'the freedom of the individual' and advised that 'behind [economic] controls' lurked 'the totalitarian state'.[20] In neighbouring Perth, Alan Gomme Duncan asked voters if they were content 'to be regimented and dragooned by officials under a Socialist system of Government which would result in tyranny and stagnation'.[21] Priscilla Grant, contesting the Labour stronghold of Aberdeen North for the Unionists, declared that her party valued 'the independent character of our people': she was, therefore, opposed to 'the Labour policy of Nationalisation', which would 'stifle personal initiative' and give 'to the few' an 'unassailable authority over the many.'[22]

Traditionally, the scale of the Conservative defeat in 1945 was understood to have prompted the party to revise its stance on economic and social questions, and to accept a new political settlement in which the primary role of government was to manage a mixed economy in a way that prioritised full employment.[23] In this reading, this pivot to the political centre, symbolised by the publication in 1947 of the *Industrial Charter*, laid the foundation for the party's return to office in 1951, and guided the Conservative approach to economic management and industrial relations in the decade that followed.[24] This cross-party consensus was commonly held to have survived until the early 1970s, before it collapsed as a result of internal and external economic pressures, and the Conservatives, under the leadership of Margaret Thatcher, turned to the right.[25] Yet, as a number of subsequent studies have demonstrated, such a narrative obscures the extent to which large sections of Conservative opinion remained unreconciled to the welfare state and the mixed economy after 1945. Instead, critiques of rationing, redistributive tax-ation, and universalism in the provision of social services continued to play an important role in Conservative appeals to the electorate during the 1950s.[26] Perceptions of public opinion, and the electoral calculations they prompted, may well have placed limits on how far Conservatives were willing to go in undoing Labour's reforms; still, grudging tolerance should not be mistaken for genuine support. As Ewen Green remarked drily, the Conservative slogan in this era was 'Set the People Free', not 'the welfare state and the mixed economy are safe in our hands.'[27]

In Scotland, Unionists certainly remained attached to an appeal to individual freedom after 1945. Vital to Unionism's post-war pitch to the electorate was the claim that the Labour Party posed an existential threat to liberty and even to democracy. Such a contention represented, in many respects, a straightforward rephrasing of arguments first advanced in the 1920s, when Unionists had exploited concerns regarding the alleged threat posed by socialism to attract the support of former Liberal voters.[28] This inherited anti-socialism was, however, amplified first by the experience of war and then by the arrival of the first majority Labour government, and was often expressed in alarmist terms. In November 1946, for example, William McNair Snadden, who had successfully held Kinross and West Perthshire for the Unionists the previous year, spoke at the annual meeting of his constituency association. Snadden informed those present that the Labour government's ultimate intention was the enactment of an irreversible programme of social and economic reform: they were, he claimed, aiming to ensure that it would be 'impossible . . . to unscramble the eggs'. Condemning what he believed to be Labour's desire to 'level down . . . incomes', Snadden urged all 'anti-socialists' to work together to combat the 'alien doctrine of Marx'; were they to fail, he concluded, they would witness the triumph of 'the very thing they had fought for six years to destroy – the Totalitarian State.'[29] Addressing the same audience two years later, Snadden repeated his warnings. After criticising the Labour government's imposition of what he termed 'penal' rates of taxation, as well as the 'avalanche of forms, regulations, and restrictions' that he suggested were the inevitable consequence of socialism, Snadden arrived at what he believed was the central issue: Labour's desire to see 'the final establishment of the complete Socialist State within these Islands.' Snadden left his audience with a final, unset-tling, prediction: if the Labour government were to be returned for a second term, he would 'not be surprised if that General Election were the last we would see in this country.'[30] Snadden's comments were patently ridiculous; still, they were not untypical. Alan Gomme Duncan,

now the Unionist MP for Perth, used similar language at a public meeting in Doune in December 1948, warning those in attendance that, if
Labour won a second term, the next general election would be the 'last'
they would experience 'in this country'.[31] Earlier that year, James Reid,
Unionist MP for Glasgow Hillhead, told an audience of more than 5,000
at a Unionist rally at Callendar House in Falkirk that the 'next election
would be vital for the future of this country' since, if Labour remained in
office, 'freedom and prosperity would be so far gone' that it would take
at least a 'generation' to recover.[32]

Of course, it may be reasoned that this was an internal mode of
expression, a knowingly exaggerated rhetorical style designed to rouse
gatherings of Unionist members. Certainly, we may be doubtful as to
whether the politicians who delivered these speeches really believed what
they were saying. This is, though, a relatively unimportant issue: these
statements were, to borrow Maurice Cowling's influential formulation,
intended as 'a form of exemplary utterance', an 'attempt to provide new
landmarks' for those in the audience.[33] Even if Unionist politicians were
not entirely sincere in their rhetoric, they were nonetheless sure that an
explicit rejection of Labour's programme of reform, and the cultivation
of a binary political contest structured around opposition to socialism,
offered their best hope of recovering power. Crucially, this emotive language was not limited to internal party events but was repeated in both
official party reports and Unionist election literature: it was designed
to stir a wider audience. As the introduction to the 1948 annual report
issued by the party's Western Divisional Council characterised matters,
Scots faced a stark choice 'between the Unionist policy of a free economy and the democratic way of life on the one hand, and Socialist State
monopoly and eventual servitude on the other.'[34]

An important influence here, and one especially difficult to recover in
retrospect, was the onset of the cold war, which added a new urgency to
Unionist accusations that Labour's socialism would prove a precursor
to communism. While similar assertions had been made in the inter-war
period, the post-war rhetoric was intensified by the confrontation with a
Soviet Union that had gained prestige as a result of its contribution to the
defeat of Nazi Germany, and, later, by the fears created by the prospect
of nuclear conflict. At a Unionist meeting in Dunblane in late 1948, Alec
Douglas-Home, the future Conservative Prime Minister, maintained that
there was little practical difference between socialism and communism,
and charged Labour with having attempted to introduce 'the Soviet
system into Britain'.[35] Suggestions of a basic affinity between socialism and communism remained an important element within Unionist

propaganda into the early 1950s. At the Glasgow Gorbals by-election in September 1948, the Unionist candidate claimed that Labour was 'ill-equipped' to combat the communist threat as '. . . it is too close to it. Too many of its members are "fellow travellers", or secret sympathisers'.[36] During the 1950 general election, Archibald Tennant, the Unionist candidate in Aberdeen North, argued that the Labour government had dragged Britain 'halfway towards Communism'; the Unionists, in contrast, offered a 'bulwark against totalitarianism'.[37] In the neighbouring constituency of Aberdeen South, Priscilla Buchan, defending a seat she had held for the Unionists at a by-election in 1946, informed voters that 'socialism, whether quickly or slowly, must end in Communism.'[38] Eighteen months later, during the 1951 election campaign, the Unionist candidate in Stirling and Falkirk Burghs, Colonel William Forbes, told a meeting at Stirling's Albert Hall that socialism existed merely to pave the way for communism.[39]

Unionist criticisms of Labour were, to be sure, not always framed in such dramatic terms. At a more prosaic level, the party hoped to exploit popular frustration with the continuation – and, indeed, extension – of wartime controls after 1945. This most often found expression as a general opposition to the regulations and restrictions that accompanied the post-war regime of rationing and economic controls. An example of such sentiments could be found in the newsletter produced by the Aberdeen North Unionist Association. Here, in November 1946, it was stated that 'new regulations' were being issued by the government at such a rate that individuals could no longer be sure if they were complying with the law. There was a sense too of exasperation (and, perhaps, a hint of injured class pride) at the growing number of bureaucrats charged with administering the new rules, who were described as 'pettifogging clerks', inexplicably now 'entitled to rule you and me'.[40] Similarly, during the 1950 campaign in Aberdeen South, Priscila Buchan emphasised her commitment to helping the 'Little Man' navigate 'the many intricacies and difficulties caused by the restrictions and controls imposed by a Socialist Government'.[41] Unionists at times concentrated on more specific grievances, as when, in early 1946, members of the Dundee Unionist Association recorded their opposition to the creation of a national health service on the grounds that it would 'prejudice the patient's right to an independent family doctor' and would result in 'the medical profession becoming full-time salaried servants of the State'.[42]

The principal focus of Unionist attacks on the Labour government was a sustained condemnation of the policy of nationalisation. At a practical level, nationalisation was depicted as simply misjudged: a poor alternative to the free market, it would encourage a misallocation of resources and result in a reduction in consumer choice. A party pamphlet from the late 1940s provided an inventory of the failings attributed to state-run industries, including 'red tape', bureaucratisation, an aversion to risk-taking and innovation, and the danger that investment decisions would be based upon political rather than economic considerations.[43] This pragmatic analysis was echoed at a local level: in early 1951 the Stirling and Falkirk Burghs Unionist Association called for a committee to be created to consider which, if any, of the nationalised industries should remain in public ownership 'on grounds of efficiency and accountability'.[44] But Unionists were often more comfortable when denouncing nationalisation on ethical and moral, rather than narrowly economic, grounds. By involving the state directly in the management of large sections of the economy, Unionists alleged that Labour had fundamentally altered the relationship between the government and the public. Unionists rejected any suggestion that nationalisation was equivalent to democratic or public control, instead insisting that the 'state' was not synonymous with the public in any meaningful sense. Influential here was the longstanding Unionist belief in the idea of a property-owning democracy, voiced first by Noel Skelton in the 1920s.[45] The vision of a society in which property ownership, and, therefore, it was held, political independence and an interest in social stability, was diffused widely, was contrasted with, to take one Unionist voice, Labour's alleged belief in 'the concentration of all property in the hands of the State'.[46] Priscila Buchan adopted near-identical language in 1950, asserting that Unionists believed in 'spreading . . . ownership of property and, therefore, the spreading of power'; she rejected the policy, which she attributed to Labour, of 'concentrating all power and all ownership in the hands of the State'. The state was, in Buchan's view, in truth nothing but 'a few men at the head of Government'.[47]

There was a related, deeper concern underpinning these denunciations of state control. Unionists maintained that the creation of what were, in effect, publicly directed monopolies in key sectors of the economy posed a series of critical threats to liberty and to the functioning of democracy. First, nationalisation would mean that in certain industries the government would be the sole employer, thereby creating a class of workers wholly reliant upon the state for their livelihoods; their dependent status would, it was alleged, act as a check on the expression of political opinions. As James Hutchison, the Unionist MP for Glasgow Central, stated in 1948, 'the nationalised industries were creating a race of sycophants – people who were always wondering if the man [sic] above was satisfied.'[48] For Priscila Buchan, nationalisation had facilitated 'the greatest monopoly' that it was possible to envisage, with workers in state-run industries having little say over where they worked. 'Instead of finding that he can sack the boss and go elsewhere' if unhappy at work, Buchan warned, employees in the nationalised industries would find 'that there is, in fact, but one boss, and one so remote that [there is] no chance of walking into his office and telling him what he thinks of him [sic].'[49] Second, there was a fear regarding the assumed negative impact of nationalisation on inflation and the cost of living. While this drew on the general belief that monopolies inflated prices and reduced consumer choice, there were additional factors at work. The Labour government had, in 1946, repealed the 1927 Trade Disputes and Trade Unions Act. Passed in the wake of the 1926 general strike, the Act had barred sympathy strikes and prohibited civil service unions from affiliating to the Trades Union Congress; the legislation also required union members to explicitly 'opt-in' to contributing to their union's political fund, affecting the financial support unions could offer the Labour Party.[50] The reversal of these measures prompted concerns on the political right that the trades unions, and especially those representing workers in the public sector, would enjoy undue influence over the Labour government, with generous wages and conditions in the nationalised industries being used to reward and secure political support. Popularising such suspicions during the October 1948 Stirling and Falkirk Burghs by-election, the Unionist candidate, William Forbes, called for an end to this alleged programme of 'Jobs for the Boys'.[51]

This framing, in which nationalisation represented a form of collusion between the Labour government and the unions that would result in higher taxes and rising prices, accompanied right-wing criticisms of rationing as an unfair burden on consumers. Ina Zweiniger-Bargielowska has argued that this appeal to the interests of the consumer was intended to reach female voters in particular, and was an important factor in the Conservative recovery at the 1950 and 1951 general elections.[52] It is difficult to measure the precise electoral impact of this rhetoric in Scotland; there is, however, some anecdotal evidence that it did persuade female voters to back the Unionists. Internal party reports offer suggestive accounts that popular concern over the cost of living was inspiring an increase in support for the Unionists, even in areas considered traditional Labour strongholds. In July 1950, it was reported that rising 'housekeeping costs' were encouraging some working-class women to look to more favourably upon the prospect of 'an anti-Socialist government'. By the following February, party officials were convinced that support among female electors was increasing; in April 1951 it was suggested that there had been 'a distinct change of heart in the woman who has always followed her husband in voting "Labour"', with it being reported excitedly that it was likely that 'some women' would 'vote independently of what their husbands do.'[53]

At certain moments, the Unionist critique of nationalisation could assume a subtler, more pacific, and perhaps contradictory tone, which was designed to appeal not to consumers but rather to those now employed in state-run industries. Here the emphasis was placed upon the extent to which nationalisation would threaten the bargaining position of organised labour by blurring the distinction between employer and government, and throwing into question the ability of workers to pursue industrial action. At the November 1946 Aberdeen South by-election, Priscila Buchan compared the position of the unions in the nationalised industries to that which had prevailed in Fascist Italy a decade earlier; the right to strike, she predicted, would soon disappear.[54] Robert Allan, the Unionist candidate at the April 1950 West Dunbartonshire by-election, declared boldly that his party would 'free Trade Unions from their present subservience to the Government and allow them to perform their proper function of safeguarding the rights and interests of their members'.[55] James Hutchison, speaking at a Unionist rally in Falkirk the following year, warned that nationalisation was a threat to the independence of trade unions; how, he wondered, could they pursue industrial action against a government that they not only supported, but also funded?[56]

This defence by Unionists of the right to strike was, it might be speculated, not wholly honest; it was, though, part of a general effort to exploit any form of disillusionment with the Labour government. Since nationalisation had not only retained management structures from the private sector but had, in Scotland, arguably made them more remote, this allowed Unionists to once again depict Labour not as the party of the working class, but as a vehicle for self-regarding middle-class pseudo-intellectuals.[57] As the 1950 general election approached, Patrick Blair, the Unionist Party's Political Secretary, supplied all candidates and election agents with talking points for use at public meetings. Prominent was a rejection of Labour's claim to speak for the working class: this was dismissed as nothing more than 'arrogance and falsehood'; it was suggested that it should be pointed out that 'many "Labour" politicians are much more "capitalists" than millions of "Tory" voters.'[58] At the rerun a year later, Priscila Buchan's platform notes for her campaign in Aberdeen South included reminders to emphasise that Labour had 'long ceased' to be a 'Working-Man's Movement'. Instead, it was to be suggested, 'so-called intellectuals [had] gained control', with their notion that the state 'should have [the] power to organise everything and everybody'. This was, then, a 'Socialist' not a 'Labour' party, one in which the 'intellectual and company director' were 'well represented'.[59] This insistence on referring to Labour as the 'Socialist' party was, of course, a longstanding tradition, and indicated Unionists continued to believe that 'socialism' could profitably be used to evoke the spectre of a foreign, extremist ideology inclined towards totalitarianism.[60]

These renderings of socialism as an ideological threat to individual liberty drew particular strength from the decision of the Labour government to impose what came to be described as 'direction of labour' in the autumn of 1947. The post-war years were marked by the continuation of measures of rationing and resource management. By 1947, however, there were concerns that prospects of an economic recovery were being hampered by labour shortages in key industries, such as textiles, agriculture, and mining. The government responded with the introduction of the 'Control of Engagement Order', which allowed the unemployed, and those deemed to be involved in 'useless occupations' such as gambling, nightclubs and street-trading, to be directed towards vacancies in essential or export-earning sectors.[61] In practice, the power to direct labour in this way was rarely exercised, and quickly fell into disuse. Nevertheless, Unionists, and the Conservatives in England and Wales, soon seized upon the policy as evidence of the government's intention to expand the power of the state in new, and more authoritarian, directions. There was a certain hypocrisy in such attacks, since right-wing critics of the Labour government's economic policy had long complained that labour had been exempt from the controls applied to goods and services, a result, it was claimed, of the government's unwillingness to confront the unions.[62] Undaunted, Willian McNair Snadden informed an audience at an event in his Kinross and West Perthshire constituency that 'for the first time . . . the fundamental right of the citizen to choose his [sic] own work was being taken away'. Through the policy of 'labour direction', the government was, he concluded, 'trying to take away the last vestige of freedom' by relegating workers to a position of 'permanent slavery'.[63]

The question of labour direction was prominent during the Glasgow Camlachie by-election in January 1948, where the Unionist candidate, Charles McFarlane, wrote that the Labour government had robbed workers of 'their cherished liberty to choose their own jobs'.[64] The contest in Camlachie was an intriguing one. Barring a brief interlude between 1931 and 1935, the seat had been represented since 1922 by

Reverend Campbell Stephen of the Independent Labour Party (ILP); Stephen had remained within the ILP following the party's disaffiliation from the Labour Party in 1932. The 1948 poll was triggered by Stephen's death, and saw the entry of competing Labour and ILP nominees, as well as candidates from the Unionists, the Liberals, and the SNP, alongside an independent socialist. The competition between Labour and the ILP allowed McFarlane to secure the seat for the Unionists.[65] It would be an exaggeration to suggest that hostility towards direction of labour was a decisive issue in the campaign. Still, it is notable that it was not only the Unionists who made plain their opposition to the policy. The ILP candidate, Annie Maxton, criticised the policy from a left-wing standpoint, declaring that 'the right to choose his [sic] own job is a worker's prize possession. To have that right denied him and to be directed into industry by the State is the first step to Totalitarianism'.[66] Robert Wilkie, contesting the seat for the SNP, likewise complained that Scots were being 'denied liberty', and reduced to the status of a 'subject people' by 'London politicians' who had arrogated to themselves 'the right to conscript you and direct you industrially'.[67] Despite the policy's marginal practical impact, attacks on direction of labour would remain a recurring theme in Conservative and Unionist rhetoric into the early 1950s, featuring in the material issued to local activists during the 1950 and 1951 general elections.[68]

BUILDING AN ANTI-SOCIALIST COALITION

Post-war Unionism was, then, characterised by a profound antagonism towards socialism, which, in an extension of a tendency evident on the political right since the 1920s, was condemned as merely a staging post on the road to communism. It should be recognised, though, that Unionist hostility towards the Labour Party did not produce a narrowly partisan outlook. Rather, the urgency of the threat allegedly posed by Labour inspired attempts to construct a coalition of all those opposed to socialism. The clearest example of this approach was the 1947 pact with the National Liberals, which saw the Unionists, and in England and Wales the Conservatives, establish joint constituency parties in a number of seats.[69] As the Unionist and National Liberal leaderships declared in a joint statement issued following the conclusion of the agreement, there was 'one fundamental political issue' facing the country, namely 'whether the principles of liberty of the individual' and 'freedom and enterprise' would survive, 'or whether the Socialist doctrine of regimentation, state-ownership and centralised control [would] prevail'.[70]

The National Liberal party, established by those Liberals who remained within the National Government following the abandonment of free trade in 1932, has been largely dismissed by historians, with the 1947 alliance generally treated as having signalled the end of the party's independent existence.[71] Such a narrative is perhaps accurate in an English context, where Conservatism was a more dominant political presence. In Scotland, however, National Liberalism survived the agreement with Unionism, and remained a distinctive political identity for another decade. Of the sixty constituencies where joint associations were established prior to the 1950 general election, fifteen were in Scotland, while the number of candidates adopting some version of the National Liberal label in Scottish seats increased in the next decade.[72] Indeed, candidates standing as National Liberals secured just under ten per cent of the Scottish vote at general elections during the 1950s. But even this overall figure understates the regional importance of National Liberalism, which was especially pronounced in the north east, south west and the Highlands, areas of historic Tory weakness where inter-war Unionism relied to a significant extent on the Liberal element of its inheritance. The prominence of Scottish MPs in the National Liberal leadership should also be noted, as should the number of National Liberals appointed to ministerial roles at the Scottish Office after the Conservatives returned to office in 1951. Between 1947 and 1964, the position of National Liberal Chairman was held exclusively by Scottish MPs, while John Maclay, National Liberal MP for West Renfrewshire, served as Secretary of State for Scotland between 1957 and 1962; Niall MacPherson and James Henderson-Stewart, who sat as National Liberals for Galloway and East Fife respectively, were both junior Scottish Office ministers in this period.[73] The National Liberals were not, as has been suggested, merely 'absorbed' by the Unionists in 1947.[74]

In England, onetime Liberals were, in Ewen Green's phrase, enlisted by the Conservatives as 'subaltern anti-socialists'; in Scotland, however, the relationship between Unionism and Liberalism was more equal, and therefore more complex.[75] The value of the alliance with the National Liberals for Unionists went beyond just electoral support, or a handful of additional MPs in the Commons. If the critical cleavage in postwar Scottish politics was between socialists and their opponents, then National Liberalism infused Unionism with the traces of an ideological tradition that had long claimed to be the guardian of individual liberty: through an association with National Liberalism, Unionists could tap a liberal language of freedom. Post-war Unionism is, then, best understood as a composite, an anti-socialist coalition in which National

Liberals played an important part by providing former Liberal voters with an ideological justification for shifting their allegiances. Such an understanding was expressed in September 1949 by John Maclay, then the National Liberal MP for Montrose Burghs. Addressing a constituency meeting in Forfar, Maclay argued that Liberals and Unionists were alike concerned with the 'value' of the individual: the two creeds were, he suggested, 'fundamentally the same', while socialism 'was the absolute antithesis'. For Maclay, it was no use clinging to 'the old cries and outdated party prejudices'; 'a pooling of knowledge and experience' was necessary. Two months later, James Henderson-Stewart echoed this perspective when addressing the same audience. Warning that if Labour was returned to power for a second term then liberal values might vanish 'for a generation', Henderson-Stewart urged Liberals to support what he termed the 'coalition led by Mr Churchill', convinced that if there was 'a straight fight in every constituency' then Labour 'would be thrashed'.[76]

The union between the Unionists and the National Liberals was originally envisaged as a precursor to a broader electoral pact that would also embrace the Liberal Party. Although a formal agreement proved elusive, attracting the support of traditional Liberal voters was a vital element within Conservative and Unionist electoral strategy after 1945, and was pursued with some success. Clearly, in areas where the Liberal Party infrastructure was weak, it was relatively straightforward for the Unionists to offer a home to those seeking a more credible vehicle for combating socialism. To take one voice as an example, in late 1949 George Ramsay, a member of the executive committee of the Unionist Association in Central Ayrshire, wrote to Lord Woolton, the Conservative Party Chairman, to commend the efforts to secure a formal coalition with the Liberals. Strikingly, despite his prominent role in local Unionist politics, Ramsay described himself as a lifelong Liberal; critically, though, he was, he claimed, 'better known' locally 'as an anti-socialist', active in Unionist politics as it was the only party in the constituency that was 'fighting socialism'.[77]

Unsurprisingly, the Liberal leadership, desperate to ensure that their party survived as a distinct entity, contested Unionist and National Liberal claims to represent all those who opposed the Labour government. Tentative discussions were held in the immediate aftermath of the war regarding a potential reunion with the National Liberals, but these collapsed when it became clear that the latter were intent on a broader agreement that would include the Conservatives and Unionists.[78] But, in truth, it must have been a challenge for contemporary electors to discern what, barring a commitment to constitutional reform, distinguished

Liberalism from Unionism in the late 1940s, so convincing was the latter's espousal of the rhetoric of individualism. Scottish Liberals opposed Labour's 'planned economy' and nationalisation, which, they claimed, would 'result in the establishment of totalitarianism'; equally, they supported tax reductions.[79] Liberals were also troubled by the repeal of the 1927 Trades Disputes Act, and complained that forcing union members to 'opt-out' of contributing to the political levy was an affront to personal liberty.[80] Yet the problem for Liberals was stark: if the outlook was as ominous as such claims suggested, if the policies of the Labour government really did contain the seeds of totalitarianism, then it was difficult to see why voters – or, indeed, Liberal Party members – who were concerned about such developments should not respond to the Unionist appeal for anti-socialist solidarity. It was hardly surprising that, in seats where independent Liberalism had little presence, local Unionist associations reported that former Liberals were enthusiastically joining their ranks.[81]

In those areas where the Liberal Party did remain electorally competitive, the Unionist preference was to reach an accommodation with local Liberals, whatever the attitude of the Liberal hierarchy. The clearest instance was in Dundee, where a degree of electoral collusion between Liberals and Unionists had existed since the 1920s, a legacy of the city's status as one of the few double-member constituencies to survive into the twentieth century. When this situation changed after the 1948 Representation of the People Act, which saw Dundee divided into eastern and western constituencies, the old agreement, under which the parties had each nominated a single candidate, became obsolete; matters were complicated further by the agreement between the Unionists and the National Liberals. Throughout 1948 and 1949, as a general election approached, the Dundee Unionist Association, now allied, of course, with the local National Liberals, encouraged the Dundee Liberal Party to agree to a pact. In practice, however, the Unionist understanding of compromise was the nomination of a National Liberal candidate in both Dundee seats.[82] Initially, the Liberals refused, and, in the run up to the 1950 general election, maintained that they would contest the new Dundee West constituency, nominating the journalist John Junor and condemning the Unionists for creating a 'situation where two anti-Socialist candidates are going forward in the Western division'. There was, though, little local support for separate Liberal and Unionist candidacies and an 'Anti-Socialist Association' was formed three weeks prior to polling to promote an agreement. Similar calls for anti-socialist unity emanated from the Dundee Housewives' Association, an organisation launched to campaign for an end to rationing.[83] Junor duly agreed to step down on the condition that, if the Unionist candidate failed, then the Liberals would be granted a chance to contest Dundee West at the next election. This compromise was not sanctioned by the Liberal leadership, who despatched a last-minute replacement candidate. Nevertheless, this effort was bluntly ignored by local activists, who chose to prioritise trying to defeat the Labour candidate. In other localities, where the balance of forces was reversed, such agreements could operate in the opposite direction, as in Greenock, where in 1950 the Unionists granted the Liberals a free run. Likewise, in Ross and Cromarty the Unionist Association supported Jack Macleod, first elected in 1945 as an independent Liberal, stating that, so long as he opposed socialism, they were not concerned what label he adopted.[84] Of course, these alliances were no guarantee of success: Labour held Greenock and both Dundee seats throughout the post-war era.

Assertions that 1945 marked a return to partisan politics after an era of coalitions, or that post-war elections in Scotland were two-party affairs, require some qualification. While Unionism was certainly the dominant identity on the centre-right, it was not necessarily understood by activists and voters as an exclusive one; it was more contingent and provisional than that. The 'culture of coalitionism' identified by Michael Dyer as prevailing on the centre and right of Scottish politics during the 1930s, but which he argues faded after 1945, was, in truth, revitalised by the hostility many felt towards the first majority Labour government and by the context of the cold war, which generated new forms of anti-communist rhetoric and granted warnings of a drift towards totalitarianism a certain credibility, however ludicrous they might now appear.[85] This interpretation of Scottish politics informed contemporary commentary, with the need for Labour's opponents to work together being voiced repeatedly. When the Liberal Party attempted to revive its fortunes at the 1950 general election by contesting an increased number of constituencies, the response in right-leaning newspapers was to declare that such a move was reckless.[86] An editorial in *The Scotsman* expressed regret that the Liberal leadership had not followed the example set in Dundee in uniting with the Unionists to oppose Labour, a party described as 'the negation of true Liberalism'. This was especially regrettable since it was 'difficult to see much' in the Liberal platform 'that differs from contents of the Conservative manifesto': both were in favour of tax cuts, opposed nationalisation, and supported 'the freedom of the individual against the power of the state.'[87] The *Aberdeen Press and Journal* urged Liberals to support the Unionists in order to prevent a Labour victory, and invoked the memory of the 1923 and 1929 general elections, when revivals in Liberal support had allowed Labour to enter office.[88]

The Liberal attempt at electoral recovery in 1950 failed; although the party's share of the vote increased slightly, more than 300 deposits were lost, and the number of Liberal MPs fell to nine, down from twelve in 1945.[89] With Labour returned to power with a Commons majority of just five, the lesson seemed clear: Liberals who opposed socialism needed to work with Conservatives and Unionists. In the period between the 1950 election and the Conservative victory at the 1951 sequel, it became evident that Liberal voters in Scotland were transferring their support to the Unionists and National Liberals as opposition to Labour, and electoral reality, overrode older loyalties. In July 1950, Patrick Blair noted that a number of Unionist constituency associations were reporting that they had 'been enrolling former supporters of the Liberal Party', and that the general opinion was 'that there will be a falling off in the Liberal vote at the next General Election.' The Unionist branch in Berwickshire and East Lothian claimed that 'people who voted in all good faith for the Liberal candidate at the last election now appreciate that the Liberal Party is dead'.[90] John Maclay made similar claims the following year, informing Unionist and National Liberal MPs that there had been 'a marked tendency during the last six months for supporters of the independent Liberals to turn towards the National Liberal and Liberal-Unionist Party.' As a National Liberal, he offered to help any 'Unionist members who felt that this trend could with advantage be encouraged in their constituencies'.[91]

At the 1951 general election, which saw the number of Liberal candidacies collapse, the Unionists were, in tandem with their National Liberal allies, positioned as the dominant political force in rural and provincial Scotland; they were also the only viable threat to Labour in the urban and industrial centres. This achievement rested upon an accommodation with the Liberal tradition at once formal and informal: at the 1951 contest there were explicit 'anti-socialist' compacts, whether with the National Liberals or Liberals, in twenty of Scotland's seventy-one constituencies.[92] The outcome was impressive: the Unionists and National Liberals together received almost forty-nine per cent of the Scottish vote in 1951, and, famously, just over fifty per cent at the 1955 general election, outpolling the Labour Party both times, and, in the latter case, securing a majority of Scottish seats as well as votes. Yet this level of popular support concealed the extent to which Unionist success in the early 1950s was conditional, and more fragile than it appeared. Unionism's mid-century ascendancy was dependent upon two claims: first, that Labour presented a genuine threat to individual liberty; second, that the Unionists were best placed to check and reverse the socialist advance. The question was always how long such an ultimately negative, defensive electoral coalition could last, and whether it would survive the transition from opposition to government.

APPEALING TO THE NATION: POST-WAR UNIONISM AND THE CONSTITUTIONAL QUESTION

An appeal to liberal sentiments was the essential element in the construction of Unionism's electoral coalition after 1945; it was, however, not the only rhetoric that was available to Unionists. Important too was the way in which a language of individual liberty could be used to portray socialism as threat to Scotland's perceived status as a partner nation within the United Kingdom. The clearest, and best-known, example was provided by Winston Churchill in 1950. Addressing an election rally in Edinburgh, Churchill stated that, 'if England became an absolute Socialist State . . . ruled only by politicians and their officials in the London offices', then he did not believe that 'Scotland necessarily would be bound to accept such a dispensation'. For Churchill, a parliamentary majority was insufficient to justify the imposition of 'the serfdom of Socialism' on Scots: rather, such a 'fundamental' change to the terms of the Union 'would require a searching review' of 'historical relations' between Scotland and England. Churchill's solution was for voters to forestall the prospect of a constitutional rupture by rejecting socialism.[93] The willingness of Conservatives and Unionists to adopt such a position may appear surprising. Yet, as Colin Kidd has shown, for much of the twentieth century support for the Union was accompanied by an expectation that Scotland's distinctive constitutional traditions and institutions would be respected.[94] Equally, and as Unionists were keen to reiterate, the Conservative-led administrations of the inter-war period had promoted what would come to be termed 'administrative devolution', raising the status of the Secretary of State for Scotland to that of a Cabinet Minister in 1926, and rationalising and expanding the remit of the Scottish Office a decade later.[95]

That the centralised direction of the Scottish economy had the potential to provoke opposition of a type that might prove receptive to such an appeal to national identity had been evident prior to the 1945 general election. The wartime electoral truce included only those parties represented in the coalition government, providing the SNP with the opportunity to intervene in several by-elections and provide a vehicle for discontented voters. At the February 1944 contest in Kirkcaldy Burghs, the Labour nominee was challenged by Douglas Young, then the Chairman of the SNP; Young received more than forty per cent of the vote, an impressive achievement in the context of the SNP's previous electoral results. The following year, Robert McIntyre became the first SNP Member of Parliament when he defeated the Labour candidate at the April 1945 Motherwell by-election. The support received by the SNP at these contests proved fleeting; McIntyre would lose his seat less than three months later at the July 1945 general election. Still, the results suggested that a substantial number of voters were disillusioned with the performance of the coalition government, sentiments that appeared to be directed in particular towards the Labour Party. Striking too was the emphasis that the SNP placed upon individual liberty in this period, as opposed to a narrow focus on the constitution. During the Kirkcaldy campaign Young, a classicist whose standing in the SNP stemmed from his refusal to recognise the right of the UK government to conscript Scots and the periods of imprisonment that had followed, underscored what he portrayed as the threat posed to individual freedom by wartime regulations.[96] Young condemned 'the inefficient and ruthless methods of British bureaucracy and English Labour Party bosses', and lamented that Scots were, 'from the creche to the crematorium', being 'tied up in red-white-and-blue tape' by 'an alien absentee irresponsible bureaucracy in London', who dictated 'what we shall eat, what we shall drink, and what we shall put on, what we shall do and what we shall not do'.[97] In Motherwell, McIntyre called for a 'reversal of the policy of bureaucratic centralisation and interference by Government officials in our private lives', stressing that he did not support the use of 'Government-controlled relief agencies' to meet social needs.[98]

The improved performance of the SNP at wartime by-elections, while not heralding any sustained increase in nationalist support, did indicate the electoral potential of an appeal to Scottish identity, especially if it was framed in terms of protecting Scottish interests from the dictates of a distant London bureaucracy. Unionists and National Liberals adopted this approach enthusiastically after 1945; nevertheless, these efforts to play 'the Scottish card' were never entirely straightforward.[99] Support for Scottish autonomy had to be balanced with a foundational opposition to notions of legislative devolution or home rule; opposing nationalisation on the basis that it removed economic decision-making powers from Scotland was easy enough, but advocating policies to protect Scottish institutions from Westminster overreach was more challenging. Serious discussions among Unionists regarding constitutional questions began in 1946, when the party's MPs assembled to consider potential proposals for the 'decentralisation of Scottish affairs'. The meeting was called following the Glasgow Bridgeton by-election, which had taken place two months earlier. Held as a result of the death of the ILP figurehead James Maxton, the contest was dominated by the battle between the ILP and Labour, with the former ultimately triumphing. The Unionist candidate received little more than twenty per cent of the vote; the party had gained more than a third of the vote at the previous year's general election. For Unionists the result prompted a bout of introspection; of particular concern was the fact that the collapse in Unionist support appeared to have been almost entirely due to the intervention of Wendy Wood, who polled fourteen per cent running as an Independent Scottish Nationalist.[100] Unionists concluded that the result had stemmed from a failure to exploit popular discontent with the impact of the 'Socialist schemes for nationalisation' in Scotland. The immediate need, it was felt, was to address the perception that Unionists had 'no detailed policy towards administration in Scotland'. But if there was a recognition that there needed to be 'a declaration of Unionist policy for Scotland', deciding what this policy should be proved more difficult. Indeed, the only decision reached at the meeting was negative, with those present reaffirming their opposition to any form of home rule. Instead, a sub-committee was established to explore the practicality of further measures of administrative devolution.[101]

The sub-committee began work almost immediately.[102] Legislative devolution was again rejected at the outset; rather, the recommendations that were produced in early 1947 were limited to increasing parliamentary scrutiny of Scottish affairs, creating additional junior ministerial posts at the Scottish Office, and raising the pay and status of civil servants in Edinburgh.[103] In general, these proposals were welcomed by senior Conservative figures, although the suggested pay rise for Scottish civil servants was rejected. Churchill and his deputy, Anthony Eden, were confident that a recognition of Scottish national sentiment could be combined with a broader anti-socialist rhetoric.[104] Despite this approval from the parliamentary leadership, however, Unionists remained unsure as to how to marry a discrete pitch to Scottish voters with the party's more general opposition to the Labour government. Indeed, Patrick Blair and John Cranna, secretaries of the Unionist Party's Eastern and Western Divisional Councils respectively, reported that party activists were concerned that highlighting constitutional questions risked distracting from the principal task of warning the electorate of the dangers of socialism.[105]

The central difficulty for Unionists was an engrained scepticism within the party towards the idea of a devolved Scottish assembly. From its roots in debates over Ireland, by the 1940s Unionist distrust of home rule had evolved into a more general antipathy towards reforming Scotland's constitutional position within the UK.[106] This opposition rested upon three claims. First, Unionists rejected the idea that the Northern Irish experience of devolution had any relevance for Scotland. The Stormont Parliament had, Unionists asserted, been created to reinforce the Union in the north following partition in 1921; there was no prospect of it becoming a focal point for separatist sentiments, as might occur in Scotland. Second, there was a concern that legislative devolution would entail introducing a further layer of government at a time when Unionists were arguing for a reduction in bureaucracy and state control. Lastly, and decisively, Unionists feared that any devolved assembly would soon return a Labour majority; proportional representation could be not countenanced as a safeguard, since it would risk triggering a revival in Liberal fortunes.

Unionist appeals to Scottish identity had, then, to remain principally rhetorical. Still, efforts were made to demonstrate that the party's stance was consistent. One approach was to maintain that home rule would fail to deliver real autonomy for Scotland, since any Labour members would, in any case, unthinkingly implement policies drafted in London.[107] As Alan Gomme Duncan argued, since Labour representatives would be 'controlled by Transport House whether they sat in London or Edinburgh', the issue was ideological rather than constitutional.[108] Unionists also sought at times to distinguish between the legislative and executive arms of the state; in rhetorical and geographical terms, this was symbolised by the difference between Westminster and Whitehall, with the threat to Scotland alleged to emanate from the growing power of the latter. From this perspective, legislative devolution offered little protection from the excesses of an increasingly influential central bureaucracy, what was required was an unwinding of the powers accrued by government and a UK-wide programme of decentralisation. Patrick Blair reasoned that the 'increasing administrative dictatorship' exercised 'from London' would be best countered by devolving management of the nationalised industries and returning powers to local councils; there was no need for a separate parliament, which would be little more than a 'glorified county council'.[109]

The trepidation with which Unionists viewed the prospect of home rule ensured that the party's position on the constitution evolved largely in response to external pressures. The modest proposals issued by the sub-committee in early 1947 were only augmented as a result of the growing prominence of Scottish Convention, the cross-party organisation initiated by John MacCormick in order to campaign for Scottish home rule. Established in 1942 when MacCormick exited the SNP, the party he had helped found, Scottish Convention garnered public attention with a series of National Assemblies, which began in March 1947 and culminated in October 1949 with the launch of the Covenant, a mass petition designed to demonstrate overwhelming public support for a Scottish Parliament.[110] Scottish Convention's pressure prompted the Labour government to produce a White Paper on Scottish affairs that recommended reforms to parliamentary procedure, as well as the convening of a Scottish Economic Conference.[111] As a result, it became imperative for the Unionists to address in a more convincing manner the issue of Scotland's relationship with Westminster. In March 1948, for example, Kinross and West Perthshire Unionist Association called on the party to issue a policy statement dealing with the constitutional issue 'as a matter of urgency'.[112]

A short document was issued in 1948; however, it was not until the following year that a more detailed policy appeared. In May 1949, at a Unionist rally at Glasgow Rangers' Ibrox Stadium, Winston Churchill addressed an audience of 20,000 supporters. Identifying a commitment to Scottish particularism with opposition to socialism, Churchill claimed that nationalisation, while dangerous in general, was especially damaging in Scotland, where it shackled 'not only prosperity' but also 'the independence that Scotland has exercised in so many fields'. There was, Churchill contended in comments that foreshadowed those he would make at the 1950 general election, 'no sharper challenge to Scottish national sentiment' than that posed 'by the Socialism of Whitehall'. To this threat he contrasted the Unionist promise to halt, and in some cases reverse, nationalisation; further, Churchill hinted that where industries remained in public ownership, separate Scottish management structures would be created. He concluded with a clear instruction to those present: 'the quickest and surest way for the people of Scotland to regain a proper control over their own affairs', he stated, was 'to dismiss the Socialists from public office'.[113]

Churchill's set-piece appearance had been preceded by the annual Unionist conference, which was held earlier the same day. Here Churchill's deference to Scottish identity, and rhetorical vilification of Whitehall, had been anticipated. D. W. Duncan, Chairman of the Stirling and Falkirk Burghs Unionist Association, had summarised what he believed were the options open to Scots now that they were confronted with a majority Labour government: to continue to be treated as a 'marginal land', administered by 'well-meaning gentlemen in London'; to campaign for independence alongside the SNP; or, in Duncan's preferred option, to seek greater autonomy for Scotland within the Union. 'England and Scotland', he stated in a revealing comparison, 'should be regarded as a business partnership. In a partnership they pooled their finance, brains and energies, but they did not ask the other partner to come in and run their domestic and family affairs'. Duncan's assessment drew widespread support, and it was agreed that a revised policy statement would be produced.[114]

This statement, *Scottish Control of Scottish Affairs*, arrived in November 1949, with publication brought forward to meet the challenge posed by the launch of the Covenant campaign the previous month.[115] The statement opened with a declaration that the Union of 1707 had been intended as a partnership of equals: 'Union', it was stressed, 'is strength . . . but Union is not amalgamation'; Scotland remained unquestionably 'a nation'. And while home rule was once again dismissed as an option, the growing authority of Whitehall in Scotland was decried as an 'unnatural state of affairs', one produced by a socialist ideology that denied 'individuality either in men or in nations'. The statement promised a range of measures, including the appointment of new Minister of State and an additional Under-Secretary of State at the Scottish Office, the latter to be a member of the House of Lords, the establishment of a Royal Commission to examine Scotland's constitutional status, and increased protections for local government.[116]

By the close of the 1940s, Unionists had seemingly alighted on an idiom that fused a sympathy for Scottish sentiments with the defence of individual liberty that underpinned the party's appeal across Britain. If this commitment to defending Scottish interests had been constructed rather hastily, the underlying distrust of bureaucracy nonetheless provided a credible justification for Unionism's unwillingness to consider the option of home rule. Unionists and Liberals were, to be sure, the primary audience for this rhetoric; it can, however, be ventured that the willingness of the Unionists to give voice to fears that the arrival of socialism would see the Scottish nation subsumed into a homogenous British state was a factor in ensuring that the SNP was an electoral irrelevance in this period. As the popular support for the Covenant campaign revealed, a strong sense of national identity was certainly present in post-war Scotland. But the position of the SNP during the 1940s and 1950s was a curious one. While the party believed, unsurprisingly, in self-government for Scotland, and had, at least since the rift in 1942 that had triggered MacCormick's departure, understood this as the creation of a sovereign, independent Scottish state, the mid-century SNP adopted an intensely individualist stance, building upon the positions the party had adopted during the Second World War. The post-1945 nationalist worldview was haunted by similar fears of a drift towards totalitarianism as informed Unionism's anti-socialism.[117] At times, this outlook was expressed in predictable ways, as when the SNP expressed disapproval of nationalisation and called for the traditional independence of local government to be defended. Yet the nationalist embrace of individualism could go further: in 1946, the nationalist newspaper, the *Scots Independent*, reprinted lengthy excerpts from Hayek's *Road to Serfdom* in its editorial column.[118] Such libertarian leanings were enhanced by the empathy that many leading figures within the SNP, most notably Robert McIntyre, felt for the small nations of eastern Europe that had been occupied by the Soviet Union after 1945, a development that fostered anti-communist sentiments. Self-government was, in consequence, often envisioned in near-instrumental terms, as a buttress against a Labour government believed to harbour authoritarian tendencies. As the SNP's 1947 policy statement argued, the conflict between capitalism and socialism had been rendered meaningless by the triumph of the state, whatever label it assumed. The task now was to defend individual freedom and the rule of law, and to resist the rise of a 'despotism ruling over an irresponsible proletariat': Scots must choose 'either the road to tyranny or the way to freedom'.[119]

Yet the fundamental contest in Scottish politics after 1945 was between collectivism and individualism; constitutional questions occupied a subordinate position. As was the case for the Liberals, this hierarchy imposed a basic limitation on the potential appeal of the SNP: if, setting incredulity aside, socialism really was as dangerous as alleged, if a British form of totalitarianism really was a plausible prospect, then surely only the Unionists offered a realistic means of removing Labour from office. Political sentiments and rhetoric that might, in a different context, have encouraged support for Scottish nationalism became, accordingly, secondary elements within Unionism's anti-socialism. This was most apparent at the February 1948 Paisley by-election, which saw John MacCormick, then in the midst of the Scottish Convention campaigns, confront the Labour candidate Douglas Johnston. MacCormick, by now a member of the Liberal Party, stood unsuccessfully as a 'National' candidate, maintaining that he had been able to unite Unionists, Liberals and nationalists on a shared platform of opposition to centralisation and support for home rule. MacCormick claimed that the use of the 'National' label demonstrated the cross-party appeal of his constitutional vision and even suggested that the Paisley contest had hinted at the potential for a broader realignment of Scottish politics on the question of home rule. For MacCormick, this prospect had been stymied only by the refusal of the Liberal hierarchy to abandon their attachment to obsolete party labels and support his candidacy.[120] Yet, as Michael Dyer has noted, the final say lay in reality with the Unionists, who, not content with 'consuming the remnants of Scottish Liberalism' had also co-opted 'the most significant figure in the Scottish national-ist cause'.[121] Certainly, the platform agreed by the joint committee sup-porting MacCormick's candidacy granted greater space to criticisms of the 'tyranny of State Socialism' than to constitutional questions.[122] Nevertheless, while Dyer views Paisley as marking the end of the infor-mal alliances that had characterised relations on the centre-right prior to 1945, and the reassertion of partisan divides, the contest might equally be viewed as suggesting the continued suppleness and flexibility of the Unionists, and their willingness to support informal anti-Labour alli-ances where appropriate. Revealingly, when endorsing MacCormick, the Unionist Western Divisional Council referred to him as the 'anti-Socialist', and not the 'National', candidate.[123]

UNIONISM IN OFFICE AND THE LIBERAL REVIVAL

In a Scottish context the 1951 general election, which saw the Conservatives return to power at a UK level, confirmed the continued viability of an electoral appeal founded upon anti-socialism. Still, the transition from opposition to office presented challenges for the Unionists and their National Liberal allies: the stringency of the individualist lan-guage which had been used to attack the Labour Party was always likely to prove difficult to sustain once in government. Nevertheless, some electoral commitments were delivered: the iron and steel industries were returned to the private sector, and Labour's proposals for the nationali-sation of road haulage were abandoned; there were reductions in income tax and rationing was abolished in 1954. Taken together, such measures could be presented as evidence that the government had kept its prom-ises 'to restore freedom, to reduce the burden of taxation and to give individual men and women a better chance to live a decent life'.[124] In Scotland, Unionists could point to the fulfilment of many of the prom-ises of extra protections for Scottish autonomy made in the 1949 policy statement: additional ministers were allocated to the Scottish Office, and a Royal Commission on Scottish Affairs commenced work in 1952.[125]

For the Conservative and Unionist leadership, however, this approached the limits of the possible: further dismantling of the nationalised industries, or shrinking of the welfare state, presented too great a political risk.

Initially, this approach appeared to satisfy Unionist opinion. A little more than a year after the 1951 election, for example, the *Perthshire Advertiser* praised the new administration for demonstrating their 'intention to abolish costly and unnecessary controls'; while only 'a beginning' had 'been made in this direction', the *Advertiser* welcomed 'the fresh wind of freedom' it detected 'in these islands'.[126] Indeed, in the early to mid-1950s, Unionist and National Liberal electioneering was dominated by claims that the socialist threat had been repelled, even if these declarations were accompanied by stern warnings that any Labour revival 'would mean a return to rationing and to the theory that the man in Whitehall knows what is best for you.'[127] The increased majority achieved by the Conservatives and Unionists at the 1955 general election demonstrated that this rhetoric retained its political effectiveness.

But such triumphs masked a growing sense of frustration amongst activists and voters on the political right who believed that the government had been too cautious, especially in avoiding confronting the trades unions, who, it was believed, were pursuing inflationary wage demands.[128] In Scotland, grumblings that the government had failed to act swiftly enough to undo the economic settlement inherited from the outgoing Labour government, and, in particular, to reduce the influence enjoyed by the trade unions, surfaced within months of the 1951 victory. In April 1952 Patrick Blair, in his capacity as the Unionist Party's Political Secretary, recorded complaints from party members to the effect 'that too much [was] being done for the working classes'; the following year, he reported widespread demands for 'more evidence of the intention to reduce the government's expenditure of the taxpayer's money'.[129] These grievances were aired with greater frequency after the 1955 victory, seemingly interpreted by some within the party as having provided a mandate for more radical reforms. In October 1955, Blair advised that there was a pervasive 'feeling' within the party that the government had not demonstrated a sufficient commitment to reducing public expenditure; many Unionist supporters felt, he warned, that the government was 'too much afraid of voters who will not support it anyhow at any time', and was doing 'too little' to assist 'the really stabilising element of the population', the salaried middle classes. Unionist voters, Blair stated, were beginning 'to say that it does not matter which party is in office – they are equally bad'.[130] It is unclear how widespread such sentiments were, nor how heavy was Blair's editorial hand; equally, these criticisms need to be considered in the context of the 1950s, and not viewed merely as evidence of early instances of 'Thatcherite' tendencies. Nevertheless, the comments relayed by Blair remain revealing, suggesting as they do that perceptions of a 'consensus' between the national leaderships of the major parties, and the unease this generated on the political right, was not just a product of the political atmosphere of the 1970s but were in fact embedded within Scottish and British politics from the very creation of the welfare state. By 1956, Blair was informing his colleagues that Unionist voters were demanding further reductions in the tax burden and in the level of government spending, amid 'complaints' that inflation was leading to the 'slow torture of the middle classes'; there were accounts of supporters threatening to abstain at the next election, or, worse, vote Liberal.[131] As the annual report of the party's Western Divisional Council noted that year, the challenges facing the 'Middle Classes' were being 'frequently and vigorously stressed'.[132] By July 1956, the Unionist President, William Sinclair, was protesting that he 'found himself continually defending the Government not against recognised opponents but against declared Unionist Electors, some of whom were threatening to withdraw their support from the Party'. This anger, Sinclair made clear, was driven by concerns over 'the cost of living, inflation and the lack of resistance to Trade Union demands for more and more wages not covered by corresponding increases in production'.[133]

The most visible short-term result of this discontent on the political right was the arrival of the Middle Class Alliance (MCA) and the People's League for the Defence of Freedom (PLDF), pressure groups that called for reductions in public spending, with the savings to be used to fund tax cuts, and, in the case of the PLDF, for the removal of the legal privileges enjoyed by the trades unions. This 'middle-class revolt' has been considered from a British perspective, primarily in the context of the Liberal revival in the late 1950s, confirmed by the party's victory at the March 1958 Torrington by-election.[134] The emergence of the MCA and PLDF have, when placed alongside the January 1958 Treasury resignations, when the Chancellor Peter Thorneycroft and two junior treasury ministers, Nigel Birch and Enoch Powell, quit in protest at the Cabinet's refusal to pursue deflationary spending cuts, been viewed as a premonition of the central role that inflation would come to play in British politics by the 1970s.[135] The presence that the MCA and PLDF enjoyed in Scotland should encourage a similar reconsideration of Scottish politics in the 1950s, and an examination of the political divisions created by the post-war reforms; the Unionist leadership were certainly concerned that the energies of party members were being dissipated by participation in these organisations.[136] Blair instructed Unionists that they should not be misled by the combative position adopted by the PLDF: he dismissed that organisation's demand that trades unions be made liable for losses caused by industrial action, cautioning that such a policy would create a 'tremendous surge of ill-feeling' that would damage the party's electoral position. Yet Blair was sure to reassure Unionists that the government was still trying its utmost 'to arrest inflation and maintain the value of money'.[137]

By the second half of the 1950s, however, it was proving ever harder to reconcile the pragmatism of the party hierarchy with the animosity towards state intervention and organised labour evident among Unionist and National Liberal voters. As a result, the anti-socialist coalition instituted in the late 1940s began to crumble, facilitating a return of independent Liberalism. Between 1957 and 1959 the return of independent Liberal candidates at by-elections in seats not contested by the party since 1950 split the previously unified anti-Labour vote; while there was no Scottish echo of Torrington, the Unionist share of the vote slumped by between fifteen and twenty-five percentage points at the contests in Edinburgh South, Argyll, Aberdeenshire East, and Galloway, each time as a result of Liberal intervention. In March 1958, Glasgow Kelvingrove was lost to Labour, largely due to the presence of an independent Liberal. The humiliation of the Suez crisis, which ended the career of Anthony Eden, Churchill's successor as Prime Minister, was no doubt partly responsible for the fall in Unionist support in this period, but there were other determinants. At Edinburgh South in May 1957, the Liberal candidate secured almost a quarter of the vote; the Unionist post-mortem attributed this result to 'disgruntlement' among 'middle-class voters' and a 'feeling that [the] government was not sufficiently Tory', a reference, presumably, to the failure of the government to pursue further economic reforms.[138] This was the conclusion reached by Lord John Hope, a junior minister at the Scottish Office and the MP for Edinburgh Pentlands. While Hope accepted that the 'cost of living' was an issue, he nonetheless suggested that 'something else' had caused 'discontent' to 'develop into anger'. There was, he sensed, 'a widespread feeling that the only people who had been insulated against rises in the cost of living were the people who had caused it – the Trades Unionists with their endless wage demands'.[139] Comparable sentiments were visible elsewhere: in a letter to the Conservative Chairman Lord Hailsham composed in early 1958, Gordon Murray, secretary of Dundee Unionist and National Liberal Association, recorded local support for the recently departed Treasury ministers, and expressed his hope that the 'prosperity of the country [would] not be jeopardised in pandering to unjust and unrealistic demands, from whatever section they may come'.[140]

The policy platform espoused by the Liberal Party in this period is also suggestive. Jo Grimond, the MP for Orkney and Shetland who assumed the party leadership in 1956, steered the Liberals towards offering a progressive alternative to Labour's state socialism.[141] All the same, Grimond's defence of individual liberty, hostility towards nationalisation and the welfare state, and support for further reductions in personal taxation, represented a refashioning of post-war anti-socialism and individualism rather than a rejection of it. Revealingly, Conservatives and Unionists found themselves attacked by Liberals for having failed to deliver on the promises they had made a decade earlier: Liberals accused the Conservatives of having been too timid, too willing to accept the mixed economy inherited from Labour. Grimond complained that the Conservatives had only been 'conserving Socialism', and had failed to undo the excessive taxes and government spending he believed to be the 'most damaging legacy of Socialism'. To those who suggested that a vote for the Liberals would allow Labour to regain power, Grimond offered his own early interpretation of the notion of a post-war consensus, retorting that 'surely there is no point in keeping a Conservative Government in power unless it is going to be something different *in kind* from a Socialist Government'.[142]

Such rhetoric was, it may be assumed, intended to appeal principally to disgruntled Unionist supporters. It met with some success: in May 1958 there were reports from Unionist agents across Scotland of a Liberal revival driven by a suspicion that the government was 'pandering too much to Socialism' with the result that 'too much is being spent on the Welfare State'.[143] At the June 1958 Argyllshire by-election, the Liberal candidate William McKean, who secured almost thirty per cent of the vote, told the public that, although new to the Liberal Party, 'he felt he must take a stand now against the two major parties. If we did not the individual would be crushed'. He offered a programme of tax cuts and restrictions on public and private monopolies. Speaking in his support John Bannerman, the Chairman of the Scottish Liberal Party, reaffirmed McKean's individualism, declaring that his party would return the state to its proper role as 'servant of the people', and would always 'look to the individual's interest'.[144]

The first signs of growing support for the SNP were, at least in hindsight, also visible in the second half of the 1950s. While the party remained on the margins of Scottish politics, fielding only two candidates at the

1955 general election, Robert McIntyre had finished second that year in Unionist-held Perth and East Perthshire, receiving almost a quarter of the vote, and outpolling the Labour candidate. As the 1959 general election approached, there was a growing recognition among local Unionist associations that the SNP was beginning to offer a more serious challenge than in the past, especially in parts of rural and provincial central Scotland, areas where the party would eventually enjoy some electoral success during the 1970s.[145] Significantly, the SNP's blend of individualism and nationalism survived the 1950s largely intact, finding an outlet in criticisms of the welfare state, which, from a nationalist perspective, appeared to be little more than a bribe intended to induce loyalty to the British state.[146] The SNP's 1957 conference programme duly dismissed the post-war settlement as 'a mass of taxes designed to make the individual look to the state for his needs'; policies that appeared to be motivated by compassion were in truth just 'a vote-catching fraud'. The SNP, in contrast, promoted 'independence for the individual Scottish citizen as well as for the Scottish nation'.[147]

CONCLUSION

In the years following the Second World War, Scottish Unionists assembled a successful electoral coalition held together by a shared opposition to what was understood as the threat posed by socialism. By the 1950 general election much of the ground lost to the Labour Party five years earlier had been recovered; at the 1951 and 1955 contests the Unionists, with National Liberal support, emerged as the pre-eminent political party in Scotland. Unionist anti-socialism was an instrument that, viewed cynically, was intended to exploit opposition to nationalisation and rationing, and fears that the Labour Party posed a threat to Scotland's privileged position within the Union. But the nature of the socialist threat conjured by Unionists was not necessarily easy to control, or to contain; in practice, the division between economic and constitutional questions was difficult to uphold, and it was not always clear whether it was only Labour administrations that needed to be opposed, or whether all attempts to govern Scotland from a distance were suspect. Unionist condemnations of centralised bureaucracy and of government from Whitehall relied upon essential criticisms of Scotland's constitutional position that could, were circumstances to change, be levelled at future Conservative governments.

It was in the late 1950s that Unionism's monopoly over such a critique first began to loosen. The record of the Conservative government returned to office in 1951 had, unsurprisingly, failed to match the heights of the party's rhetoric in opposition. Equally, the Liberal revival after 1955, however limited and lacking in parliamentary success, suggested that the longer the Unionists and National Liberals remained in government, the more that other parties might be able to deploy the very language of liberal individualism that had been so central to the party's electoral success in the early 1950s. What followed was a fragmenting, gradual at first, of the post-war anti-socialist alliance. While the results of the 1959 general election were not disastrous for the Unionists, and the feared Liberal revival did not materialise, the party surrendered four seats to the Labour Party, a performance that contrasted with the outcome in England, where a strong Conservative performance ensured that the party was returned to office with an increased majority. In retrospect, 1959 might be said to have marked the beginning of Unionist decline in Scotland, and, conversely, the establishment of a Labour ascendancy in Scotland that would last for the remainder of the twentieth century. But this was not the inevitable outcome of social and economic differences between Scotland and England. Rather, as will become apparent, the Unionist response to this initial electoral setback helped to shape the ensuing realignment of Scottish politics by creating the conditions in which other parties could adopt, and adapt, an appeal to individual liberty and a critique of distant and unfeeling bureaucracies.

NOTES

1. On politics during the Second World War, see: Harvie, 'Labour and Scottish government' and 'Labour in Scotland during the Second World War'. A suggestive assessment of post-war political culture can be found in: Hutchison, 'The Scottish Young Conservatives: A Local Case Study'.
2. Cameron, *Impaled upon a Thistle*, p. 263.
3. On the changing nature of inter-war politics, see: Knox and McKinlay, 'The Remaking of Labour'; Lawrence, *Electing our Masters*, Chapter 4; Beers, *Your Britain*; Petrie, *Popular Politics and Political Culture*.
4. Edgerton, *The Rise and Fall of the British Nation*.
5. Mitchell, *Conservatives and the Union*, pp. 48–50; Cragoe, 'We like local patriotism'; Torrance, 'Standing up for Scotland'.
6. Greenleaf, 'Modern British Conservatism', pp. 181–2; Greenleaf, *The British Political Tradition, II: The Ideological Heritage*, pp. 263–346.
7. See: Ramsden, *Age of Churchill and Eden*, pp. 166–76; Green, *The Ideologies of Conservatism*, pp. 192–239.
8. Finlayson and Martin, 'It Ain't What You Say . . .', p. 451.

9. National Library of Scotland (NLS) Acc. 10424/54: Notes on Meeting of the Scottish Unionist Association (SUA) Central Council, 27 Feb. 1942.
10. On Elliot, see: Ward, *Unionism in the United Kingdom*, pp. 21–40.
11. NLS Acc. 10424/54: Notes on Meeting of the SUA Central Council, 27 Feb. 1942.
12. Cameron, *Impaled upon a Thistle*, pp. 163–8.
13. NLS Acc. 10424/64: SUA Central Council Minutes, 30 Oct. 1942. Capitalisation in original.
14. Thorpe, *Parties at War*, Chapter 5.
15. Bodleian Library (Bod. Lib.) Conservative Party Archive (CPA) Scottish Unionist Members' Committee (SUMC) 1/46: SUA Western Divisional Council, Meeting of Constituency Chairmen, 17 Mar. 1944. Capitalisation in original.
16. Toye, 'Winston Churchill's "Crazy Broadcast"'.
17. For accounts that stress Hayek's influence on the Conservative campaign, which came seemingly via the party Chairman, Ralph Assheton, see: Cockett, *Thinking the Unthinkable*, pp. 91–9; Green, *The Ideologies of Conservatism*, pp. 219–20. For a more sceptical reading, see: Freeman, 'Reconsidering "Set the People Free"'.
18. McKibbin, 'Class and Conventional Wisdom'; Jarvis, 'British Conservatism and Class Politics in the 1920s'.
19. Bod. Lib. CPA Published and Printed Material: Notes for Speakers and Workers 1945, p. 19. Capitalisation in original.
20. Perth and Kinross Council Archives (PKCA) MS 152/2/4/1: *General Election 1945, Kinross and West Perthshire Division: William McNair Snadden, Unionist & National Government Candidate*. Snadden had represented the seat since 1938.
21. NLS Acc. 11368/68: *To the Electors of Perth Parliamentary Division: Colonel Alan Gomme Duncan, Unionist Candidate*. Capitalisation in original.
22. NLS Acc. 11884/1: *General Election 1945 North Aberdeen: Priscilla Grant*. Capitalisation in original.
23. For some influential interpretations, see: Addison, *The Road to 1945*; Ramsden, 'A Party for Owners or a Party for Earners?'; Lowe, 'The Second World War, Consensus and the Foundation of the Welfare State'; Kavanagh, 'The Post-War Consensus'.
24. Conservative and Unionist Central Office, *The Industrial Charter*.
25. Harrison, 'The Rise, Fall and Rise of Political Consensus'.
26. Zweiniger-Bargielowska, 'Rationing, Austerity and the Conservative Recovery after 1945'; Jones, 'A Bloodless Counter-Revolution'; Green, 'The Conservative Party, the State and the Electorate, 1945–1964'.
27. Green, *The Ideologies of Conservatism*, p. 220. For a considered critique of this stance, see: McKibbin, *Parties and People*, pp. 164–76.
28. On this approach, see: Smyth, 'Resisting Labour'; Cameron, *Impaled upon a Thistle*, pp. 163–8; Petrie, 'Contests of Vital Importance'.

29. PKCA MS 152/2/1/3: Kinross and West Perthshire Unionist Association Minutes, 30 Nov. 1946. Capitalisation in original.
30. PKCA MS 152/2/1/3: Kinross and West Perthshire Unionist Association Minutes, 27 Nov. 1948. Capitalisation in original.
31. *Grangemouth Advertiser*, 12 Dec. 1948.
32. *Grangemouth Advertiser*, 24 Jul. 1948.
33. Cowling, *The Impact of Labour*, p. 5.
34. NLS Acc. 10424/27: SUA Western Divisional Council, *Annual Report: 1948*, pp. 2–3. Capitalisation in original.
35. *Stirling Journal*, 11 Nov. 1948. As Lord Dunglass, Douglas-Home had served as the MP for Lanark between 1931 and 1945; he would regain the seat at the 1950 general election, before entering the House of Lords the following year after succeeding his father as the Earl of Home.
36. Bod. Lib. CPA PUB 229/1/10: *Gorbals Division Parliamentary by-election 30 September 1948: Election Address of Willis Roxburgh*.
37. *Aberdeen Press and Journal*, 17 Feb. 1950.
38. NLS Acc. 11884/5: *Aberdeen South Parliamentary Election 1950: The Unionist Candidate, Lady Tweedsmuir*. Capitalisation in original. Buchan had contested Aberdeen North in 1945 under her previous surname of Grant.
39. *Stirling Observer*, 23 Oct. 1951.
40. University of Aberdeen Archives (UAA) MS 3179/10/6/4: Aberdeen North Unionist Association, *North Aberdeen Gleanings*, 1 Nov. 1946.
41. NLS Acc. 11884/5: *Lady Tweedsmuir: 'Vote for me and I shall work for you'* (Aberdeen, 1950). Capitalisation in original.
42. University of Dundee Archives (UDA) MS 270/1/12: Dundee Unionist Association Minutes, 26 Apr. 1946. Capitalisation in original.
43. NLS Acc. 11765/48: *6 Questions that concern you* (n.d. 1947–8).
44. Falkirk Council Archives (FCA) A1703/2: Stirling and Falkirk Burghs Unionist Association Minutes, 28 Mar. 1951.
45. Cameron, *Impaled upon a Thistle*, pp. 167–8.
46. UAA MS 3179/10/6/4: Aberdeen North Unionist Association, *North Aberdeen Gleanings*, 1 Dec. 1946. Capitalisation in original.
47. NLS Acc. 11884/5: Lady Tweedsmuir, Campaign Notes, 1950. Capitalisation in original.
48. *Falkirk Herald*, 27 Nov. 1948.
49. NLS Acc. 11884/5: Lady Tweedsmuir, *Notes on Nationalisation: General Election 1950*, pp. 1–2.
50. Williamson, 'The Trade Disputes and Trade Unions Act 1927 Reconsidered'.
51. Bod. Lib. CPA PUB 229/1/10: *Stirling and Falkirk Burghs by-election, 7 October 1948: Election address of Lt. Col. William Forbes, the Unionist Candidate*. Capitalisation in original.
52. Zweiniger-Bargielowska, *Austerity in Britain*, pp. 203–55.
53. Bod. Lib. CPA Conservative Central Office (CCO) 2/2/18: Scottish Intelligence Reports, Jul. 1950 and Feb. and Apr. 1951.

54. NLS Acc. 11884/5: Lady Tweedsmuir, Political Notes for 1946 by-election, 'The Closed Shop'.
55. Bod. Lib. CPA PUB 229/1/10A: *A personal word from Robert Allan, the Unionist candidate, to the electors of West Dunbartonshire* (1950). Capitalisation in original.
56. *Falkirk Herald*, 31 Mar. 1951.
57. On the lineage of this critique, see: Freeman, 'Reconsidering "Set the People Free"'.
58. Bod. Lib. CPA CCO 2/1/18: Memorandum from Colonel Blair to Candidates and Election Agents in Scotland, 13 Feb. 1950.
59. NLS Acc. 11884/7: Lady Tweedsmuir Papers, *The Socialist Party: General Election 1951*, pp. 2 and 5. Capitalisation in original.
60. On inter-war anti-socialism, see: McKibbin, *Parties and People*, Chapter 2. For the Scottish context, see: Hutchison, 'Scottish Unionism between the two world wars'.
61. Cairncross, *Years of Recovery*, pp. 393–9.
62. Tomlinson, *Democratic Socialism and Economic Policy*, pp. 174–8.
63. PKCA MS 152/2/1/3: Kinross and West Perthshire Unionist Association Minutes, 29 Nov. 1947.
64. Bod. Lib. CPA PUB 229/1/10: *Parliamentary by-election 1948, Camlachie Parliamentary Division: Charles S. McFarlane, Unionist Candidate.*
65. McFarlane polled 395 votes more than the Labour candidate; Annie Maxton, the ILP candidate, received over 1,600 votes.
66. Bod. Lib. CPA PUB 229/1/10: *Parliamentary by-election 1948, Camlachie Division: The Candidature of Annie Maxton*. Capitalisation in original. Maxton was the sister of James Maxton, the former leader of the ILP and MP for Glasgow Bridgeton, who had died two years earlier.
67. Bod. Lib. CPA PUB 229/1/10: *A message to the electors of Camlachie from Robert Blair Wilkie MA, Scottish National Candidate.*
68. Bod. Lib. CPA PUB: *General Election 1950: The Campaign Guide*, pp. 12–13 and 162–7; *General Election 1951: The Campaign Guide*, pp. 94–102.
69. Ramsden, *Age of Churchill and Eden*, pp. 197–205.
70. NLS Acc. 11368/4: SUA Central Council (CC) Minutes, 2 Sept. 1947. Capitalisation in original.
71. The only full-length study is: Dutton, *Liberals in Schism*.
72. Hutchison, *Scottish Politics in the Twentieth Century*, pp. 76–9.
73. From 1947 until 1956 John Maclay served as National Liberal Chairman; Maclay was succeeded by James Duncan, MP for South Angus, James Henderson-Stewart, MP for East Fife, and Colin Thornton-Kemsley, who represented North Angus and Mearns. The east coast bias should also be noted.
74. MacDonald, *Whaur Extremes Meet*, p. 205.
75. Green, 'The Conservative Party, the State and the Electorate, 1945–1964', p. 192.

76. UDA MS 309/2/2/3/1: South Angus Unionist and National Liberal Association, Forfar Branch Minute Book, 9 Sept. and 11 Nov. 1949.
77. Bod. Lib. CPA CCO 4/3/43: George Ramsay to Lord Woolton, 27 Nov. 1949.
78. NLS Acc. 11765/45: Scottish Liberal Party, *Annual Report of the Executive Committee, 1946–1947*, pp. 3-4.
79. NLS Acc. 11765/56: Scottish Liberal Party, Executive Committee Minutes, 23 May 1946.
80. UAA MS 3179/10/6/2/1: Scottish Liberal Party, Executive Committee Minutes, 30 Jan. 1946.
81. PKCA MS 152/2/1/3: Kinross and West Perthshire Unionist Association Minutes, 31 Jan. 1947.
82. UDA MS 270/1/1/2: Dundee Unionist Association Minutes, 10 Feb., 30 Mar. and 24 Sept. 1948, 25 Nov. 1949.
83. *Dundee Courier and Advertiser*, 31 Jan., 3 and 7 Feb. 1950. On the phenomenon of the housewives' groups, see: Hinton, 'Militant Housewives'.
84. *Aberdeen Press and Journal*, 15 Oct. 1951.
85. Dyer, 'The Evolution of the Centre-Right and the State of Scottish Conservatism'.
86. The Liberal Party contested 475 seats in 1950 compared to 306 in 1945.
87. *The Scotsman*, 11 Feb. 1950.
88. *Aberdeen Press and Journal*, 17 and 23 Feb. 1950.
89. In Scotland, the Liberals did gain Orkney and Shetland, and Roxburgh and Selkirkshire, both from the Unionists.
90. Bod Lib. CPA CCO 2/2/18: *Scottish Intelligence Summary*, Jul. 1950. Capitalisation in original.
91. Bod. Lib. CPA SUMC 2/5: Minutes, 24 Jul. 1951.
92. See the list in: Bod. Lib. CPA CCO 4/3/319: *A United Front Against Socialism*, 16 Apr. 1951.
93. *The Scotsman*, 15 Feb. 1950. Capitalisation in original.
94. Kidd, *Union and Unionisms*, especially Chapter 1.
95. Mitchell, *Devolution in the United Kingdom*, Chapter 2.
96. On Young, see: Pentland, 'Douglas Young'; Kidd, *Union and Unionisms*, pp. 293–5.
97. NLS Acc. 10090/17: *Douglas Young: To the Electors of Kirkcaldy Burghs* (1944).
98. NLS Acc. 10090/17: *Motherwell and Wishaw by-election: Robert McIntyre demands a Scottish Policy for Scotland* (1945).
99. Cameron, *Impaled upon a Thistle*, p. 272; Mitchell, *Devolution in the United Kingdom*, p. 25.
100. *The Scotsman*, 31 Aug. 1946. On Wood, a prominent activist in the independence movement, see her memoir *Yours sincerely for Scotland*.
101. Bod. Lib. CPA SUMC 1/11: Devolution of Scottish Affairs, 22 Oct. 1946. Capitalisation in original.

102. The committee was composed of eight members: seven Unionist MPs (William Darling, Tam Galbraith, Alan Gomme Duncan, James Hutchison, James Reid, William McNair Snadden and Arthur Young) and one member of the Lords (Lord Tweedsmuir).
103. Bod. Lib. CPA SUMC 1/51: Sub-Committee on Scottish Affairs, 30 Oct., 5, 14, 21 and 28 Nov. 1946, 27 Feb. 1947; CPA SUMC 1/11: Devolution of Scottish Affairs, 25 Feb. 1947.
104. Bod. Lib. CPA SUMC 1/11: Devolution of Scottish Affairs, 27 Feb. 1947; CPA SUMC 1/51: Sub-Committee on Scottish Affairs, 19 Mar., 1 Apr. and 7 May 1947.
105. Bod. Lib. CPA SUMC 1/11: Devolution of Scottish Affairs, 16 and 18 Jul. 1947.
106. Torrance, 'Standing up for Scotland', pp. 170–2; Burness, *Strange Associations*.
107. Scottish Unionist Association, *Scotland and the United Kingdom* (Edinburgh, 1948), pp. 16–18.
108. Bod. Lib. CPA SUMC 1/11: Special Meeting of the SUMC, 15 Feb. 1949. Transport House, located in London, housed the headquarters of both the Labour Party and the TUC.
109. Bod. Lib. CPA SUMC 1/11: Special Meeting of the SUMC, 15 Feb. 1949.
110. MacCormick, *The Flag in the Wind*, pp. 114–24; Levitt, 'Britain, the Scottish Covenant movement and Devolution'.
111. *Scottish Affairs* (Cmnd. 7308, 1948).
112. PKCA MS 152/2/1/3: Kinross and West Perthshire Unionist Association, 27 Mar. 1948.
113. *The Scotsman*, 21 May 1949. Capitalisation in original.
114. *The Scotsman*, 21 May 1949.
115. Bod. Lib. CPA SUMC: Minutes, 18 Oct., 1 and 15 Nov. 1949.
116. Scottish Unionist Association, *Scottish Control of Scottish Affairs* (Edinburgh, 1949), pp. 1–2.
117. On SNP ideology in this period, see: Jackson, *The Case for Scottish Independence*, pp. 16–34.
118. *Scots Independent*, Dec. 1946, p. 4.
119. *Aims and Policy of the SNP* (Glasgow, 1947), p. 3.
120. MacCormick, *The Flag in the Wind*, p. 119. MacCormick's candidacy was supported by local Liberals, but not by the Liberal Party leadership.
121. Dyer, 'A Nationalist in the Churchillian Sense', pp. 287 and 307.
122. Bod Lib. CPA PUB 229/1/10: *Parliamentary Burghs of Paisley, Parliamentary by-election 1948: Candidature of John MacCormick, MA LLB*. Capitalisation in original.
123. NLS Acc. 10424/34: SUA Western Divisional Council Minutes, 4 Feb. 1948.
124. Conservative and Unionist Party, *General Election 1955: The Campaign Guide* (1955), p. 1.

125. Mitchell, *The Scottish Question*, pp. 79–85.

126. *Perthshire Advertiser*, 10 Dec. 1952.

127. Such warnings were commonplace in this period. This example is taken from: Bod. Lib. CPA PUB 229/1/11: *It's Sloan for Motherwell* (1954).

128. On the position in England, see: Green, *The Ideologies of Conservatism*, p. 220; Ramsden, *Age of Churchill and Eden*, pp. 294–303.

129. Bod. Lib. CPA CCO 2/2/18: Scottish Intelligence Summaries, Apr. 1952 and Feb. 1953.

130. Bod. Lib. CPA CCO 2/2/18: Scottish Intelligence Summaries, Oct. 1955.

131. Bod. Lib. CPA CCO 2/2/18: Scottish Intelligence Summaries, May 1956.

132. NLS Acc. 10424/27: SUA WDC, *Annual Report 1956*, p. 3. Capitalisation in original.

133. NLS Acc. 11368/4: SUA Central Council Minutes, 4 Jul. 1956. Capitalisation in original.

134. Ramsden, *Age of Churchill and Eden*, pp. 294–303. On Liberal attempts to exploit middle-class discontent, see: Sloman, *The Liberal Party and the Economy*, pp. 209–12.

135. Green, 'The Treasury Resignations of 1958'.

136. NLS Acc. 10424/36: SUA WDC Education and Propaganda Committee Minutes, 25 Sept. 1956; Acc. 10424/50: SUA Eastern Divisional Council (EDC) Minutes, 12 Dec. 1956; Acc. 11368/22: SUA EDC Minutes, 11 Apr. 1958.

137. NLS Acc. 11368/22: SUA EDC Minutes, 5 Oct. 1956.

138. NLS Acc. 11368/24: SUA EDC Executive Committee Minutes, 17 Jun. 1957.

139. NLS Acc. 11368/22: SUA EDC Minutes, 4 Oct. 1957.

140. Bod. Lib. CPA CCO 1/12/552-3: Area Files, Dundee: Gordon Murray to Lord Hailsham, 17 Jan. 1958.

141. Sloman, *The Liberal Party and the Economy*, pp. 204–29.

142. Grimond, *The New Liberal Democracy*, p. 17. Emphasis and capitalisation in original.

143. Bod. Lib. CPA CCO 2/2/20: Scottish Intelligence Summary, May 1958. Capitalisation in original.

144. Bod. Lib. CPA CCO 1/12/556/1: Area Files, Argyll: Report of Meeting, Victoria Hall, Campbeltown, 29 May 1958.

145. See the reports in: PKCA MS 152/2/1/4: Kinross and West Perthshire Unionist Association Minutes, 3 Nov. 1956, 2 Nov. 1957, 23 Jul. and 8 Nov. 1958; FCA A1703/4: Stirling, Falkirk and Grangemouth Burghs Unionist Association Minutes, 25 Jun. 1959; *Stirling Sentinel*, 29 Sept. 1959.

146. *Scots Independent*, 13 Oct. 1956.

147. NLS Acc. 10090/26: *Scottish National Party: Annual National Conference, 18–19 May 1957*, pp. 29–30.

2

Too Complex, Too Remote?
Scottish Politics in the 1960s

IN OCTOBER 1967 JOHN MACKINTOSH, the Labour MP for Berwick and East Lothian and a Professor of Politics at Strathclyde University, reflected on the rise in popular support for the SNP that had taken place since the start of the decade. Published in the *Political Quarterly*, Mackintosh's assessment arrived a month before the SNP's landmark electoral victory at the Hamilton by-election, when Winnie Ewing famously overturned what had been the largest Labour majority in Scotland. If Ewing's triumph has come to be remembered as a seminal moment in post-war Scottish politics, one which signalled the onset of a new period in which the constitutional question would become increasingly unavoidable, Mackintosh's prescient consideration of the SNP's appeal offers a reminder that contemporaries were becoming conscious of the growing political significance of the SNP even before Hamilton.[1] Certainly, by the mid-1960s it was evident that the SNP could run credible, if not yet successful, by-election campaigns. Further, as party membership rose, from around 2,000 in 1962 to perhaps 42,000 by late 1966, it became financially and logistically feasible for the SNP to contest general elections on a broader basis.[2] At the 1955 general election there were just two SNP candidates; four years later the party was still only able to contest five constituencies. By the time of the 1966 general election, there were SNP candidates in twenty-three seats, and the party received five per cent of the Scottish vote. While not yet a serious political force, by the second half of the 1960s the SNP clearly enjoyed a support that was larger and more secure than it had been at any time since the party's foundation.[3] That the new, still minor, influence enjoyed by the SNP might have wider political consequences had been apparent since the March 1967 Glasgow Pollok by-election, when the party's candidate, George Leslie, had polled twenty-eight per cent of the vote, a performance that enabled the Conservatives to record a rare gain from Labour in Scotland.[4]

For Mackintosh, the paradox that required explanation was that the rise in support for the SNP had occurred during a period in which Scotland had, in social and economic terms, become ever more like the rest of Britain. Perhaps surprisingly, however, Mackintosh dismissed suggestions that Scotland's comparatively weak recent economic performance might account for the SNP's newfound popularity; while 'such trends' may have encouraged some to vote for the SNP, 'the key' to understanding the new attraction of nationalism was, he proposed, 'a sense of humiliation, of loss of identity, of domination from a distance.' Mackintosh acknowledged that these sentiments were not unique to Scotland and that similar complaints could be heard elsewhere in Britain. Nevertheless, he noted shrewdly that what in England was criticised as 'remoteness' or 'bureaucracy' was in Scotland transposed into constitutional terms, discussed as a question of 'English or Whitehall domination'.[5]

The SNP's emergence during the 1960s, and the subsequent reshaping of electoral politics in Scotland, has, of course, attracted analysis. Yet Mackintosh's insightful comments on the importance of popular perceptions of a growing gulf between the people and their government have found few echoes in the historiography. Instead, the rise of the SNP, and the parallel decline in support for Unionism, has been viewed primarily from two overlapping perspectives. First, social and economic developments, most notably secularisation, the weakening of established class identities among younger voters, and the perceived economic failings of successive UK governments, are alleged to have undermined traditional allegiances, eroding Unionist support in particular, and creating opportunities for the SNP. Second, the SNP's increasingly professional organisation in this period, reflected in the party's growing membership, is contrasted with the lethargy that appeared to envelop Unionist and Labour constituency activity, and which left the two main parties especially vulnerable at by-elections.[6] The intention here is not to suggest that such accounts are incorrect; it is, though, to propose that there are other viewpoints from which Scottish politics during the 1960s might be usefully considered. Focusing on the period between the 1959 general election and the SNP's rapid growth after the victory at the November 1967 Hamilton by-election, this chapter presents a reappraisal of the decline of Unionism and the rise in support for the SNP, linking events in Scotland to developments elsewhere in the UK. As Mackintosh suggested, the progress made by the SNP in this period should be viewed, at least in part, as the Scottish manifestation of a disillusionment with representative democracy that could be discerned across Britain. This sense of disenchantment could, to be sure, be attributed to a sense of national decline, visible on the political left and right alike, and which had both imperial and economic dimensions.[7] But a deeper sense of alienation and frustration was also present, a suspicion that parliamentary democracy was no longer functioning as it should, that the relationship between parliamentarians and those they were supposed to represent had somehow broken down. As will be seen, it was in this atmosphere of political dissatisfaction that the SNP proved able to seize the appeal to individual freedom and critique of central government that had been so vital to the success of the Unionists and National Liberals a decade earlier, and repurpose it in a manner that emphasised the question of Scotland's constitutional status.

The chapter opens with an examination of Unionist responses to the party's increasingly disappointing electoral performance in this period. It traces first the steady abandonment of the anti-socialist rhetoric of the 1940s and 1950s in favour of a recognition of the virtues of economic modernisation. The focus then shifts to a consideration of the emergence of nationalism as an electoral force, assessing why the SNP, and not, as may have seemed more probable, the Liberals, proved the main beneficiary of the shifting political landscape of the 1960s. The final section of the chapter explores reactions to the challenge posed by the SNP, and how the nationalist appeal was interpreted and explained by contemporaries; it also assesses the relationship between developments in Scotland and the challenges to the post-war duopoly that were present in England and Wales. Throughout precedence is given to what might be best described as the non-Labour 'half' of the Scottish electorate; Labour, still able to consistently secure the support of the between forty-five and fifty per cent of the Scottish electorate throughout the decade, will, for now, remain a largely off-stage presence. Rather, the emphasis is on the disintegration of the anti-socialist coalition established in opposition to Labour after 1945. Care must be taken not to overstate the events of the 1960s, or to be led astray by knowledge of subsequent events. It is true that the SNP remained a limited actor in Scottish politics even after the victory at Hamilton, unable to hold on to the gains made in subsequent local government elections; likewise, the party's hopes of a decisive breakthrough at the 1970 general election were frustrated, with the sole nationalist success coming in the Western Isles.[8] But if it was not until the twin general elections of 1974 that the SNP would make significant parliamentary advances, the foundations of those later successes can still, without relying too much on hindsight, be located in the political developments of the 1960s. At the 1970 general election the SNP had clearly overtaken the Liberal Party as the third force in Scottish politics in terms of vote share. The question that underlies this chapter is, then, which elements of the SNP's appeal to the Scottish electorate in the 1960s were successful, and why?

RESPONDING TO DECLINE: UNIONISM IN THE EARLY 1960S

Unionists were convinced that the loss of their pre-eminent position in Scotland at the 1959 general election, a result that compared poorly with the continued success of the Conservative Party in England, had been caused by Scotland's sluggish economic performance and relatively high rate of unemployment. The party's Western Divisional Council, based in Glasgow, concluded that the decision to campaign on a theme of rising prosperity, while perhaps appropriate in the midlands and south of England, had backfired in urban and industrial Scotland, where a widespread 'fear of unemployment', and opposition to the 1957 Rent Act, which had lifted rent controls on private lettings, had strengthened support for the Labour Party.[9] This assessment has been repeated in subsequent accounts, which have stressed the electoral significance of economic concerns in a Scottish context, and the extent to which this aided the Labour Party by increasing public support for state intervention.[10] The Unionists did, to be sure, lose four seats in west-central Scotland in 1959, all to Labour: Central Ayrshire, Lanark, and the Craigton and Scotstoun divisions of Glasgow. Yet there remains, all the same, a suspicion that the party overinterpreted these results. As Richard Finlay has observed, Labour's gains in 1959 were the result of marginal fluctuations in local vote share: in the four seats lost, the cumulative Unionist majority had been fewer than 2,000 votes; these were seats secured narrowly in the early 1950s, and the party's support had only to fall slightly for them to be lost.[11] To attempt to draw broader lessons from such results was misguided: in truth, at a national level, the Unionist vote was reasonably robust in 1959; if support for National Liberal candidates is included, the party still outpolled Labour. Indeed, even in Glasgow Unionist support among the electorate as a whole increased marginally, despite the defeats in Craigton and Scotstoun, and the party regained Kelvingrove, lost at a by-election the previous year.[12] Claims of a leftward shift in Scottish public opinion in the late 1950s are, then, overstated, and can obscure the fact that support for the Labour Party remained largely static. Where sharp falls in the Unionist vote did occur, such as in Ross and Cromarty, Argyllshire, Moray and Nairn, and South Angus, this was due chiefly to the re-emergence of independent Liberalism.

The principal challenge facing Unionists remained the weakening of the anti-socialist coalition that had proved so electorally successful in the first half of the 1950s. But Unionist opinion appeared complacent, and, initially at least, unaware of this threat; instead, support for the Liberal Party was understood, rather counterintuitively, as a continued endorsement of the Conservative government. For the *Glasgow Herald*, still firm in its support for Unionism, the Liberals were a party 'dedicated to individual liberty'; their moderate resurgence in 1959 could therefore be treated as a rejection of Labour's 'policies of restriction and control', and a signal that 'for the majority, the mixed economy now in being, and its management by Conservatism, marks the acceptable limit of government interference with the individual.'[13] There was some truth in the claim that the Liberal appeal rested upon opposition to socialism. The Liberal Party fought the 1959 election on a manifesto that demanded an end to the closed shop, cuts to inheritance tax, and for local authority tenants to be allowed to purchase their homes.[14] For his part, the Liberal leader Jo Grimond complained that nationalisation had proved to be a 'fiasco' that was 'incompatible with freedom'; he was equally sceptical of 'the promise of endless welfare benefits to be handed out by the grandmother state'. Grimond was critical too of trades unions, which he categorised as 'a well-organised producer interest' that had hindered efforts to tackle inflation. Grimond called for reform of the nationalised industries, reductions in public spending, and tax cuts: 'liberty', he argued, could not be enjoyed by those 'dependent on the charity of the State'. Strikingly, though, alongside these boilerplate criticisms of socialism, Grimond also attacked the Conservative government, which, he alleged, had accepted 'the new dispensation' established by Labour after 1945, and had proved to be 'as conservative of Socialism as once they were conservative of Liberalism'.[15] Grimond's comments indicated that, after almost a decade in office, the Unionist appeal to anti-socialism required renewal: demands for a more thoroughgoing reversal of the post-war settlement that would prioritise individual freedom were now being voiced.

If the tentative Liberal recovery in Scotland failed to produce any immediate parliamentary victories, by the early 1960s there were, nevertheless, indications that the Unionists were struggling to dominate the loyalties of non-Labour voters in the way that had proved possible during the previous decade. Between the 1959 and 1964 general elections, there were ten by-elections in Scotland; six took place in constituencies won by the Unionists in 1959, with the remaining four in Labour-held seats. The Unionist vote fell markedly at every contest, and the party lost both Glasgow Woodside and Rutherglen to Labour [see Table 2.1]. Such setbacks were perhaps to be expected. At a UK level the Conservative government was in its third term, and had been damaged by growing criticisms of its economic policy, as well as by the failed attempt to join the Common Market, the botched Cabinet reshuffle of July 1962, and, by 1963, the Profumo affair, which contributed to the resignation of the Prime Minister Harold Macmillan and his replacement by Alec Douglas-Home.[16] Moreover, a number of the contests took place in seats such as Edinburgh North, East Fife, and Kinross and West Perthshire, where the Unionists could depend upon majorities so large that, even if a substantial section of the party's support chose to register their discontent by abstaining or defecting to the Liberals, there was little serious prospect of defeat. These results might easily be rationalised as classic examples of mid-term protest voting.

Table 2.1 Vote share at parliamentary by-elections in Scotland, 1959–1964 [Figure in brackets indicates change from vote share at 1959 general election]

Date	Constituency	Unionist/ Nat. Liberal	Labour	Liberal	SNP	Result
19 May 1960	Edinburgh North	54 (-10)	30 (-6)	16 (n/a)	-	Unionist hold
20 Apr. 1961	Paisley	13 (-29)	45 (-12)	41 (n/a)	-	Labour hold
9 Nov. 1961	East Fife	47 (-22)	26 (-4)	26 (n/a)	-	Unionist hold
16 Nov. 1961	Glasgow Bridgeton	21 (-16)	58 (-6)	-	19 (n/a)	Labour hold
14 Jun. 1962	West Lothian	11 (-28)	51 (-9)	11 (n/a)	23 (n/a)	Labour hold
22 Nov. 1962	Glasgow Woodside	30 (-19)	36 (-7)	22 (+14)	11 (n/a)	**Labour gain**
7 Nov. 1963	Kinross & W. Perthshire	57 (-11)	15 (-2)	20 (n/a)	7 (-8)	Unionist hold
21 Nov. 1963	Dundee West	39 (-9)	51 (+1)	-	7 (n/a)	Labour hold
12 Dec. 1963	Dumfriesshire	41 (-18)	38 (-3)	11 (n/a)	10 (n/a)	Unionist hold
14 May 1964	Rutherglen	44 (-8)	56 (+8)	-	-	**Labour gain**

Yet elsewhere the picture was more worrying. The defeat at Woodside, for example, was the result of a sharp increase in Liberal support and the presence of a SNP candidate, which together allowed the Labour candidate to win with just thirty-six per cent of the vote. In Dumfriesshire in December 1963, the Unionists were barely able to hold on to the seat as interventions from Liberal and SNP candidates turned what had been a safe seat into a marginal. Significantly, it seemed that any rise in third party support in this period came almost entirely at the expense of the Unionists. But arguably of even greater concern was the party's feeble performance in Labour-held seats; here Unionists repeatedly found that, in constituencies where they had previously been able to mount at least a plausible challenge to Labour incumbents, they were losing support to the Liberals and the SNP. In some instances, such as the April 1961 contest in Paisley, this outcome was less surprising: Paisley was a former Liberal stronghold, and the second place achieved by the Liberal candidate John Bannerman, a former Scotland rugby international and Scottish Liberal Chairman, was hardly a shock.[17] There were, though, more troubling results: in November 1961, the SNP's national organiser, Ian MacDonald, polled almost twenty per cent at Glasgow Bridgeton; the following year, William Wolfe received twenty-three per cent of the vote for the SNP at West Lothian, finishing behind Labour's Tam Dalyell, but ensuring that the Unionist candidate lost his deposit. The result at West Lothian was especially disconcerting, suggesting as it did that the party was now unable to attract clearly disillusioned Labour voters.[18] Even in less dramatic instances, such as Dundee West, where, in November 1963, the SNP candidate James Lees polled just seven per cent of the vote, this had seemingly been drawn almost wholly from former Unionist supporters; what had been a narrow marginal in 1959 was now a safe Labour seat.

The difficulties facing the Unionists in Scotland soon elicited comment from the Conservative Party leadership. In April 1961 Lord Aldington, the deputy Chair of the Conservative Party, wrote to Rab Butler, then Home Secretary and Conservative Party Chairman, noting that he was 'getting more and more concerned about the Party in Scotland.' Foreshadowing the eventual adoption of the Conservative label in Scotland in 1965, and the closer financial and organisational links that would follow, Aldington proposed that Conservative 'Central Office should be given responsibility for the whole of Great Britain including Scotland.'[19] He recognised, however, that, given the traditional autonomy enjoyed by the Unionist Party, such a proposal would need to originate in Scotland.[20] Aldington noted too that one of the key issues in Scotland was the continued attachment of many within the Unionist Party to a coalitionist worldview that failed to take seriously the potential electoral threat posed by the Liberals. There was, Aldington reported, a 'weak attitude' being displayed towards 'the Liberals' in seats such as 'Paisley and Greenock', where 'many Unionists' were still willing to allow the Liberals to stand against Labour unopposed.[21]

By the early 1960s it was becoming increasingly anachronistic to conceive of Scottish politics as a binary contest between socialism and its opponents that aligned straightforwardly with broader British patterns. The revival of independent Liberalism, coupled with the gradual emergence of the SNP, undercut the Unionist claim to speak for non-Labour voters. There followed a process of fragmentation and regionalisation, as the Unionist share of the vote declined and political allegiances in Scotland shifted. Unionist representatives and activists were certainly aware that they were losing support; the challenge was identifying what, if anything, could be done to reverse the trend. There was, understandably, a tendency within the party to try to locate a single, simple explanation for the electoral challenges they now faced. For most, the election results simply demanded an even greater focus on economic questions, and more visible efforts from the Conservative government to tackle Scotland's relatively high unemployment rate.[22] On occasion, Unionism's diminishing appeal was blamed on events at Westminster. In June 1964 William Hunter, President of the Scottish Unionist Association, told Unionist MPs that, while he accepted that the recent by-election results had been disappointing, 'organisation' at the constituency level could only achieve so much: 'policy and leadership' were of critical importance. Hunter listed a litany of recent national setbacks, including 'the dismissal of seven Cabinet Ministers over-night, the Common Market failure, the Profumo and Vassal cases and the leadership crisis', declaring that 'these had caused dismay and distress to the voluntary workers in Scotland.' Nevertheless, Hunter still believed that the key issue was 'the fact there were fewer men at work in Scotland in 1963 than in 1951.'[23]

The result was that Unionists increasingly foregrounded their willingness to intervene in the economy, a response that mirrored the national stance adopted by the Conservative government under the leadership of Harold Macmillan.[24] This did not necessarily involve a dramatic change in policy: Conservative-led administrations had been willing to implement interventionist economic policies since at least the 1930s. There was, nonetheless, a rhetorical shift in the early 1960s, as blanket denunciations of socialism gave way to attempts to differentiate, in effect, between good and bad forms of economic planning. An important

influence here was an implicit acceptance of a narrative of British decline
that was, in the early 1960s, expressed as a left-wing critique of the
Conservative government as being dominated by a cossetted aristocratic
elite ill-suited to the task of modernising Britain's outmoded economic
base.[25] This assessment was promoted most forcefully by Harold Wilson
following his accession to the Labour leadership in 1963, and especially
once Macmillan had been replaced as Prime Minster by Douglas-Home,
whose aristocratic background was impossible to downplay.[26] By the
summer of 1964, there were concerns amongst Unionist MPs that their
public image was too 'feudalistic'.[27] In response, Unionists attempted to
promote a distinctive version of modernisation and economic planning:
the party broadly endorsed the suggestions of the 1961 Toothill enquiry
into the Scottish economy, which recommended directing investment
towards 'growth points'; in 1962, an economic development department was added to a steadily expanding Scottish Office.[28] A year later,
the Conservative government published a development plan for central
Scotland that promised a 'massive programme of national reconstruction and modernisation', and conceded that 'full employment' could
'only be maintained by conscious and far-ranging acts of policy'.[29]

By the time of the October 1964 general election, the Unionists had
discarded much of the rhetoric of freedom that had previously defined
the party's appeal to the electorate. As recently as the 1959 election
campaign, Unionist activists had been reminded to warn voters that
'"Socialist planning" really means controlling Scottish affairs from
London', underpinned by 'the idea that the "Gentleman in Whitehall"
knows what is best for Scotland'.[30] Unionist MPs were advised similarly to focus their speeches on the basic question of whether Scotland
was 'to become a Socialist State ruled by a handful of Bureaucrats in
Whitehall with Private Industry and Commerce . . . regulated, hindered
and interfered with by a Bureaucracy directed by Socialist politicians'.
Emphasis was to be placed on the likelihood that a Labour government
would pursue further nationalisations, and to stress that planning could
not deliver the rates of economic growth claimed by the Labour leadership.[31] Five years later, the basic clarity that this brusque anti-socialism
provided had been lost, dissipated amid Unionist attempts to highlight
a commitment to 'economic transformation' alongside examples of the
Conservative government's implementation of regional economic policies that benefited Scotland.[32] Douglas-Home informed voters in his
Kinross and West Perthshire constituency that he now accepted 'that
in modern conditions there must be a good deal of both central and
regional planning.'[33] That year's Unionist manifesto celebrated the

benefits of planning, and promised the creation of a 'vast new economic complex' in central Scotland.[34] Priscilla Buchan, defending her seat in Aberdeen South, admitted during the campaign that her party had now come to recognise 'far more the need for gov[ernment] to take greater responsibility to promote social and economic change'.[35] Planning was no longer rejected on principle as a socialist ploy that would result in authoritarianism; rather, a distinction began to be made between Labour and Unionist versions of planning. While the latter was depicted as more flexible and responsive, and less subject to centralised direction, this was now a difference of degree, not kind.

These attempts to renew the Unionist appeal were, however, a failure. At the October 1964 election the party shed almost a fifth of its vote; the number of Unionist and National Liberal MPs slipped from thirty-one to twenty-four, the lowest total since 1929. Indeed, the collapse in Unionist support in Scotland was critical in ensuring the return of the first Labour government in thirteen years.[36] When the surviving Unionist MPs convened a fortnight after the election, there was an acceptance that the result represented a significant setback, and that action would be required to avert the 'danger of yet another failure.' There remained, though, the sense that those present lacked any real understanding of why their party had lost support. Michael Noble, the outgoing Secretary of State for Scotland, issued a vague call for 'fresh thinking, planning and acting', but neglected to offer any actual proposals.[37] Indications that more fruitful assessments might be possible were at times discernible at the post-election meetings of the party's hierarchy in Scotland. Ian Mowat, Secretary of the Eastern Divisional Council, argued that a sense of 'boredom' had taken root among middle class electors, who had 'felt neglected' by the Conservative government.[38] Addressing the Unionist Central Council, Mowat suggested further that the 'mood of the people' had been against the party, with younger voters in particular opting to support the Liberals, most notably in the Highlands, where the Liberals had gained three seats, but also in Aberdeenshire, Angus and the Borders. In an intriguing comment that hinted at the ideological roots of Unionism's difficulties, Mowat concluded that 'the young were looking for some idealism' and that the party had come to be seen as too 'materialistic in our outlook.'[39]

If Mowat failed to explore fully the implications of these comments, others were more willing to conclude that the failure to uphold, or at least find a viable alternative to, the anti-socialism that had under-pinned Unionism's earlier appeal had been the critical factor. A resolution from the Unionist Association in Crieff, located in Douglas-Home's

Kinross and West Perthshire seat, complained that the party's election materials had not been 'positive enough', nor 'sufficiently effective and simple to convince the General Public of the dangers of a Socialist Administration'.[40] This was an echo of the pre-election concerns expressed by Lord Dalkeith, the MP for Edinburgh South. Addressing the Eastern Divisional Council in July 1964, Dalkeith had warned that the party was placing 'insufficient emphasis . . . on one of the most fundamental points of difference between the political parties'. For Dalkeith, this 'essential difference' was that, while Conservatives and Unionists 'recognised that the heartbeat of the nation was its free enterprise industry [sic]', operated 'by individuals who responded naturally to . . . conditions of opportunity . . . the Socialists . . . regarded the individual as a cog in the great state machine planned and controlled by the all-knowing man in Whitehall'. Dalkeith worried that, as Labour had been out of office for more than a decade, voters may have forgotten the risks posed by 'Socialist rule': he urged a return to 'the phrase that was heard so often around 1950 – "set the people free".'[41]

Such perspectives were, though, far from universal. Some members of the Western Divisional Council, for example, still preferred to ascribe the party's electoral defeats to narrower economic questions, such as popular opposition to the abolition of resale price maintenance.[42] By 1964, however, the default position appeared to be to highlight questions of organisation and public image. Sir John George, the Unionist Party Chairman, informed MPs that the central issue was the weakness of the party's structure in Scotland; in particular, George questioned whether the traditional division of authority between east and west was now obsolete, and whether, given the Liberal success there, the Highlands should not be granted specific attention. Those present offered various additional perspectives. Teddy Taylor, MP for Glasgow Cathcart, argued that the party needed to reassert its Scottish image, and 'identify . . . with Scottish problems.' Others felt that a clean break should be made: Michael Noble, expressing a widespread sense among MPs that the Unionist brand had come to be viewed as antiquated and obsolete, suggested that the name should be abandoned in favour of adopting the Conservative label, a recommendation implemented the following year.[43] This proposal again indicated the extent to which Unionists had internalised a distinctive Scottish version of the Labour critique of the outgoing Conservative government as being the preserve of an out of touch landed elite. Thus Patrick Wolridge-Gordon, the relatively youthful MP for East Aberdeenshire, lamented that the voters 'evidently considered us as rather superior beings who did not really bother about the ordinary people'.[44] A meeting of the party's Western Divisional Council in December 1964 concluded that the 'image of the party in Scotland was too aristocratic and Anglicised to be acceptable. It should have been much more representative of all sections of the community'. 'The party', it was felt, was considered 'too remote from the lives of the ordinary people.'[45]

There was, no doubt, some truth to these judgements; it was not especially difficult for the party's opponents to portray Unionism as an outmoded identity relevant only in Scotland's rural hinterland. Still, the measures adopted to counter such perceptions, while understandable, were often counterproductive. Most obviously, the adoption of the Conservative label in 1965 weakened Unionism's distinctive Scottish identity. But the problems posed by the name change went deeper: in agreeing to become more closely identified with their counterparts in England and Wales, Unionists found they were increasingly tied to a Britain-wide rhetoric of modernisation that jarred with the more nuanced bases of the party's support in Scotland. Edward Heath, who succeeded Douglas-Home in 1965, becoming the first Conservative leader to be elected rather than 'appointed', held a more complex political and economic outlook than later narratives would suggest; he was neither a defender of a supposed post-war consensus, nor did he abandon a fulsome commitment to market liberalism once in office. Nevertheless, Heath, grammar-school educated and at that point the youngest leader in the party's history, was identified with a modernising tendency within the Conservative Party, and his arrival as leader was interpreted as an attempt to match the meritocratic, technocratic image cultivated by Harold Wilson.[46] Conservative rhetoric therefore continued to emphasise the extent to which the Labour Party's particular interpretation of economic planning was misguided, but left open the prospect that a future Conservative government might pursue more considered forms of economic direction. The campaign guide issued to activists in advance of the March 1966 general election duly cautioned against engaging in 'crude' and 'totally sterile' arguments on the merits of 'planning' in the abstract. 'The word', it was suggested, 'can be and is used to describe a variety of activities' that ranged from those 'universally regarded as desirable', and which were entirely compatible with a 'market economy', to those that only 'the extreme Left' believed were relevant 'to the British context'. While socialist planning was obviously to be opposed, there remained 'many other types of planning which Conservatives not only accept but have been largely responsible for developing'. From a Scottish perspective, the Conservative record of directing investment towards Scotland was stressed, with the Labour government criticised for its alleged failure to build upon the Conservative government's 1963 White Paper.[47]

The prominence accorded by the Conservatives to an account of economic modernisation that could incorporate forms of planning created difficulties for the party in Scotland. Even if this shift was largely a question of presentation, it nonetheless appeared as though Conservatism's anti-socialism had softened, blurring a previously firm distinction between the two major parties.[48] A commitment to modernisation could also lead the party to defend deeply unpopular policies, most notably the rationalisation of the rail network recommended in 1963 by the Beeching report. The scheme, which involved the closure of a significant number of lines, promised to provoke opposition, especially in rural areas. Likely a factor in the Conservative defeat at the 1964 election, the closures were certainly an important issue at the Roxburgh, Selkirk and Peebles by-election in March 1965.[49] During the campaign, it was clear that the proposed closure of the Edinburgh–Carlisle line, eventually implemented in 1969, was causing the Conservatives difficulties. Prior to polling, William Anstruther-Gray, MP for the neighbouring constituency of Berwick and East Lothian and Chairman of the back-bench 1922 committee, warned of 'an infinity of damage' if the closure of the line was condoned. Yet Anstruther-Gray, a traditional Unionist first elected to Parliament in 1931, was opposed by those more convinced of the need to update the Conservative appeal in Scotland. For Teddy Taylor and Jock Bruce-Gardyne, the latter the newly elected MP for South Angus, the closures were a necessary step towards reducing the losses incurred by British Rail.[50] To the extent that Beeching could be construed as imposing discipline on a loss-making nationalised industry, Taylor and Bruce-Gardyne's stance was consistent with their position on the Conservative right. Still, if anti-socialism had been the dominant theme within post-war Unionism, it had in the past been combined with a willingness to adjust the party's appeal to local conditions and to take account of Scottish particularities. While from an economic perspective the Beeching cuts were about reducing public subsidy for the railways, viewed from rural Scotland they could appear as precisely the kind of unthinking decree from central government that Unionists had railed against in the past. As Anstruther-Gray feared, the seat was lost to the Liberals.

Scottish Conservatism's growing ideological incoherence led to a further electoral reverse at the 1966 general election. The party's share of the vote in Scotland slipped below forty per cent for the first time since the 1920s, as support for the Liberals and, at the margins, the SNP, increased, and the Labour Party secured its highest ever share of the vote in Scotland. In the aftermath of the election, Ian McIntyre, who had served as the party's Scottish Director of Information between 1962 and 1965 before unsuccessfully attempting to reclaim Roxburgh, Selkirk and Peebles at the 1966 contest, wrote to George Younger, the MP for Ayr.[51] McIntyre was, like Younger, still in his mid-thirties; he was adamant that the party's weakness in Scotland was the result of an appeal to the electorate that continued to be defined by 'landed interests' and 'agriculture'. Bemoaning the fact that an older generation of MPs still provided 'the stock image of the Party in Scotland', McIntyre believed that Scottish Conservatism was 'rapidly becoming [a] laughing stock'. He contrasted this with the appeal of the Liberals, who he felt had successfully positioned themselves as 'a party of youth, drive, opportunity, and a party in which talent gets its chance early'. McIntyre wished to eschew what he saw as easy fixes, yet his proposals ignored any questions of policy or ideology, and focused instead on overhauling the party's organisation and making efforts to recruit candidates from a broader range of backgrounds, who, he believed, might prove better able to speak to modern, industrial Scotland.[52] This continued focus on image provoked a predictable reaction from MPs of longer standing, who felt that they were being unfairly blamed for the party's decline. Tam Galbraith, who had represented Glasgow Hillhead since 1948, complained that he and other long-serving colleagues were being dismissed by Conservative Central Office as elderly 'hayseeds'.[53] Nevertheless, it was difficult to avoid the conclusion that the Conservative image was at least part of the issue. Reporting on the party's Scottish conference that year, *The Scotsman* warned that the Conservatives were 'in real danger of becoming an agrarian rump of a party . . . irrelevant to modern Scotland'; the 'uncharacteristic nature of the majority of [the party's] candidates', with their 'Eton-and-Oxbridge image', was felt to be especially problematic.[54]

By 1966, Scottish Conservatives, as they had become, had suffered three successive electoral setbacks, losing sixteen seats in the process. Moreover, this decline had affected both urban and rural constituencies, with the seats lost by the party being divided between Labour and the Liberals. Conservative efforts were, unsurprisingly, centred upon the question of how to combat these twin threats; but such an emphasis neglected the growing challenge posed by the SNP, especially in those constituencies in central and eastern Scotland where Liberal organisation was weak. As Taym Saleh has demonstrated, the party's North-Eastern Regional Council offers an intriguing case study of the difficulties

facing Scottish Conservatives in this period.[55] The Council was responsible for an area that included the four urban seats in Aberdeen and
Dundee, as well as five rural constituencies in Angus, Aberdeenshire and
Banffshire.[56] In 1964, the Conservatives had still held six of the nine
constituencies, with Labour prevailing in Aberdeen North and the East
and West divisions in Dundee. In 1966, Aberdeen South was lost to
Labour and the Liberals triumphed in Aberdeenshire West. A review of
Conservative prospects in the region in early 1967 accepted that Labour
was entrenched in Aberdeen North and Dundee West but maintained
that both Aberdeen South and Dundee East continued to be realistic
targets. The remaining seats were believed to be 'absolutely safe from
Socialism (though not from the Liberals)'; still, there was a belief that
Aberdeenshire West would be reclaimed from the Liberals at the next
election. These assertions were largely borne out at the 1970 general
election, when both Aberdeen South and Aberdeenshire West were
reclaimed. Yet the lack of consideration given to the SNP was note-
worthy: while there was some awareness that support for the SNP in the
area was rising, this was derided as being largely emotional in nature.[57]
Such dismissals would appear almost unbelievably complacent in the
aftermath of the October 1974 general election, which saw the SNP seize
Aberdeenshire East, Banffshire, Dundee East and South Angus. As Saleh
rightly suggests, the Conservatives were too slow to respond to the new
challenge posed by the SNP. But Saleh's assertion that a 'commitment
to anti-socialism' was a weakness in areas where Labour 'was a virtual
non-presence' requires qualification.[58] Rather, it was the failure to find a
meaningful alternative to the anti-socialism that had cemented Unionist
loyalties in the preceding decades that was so damaging to Conservative
support in provincial Scotland. More than this, the discarding of an
explicit appeal to individualism enabled the SNP to take charge of this
rhetoric of individual liberty, and then bend it towards constitutional
rather than economic questions.

THE ARRIVAL OF THE SNP

The growing support enjoyed by the SNP in the early 1960s drew the
attention of the media. Following the party's creditable performance at
the Glasgow Bridgeton by-election in November 1961, the journalist
Magnus Magnusson offered readers of *The Scotsman* an assessment
of what he termed the 'World of Scotnattery'. Magnusson's portrayal
of the competing grouplets within the wider Scottish nationalist movement was gently mocking, and he took some pleasure in relating the

pretensions, petty factionalism and paltry membership of not just the SNP, but also the Scottish Covenant Association, Scottish National Congress, and Wendy Wood's more militant Scottish Patriots. Beneath the wry presentation, however, Magnusson's was a measured account, and he recognised that Scottish nationalism was beginning to attract the backing of a wider section of the electorate than in previous decades. As he noted, notwithstanding the 'perpetual self-destructive bickering and feuding' that had marred relations between the various elements within the nationalist movement, these groups were 'merely symptoms', 'froth on the surface' of a 'current' in Scottish politics that was growing in influence. Further, Magnusson recognised that this rising 'current' was a largely provincial phenomenon: for all the importance of urban intellectuals in maintaining and promoting a distinctive Scottish culture, support for Scottish nationalism was strongest not in the major cities, but rather 'out in the country, in the towns and burghs, in places where there is still sufficient sense of a common culture and a common tradition to make it a meaningful proposition.'[59] The trend detected by Magnusson would become increasingly visible in the years that followed. At the close of 1966, with the SNP's pivotal electoral advance at the Hamilton by-election still ten months away, the *Daily Telegraph* acknowledged that the SNP could plausibly claim to be the fastest-growing political party in Europe, with membership having doubled annually throughout the decade, reaching over 40,000 by that stage.[60]

The rise in party membership, and the increased public profile that it stimulated, nurtured a growing optimism and confidence within the SNP in the years before the Hamilton victory. At the beginning of the 1964 general election campaign, the SNP Chairman, Arthur Donaldson, reported that the party was 'in better shape organisationally and financially than on previous occasions' and that opinion at a branch level was 'more realistic and sober'. While there was no expectation of any instant victory, there was a clear sense that a firmer popular foundation was being laid.[61] Other positive signals were also apparent. Since the 1930s, the SNP had organised annual rallies to commemorate the Battle of Bannockburn and the birth of William Wallace, held in June and August respectively. By the mid-1960s these had been transformed from modest events into mass gatherings, attracting thousands of participants as well as generating positive press coverage and, unlike in previous years, a financial profit for the SNP.[62] The newly professional tone that prevailed within the SNP in this period encouraged a more pragmatic, calculated approach to electioneering. If a commitment to a nationwide appeal unsurprisingly remained, the relatively haphazard methods of previous eras were discarded, as a language of targeted campaigning and constituency organisation entered party communications. Reports authored following the 1964 contest by Douglas Drysdale and William Wolfe, vice chairmen for Organisation and Publicity and Development respectively, stressed the need to identify target seats in advance of any future election.[63] The party President, Robert McIntyre, concluded that the 'experience of this election', at which the SNP had polled over ten per cent of the vote in the fifteen seats the party had contested, demonstrated that there was 'no political barrier' preventing the securing of 'a large number of seats . . . within the foreseeable future'; all that was required was 'better organisation . . . and . . . a steady continuity in the presentation of the Scottish case'.[64] The improved status now enjoyed by the SNP was confirmed by the airing of the party's first party political broadcast the following year. In the aftermath, Donaldson stated that he was 'greatly impressed' by the 'very great improvement in public attitude to the Party [sic]'.[65] Following the 1966 general election, at which the performance of the SNP had improved further, Donaldson felt able to conclude that the SNP had 'now definitely broken through in all areas', asserting confidently that the party had moved 'beyond the stage of regarding itself as a minority with a mission to be accomplished at some vague date.' Stressing the 'adult attitude' that he claimed predominated within SNP branches, and the extent to which the 'public' were 'now . . . beginning to look upon' the party as 'the true, even official opposition in Scotland', Donaldson believed that it was 'now obvious' that 'self-government' would be attained 'within a very reasonable time indeed.'[66]

Donaldson's assessment would prove overly optimistic. Nevertheless, subsequent events would partly vindicate his sense that the electoral position of the SNP had been transformed during the 1960s. As outlined previously, efforts to explain the new viability of the SNP in this period have focused in the main on tracing the social and economic developments held to have underlaid shifts in political allegiance. Early considerations of the electoral advance of Scottish nationalism highlighted the apparent decline of class as the primary determinant of political allegiance during the 1960s, alongside the trend towards secularisation among the Protestant community. Together, these developments, it was believed, loosened the hold of the two-party system that had prevailed since 1945 and created new constituencies of support for 'third' parties.[67] Subsequent contributions have added depth to this assessment, noting the political impact of shifting patterns of employment and the extent to which post-war housing policy, and especially the establishment of New Towns such as Glenrothes and Cumbernauld, where the

SNP enjoyed notable success at a municipal level, disrupted traditional political communities.[68]

Yet the question remains why it was the SNP, rather than, say, the Liberals, who benefited from such developments. Some attention has been granted to the tendency evident from the early 1960s onwards to treat Scotland as a discrete, and relatively deprived, economic unit. Driven, ironically, by the policy decisions of both Conservative and Labour governments at a UK level, this new Scottish 'frame' to political debate, relayed by a still-distinctive Scottish press, is deemed to have assisted the SNP.[69] Most accounts, however, point towards improvements within the SNP's internal organisation, and the arrival of a new, more professional, generation of senior figures, including Ian MacDonald, William Wolfe and Gordon Wilson, as being central to the party's ability exploit the changing political landscape of the 1960s.[70] But to observe that by the mid-1960s the SNP had a larger membership, or a stronger financial position, or even a more competent leadership group, is really to describe rather than explain political change. Left unresolved is the nature of the SNP's appeal to the public, and the question of why a growing number of Scots were willing to dedicate their time and money to the party.[71] The deeply regional nature of support for the SNP also requires reflection. Even before the results of the two general elections of 1974 offered confirmation, it was evident that the SNP's membership was weighted towards county constituencies rather than the burghs. Ian MacDonald, the party's National Organiser, noted in late 1966 that SNP membership amounted to roughly one in every 300 residents in urban areas, compared to a figure of one in every sixty of those in rural seats.[72]

The worldview that the SNP offered to the Scottish public in the 1960s remained rooted in the individualism and distrust of bureaucracy that had been so prominent in nationalist rhetoric in the previous two decades.[73] As Gordon Wilson, who served as the party's National Secretary between 1963 and 1971 before entering Parliament in 1974, reflected, despite the rapid rise in membership experienced in this period, the SNP retained the 'decentralist traditions' established during the 1940s, and was able to blend its 'previous libertarianism' with newer, more social-democratic influences.[74] The statement of aims and policy issued by the SNP after the Second World War, steeped as it was in opposition to 'State socialism', 'nationalisation', and 'irresponsible bureaucracy', remained in effect, with only minimal amendments, into the early 1960s.[75] While this programme was superseded by the arrival of *SNP & You*, the party's manifesto, first issued in 1966 and updated periodically in the years ahead, similar themes continued to predominate.

Indeed, although the vehement anti-communism of the late 1940s and early 1950s had abated, that document continued to use fear of the Soviet Union as a reference point, with it being asserted that Scotland was a 'more complete serf or satellite of England than Poland, Hungary, Bulgaria and Roumania [sic] are of the USSR.'[76] A similar strand of thought could be detected in the election literature issued that year by Robert McIntyre, who, during his campaign in West Stirlingshire, restated his belief that independence remained the 'best defence against totalitarian power', a means by which 'individual freedom' could be protected and the people of Scotland could avoid becoming 'mere cogs in a great soul-less machine.'[77] A year later, in a policy statement authored jointly by Donaldson and McIntyre, the SNP's commitment to local democracy, and opposition to centralisation, was restated: government, it was stated, 'must be the servant of the People, never their master'.[78]

The SNP's outlook also rested upon a particular reading of Scottish history. While the party attributed Scotland's contemporary economic difficulties to the nation's perceived constitutional subservience, there was, perhaps surprisingly, little sustained interest in the evolution of the Union settlement in the eighteenth or nineteenth centuries. Rather, nationalists believed Scotland's precarious economic position in the 1960s, as demonstrated by the twin measures of unemployment and emigration, to be the consequence of developments that had emerged in the wake of the First World War. As the SNP's post-war policy statement had claimed, 'during the twentieth century' Scotland had been subjected to an 'ever-increasing centralisation of government', a 'process . . . assisted and accelerated by two major wars', which had 'been disastrous for Scotland'.[79] In effect, the SNP embraced a reading of Scottish history that understood the two centuries after 1707 as a period in which a form of what Graeme Morton later labelled as 'Unionist-Nationalism' flourished.[80] An appeal for funds issued by the SNP prior to the 1964 general election noted with approval that, 'Up to the first Great War, the financial and commercial life' of Scotland had been 'quite independent of interference from the south', and had remained 'almost entirely in the hands of local people.' The impact of the First World War, and the growing centralisation of political and economic power that followed, had, however, left Scotland weakened, and in danger of being reduced to the level of 'a regional area of England.'[81] Union between Scotland and England was, then, not necessarily to be opposed as a matter of course; rather, the specific way in which the Union operated, and the degree to which Scotland retained political and economic autonomy, was key. As the Union settlement had been eroded during the twentieth century, and Westminster and Whitehall began to exert increasing influence over life in Scotland, so, the argument went, the need for Scottish independence had grown. This critical account of constitutional developments was married to the belief that, as central government had come to play an ever more influential economic role, so Scotland's needs had been disregarded in favour of those of the south of England. The result had been the regular imposition of restrictive fiscal and monetary measures designed to avert currency crises and deflate an overheating economy in the south, but which were ill-suited to a Scottish economic context where unemployment and emigration were more immediate concerns.

The parallels between this nationalist interpretation of Scotland's constitutional position and the post-war Unionist critique of socialism are obvious and need not be laboured; they are, however, significant. While Arthur Donaldson might, in his role as SNP Chairman, have claimed in 1965 that 'government from London is always unsatisfactory, whatever the party in power', the issues that drew his ire suggested that he believed that certain types of economic policy were more dangerous than others. For Donaldson, it was the willed creation of a homogenous British economy that was the greatest threat, as he decried 'Takeovers, mergers, nationalisation, centralisation, closures, suspensions, re-organisations . . . English interference,' and 'managements who do not understand their men, lightning strikes, stubborn industrial quarrels, unintelligent policies, weak and uninformed Government Departments'. These trends 'threatened' Scots 'with a future' in which they would become mere 'tenants . . . industrials serfs in our own factories, servants in our own house.'[82] The Labour government's implementation of a national plan prompted similar concerns, with a press release from the SNP declaring that such a measure would simply 'mean an even tighter grip by Whitehall on the Scottish economy', a relationship that was 'already far too tight for Scotland's economic comfort'.[83]

The tax rates required to support the expanding responsibilities of the post-war state produced further objections from the SNP. Denounced as disproportionate, the level of taxation in the UK was compared unfavourably with that prevailing elsewhere in northern Europe, with the party claiming that 'Central Government' represented 'a greater cost per head' for Scots than was the case in independent nations like 'Norway or Denmark or the Netherlands'.[84] A particular concern for the SNP was the Selective Employment Tax, introduced by the Labour government at the 1966 budget. The tax, which offered incentives for the manufacturing sector while imposing an additional levy upon those engaged in services, was designed to encourage a rebalancing of the UK economy by

aiding exports while suppressing domestic consumption.[85] For nationalists, this was an excessively blunt measure that would disadvantage
those provincial areas where the service sector predominated; it also
appeared an unfair attempt to resolve the problems of the economic core
by punishing those on the periphery. An emergency resolution condemning the tax was passed at the party's June 1966 conference.[86] Critically,
the SNP demand was for less government intervention in Scotland, not
more: regional industrial policy that offered companies incentives to
locate in Scotland was a symptom of failure, not a solution. In an interview with *The Scotsman* in 1966, William Wolfe declared that Scotland
needed 'self-effort, not dependence on charity or on being able to supply
cheap "peasant" labour'. Support for the SNP was, Wolfe claimed,
evidence that 'the people' were intent on 'exercising their democratic
rights': by supporting independence, they were 'rejecting the domination' he believed had 'been increasingly felt by Scotland', something he
attributed to 'centralising tendencies in practically every sphere of government and economic activity'.[87]

If the 1960s saw the arrival of a younger, more progressive constituency within the nationalist movement, most notably as a result of the
SNP's opposition to nuclear weapons, the party retained an instinctive
anti-state outlook.[88] At times, the traditional nationalist distrust of central government could assume curious manifestations. The party's pirate
radio station, Radio Free Scotland, had been launched in 1956, but came
to prominence in the early 1960s when Gordon Wilson assumed control
and began to make use of the platform during the Glasgow Bridgeton by-
election campaign.[89] The establishment of the unlicensed, illegal station
was intended to highlight the perceived inequity of the BBC's decision to
refuse airtime to both the SNP and Plaid Cymru at the 1955 general election on the grounds that they were not contesting a sufficient number of
constituencies; it would disappear following the reversal of that decision
a decade later. The name chosen for the station was an obvious attempt,
however facetious, to hint at an equivalence between the situation in
Scotland and the position prevailing in the Communist states of eastern
Europe. Furthermore, the issue was framed explicitly as a question of
democratic freedom: the revival of the station under Wilson's direction
was justified as a defence of the 'ideal of democracy – and the freedom
of speech that should go with it'; the broadcasts would offer 'a vision
of a new Scotland . . . alive, virile, and creative . . . a country where the
individual is more important than the State.'[90]

The SNP's foray into pirate radio was short-lived, and of little lasting
political significance. Still, by the second half of the 1960s it was evident

that the nationalist scepticism towards the state was beginning to enjoy a new credibility. It was clear too that support for the SNP was concentrated within certain regions of Scotland, and among particular sections of the electorate. Central and north-eastern Scotland were already emerging as potential areas of strength for the party, where there were active local branches able to sustain electoral campaigns. Here, as Iain Hutchison and Michael Dyer have indicated, SNP activists were able to both exploit Unionist decline and repurpose a traditional provincial radical tradition.[91] The New Towns of Cumbernauld and Glenrothes would also become sites of early nationalist breakthroughs at local government elections. And while Poujadist caricatures should be avoided, the SNP did seem to appeal disproportionately to middle and lower middle-class voters in small town and provincial Scotland. This was especially true of the SNP's leadership group. A newspaper profile of the party published following the victory at Hamilton offered a portrait of an inner circle dominated by the self-employed, small business owners, and professionals of various kinds.[92] This impressionistic assessment was supported by an analysis of nationalist candidates at the 1968 local elections conducted by the *Glasgow Herald*. This study, which examined the background of eighty-one of the 309 SNP nominees, concluded that the typical candidate was a man in early middle age, standing in the area in which he had been born, and who was either a small business owner or shopkeeper, or otherwise a skilled tradesman who was not a member of a trade union. The report concluded that the SNP gave the 'overwhelming impression' of being 'a party for the little man [sic]', who was 'neither a working class Socialist nor a wealthy Tory', but who was 'in business in a small way' and who felt 'disenfranchised by the major party machines'.[93]

In this regard, support for the SNP can be understood as a Scottish manifestation of the rise in third party support visible across Britain during the 1960s. It is clear that an important factor in enabling the initial rise in support for the SNP in the mid-1960s was the weakness of the Liberal Party across much of Scotland. While the Liberals had been able to return to relevance in the Highlands, parts of Aberdeenshire and the Borders, elsewhere the party lacked any serious electoral or organisational foothold. Here the SNP, strengthened by its expanding membership and new media profile, was able to provide an alternative third-party option for voters disillusioned with both Labour and the Conservatives. Earlier in the decade, the complementary geographical strengths of the SNP and the Liberals, and the fact that the latter were still committed to supporting a devolved Scottish Parliament, had prompted some discussion of a potential alliance. The Liberals, faced with the improved nationalist performances of the early 1960s, were open to the possibility of cooperation, with the Scottish Liberal Chairman, John Bannerman, long sympathetic to the cause of Scottish home rule, suggesting that he would be willing to hold informal talks regarding an electoral pact with the SNP.[94] Bannerman would subsequently express his frustration that the SNP's intervention at by-elections had resulted in the splitting of what he, perhaps revealingly, termed the 'Scottish' vote.[95] Some within the SNP, most notably William Wolfe and his colleagues in the West Lothian constituency party, were open to such an arrangement. However, Wolfe failed to secure the support of the party hierarchy for such a move.[96] The prospect was, in any case, soon lost, as the SNP's momentum encouraged more ambitious plans. While Wolfe continued to advocate some form of deal between the SNP and the Liberals, by the summer of 1966 he viewed this more cynically as a prelude to the ultimate absorption of the latter by the former, and suggested that any informal talks should be accompanied by efforts to increase the SNP presence 'in the "Liberal" areas'.[97] By the end of the decade, it was senior Liberals, such as Jo Grimond, who were arguing, without success, for a united front with the SNP in favour of home rule.[98]

Care should, then, be taken when interpreting the SNP victory at Hamilton in November 1967. It is, to be sure, true to describe the contest as the 'most sensational by-election' in post-war Scottish history. Likewise, Winnie Ewing undeniably fronted a hugely impressive and innovative campaign, one that produced an enduring set of images that have come to serve as a visual shorthand for the arrival of 'modern' Scottish politics, where the constitutional question plays a central role.[99] But the Hamilton result was, in an important sense, a piece of political misdirection that both obscured the roots of the SNP's newfound support and encouraged a false impression of the party's potential for subsequent growth. The rise in party membership in the preceding years had been steady, sustained, and tilted towards certain regions. Ewing's campaign drew partly on these trends, and undoubtedly benefited from the optimism and sense of novelty that surrounded the SNP. Nevertheless, if the result was more than a fluke, and represented something more significant than Robert McIntyre's victory in Motherwell a generation earlier, it remained closer in nature to an archetypal, and ultimately short-lived, by-election upset than has sometimes been claimed. The apparent failure of the Labour government's economic policy, substantiated, it seemed, by the devaluation of sterling the month before the by-election, undermined Labour support in the constituency, as did the perceived arrogance of the decision of the outgoing MP, Tom Fraser, to step down in order to take up the position of Chairman of the North of Scotland Hydro-Electric Board.[100] Labour's defeat, while still a surprise, was therefore not necessarily a complete shock, especially given the victory of Plaid Cymru at the Carmarthenshire by-election the previous year. More than this, Hamilton appeared to suggest that the SNP was able to challenge Labour in its strongholds in central Scotland; as the subsequent decade would demonstrate, this would rarely, if ever, prove to be the case. The only comparable result would be the November 1973 Govan by-election, when Margo MacDonald secured what had been a safe Labour seat for the SNP; as was the case in Hamilton, however, Labour would regain the seat at the following general election. When broader electoral success did arrive for the SNP in 1974, it would largely occur elsewhere, in the former Unionist redoubts of rural and semi-rural central, north-eastern, and south-western Scotland.

So far, the emphasis has been on the persistence within the SNP of a language of individualism and of a distrust of distant bureaucracies, and upon the constituencies, both physical and social, that began to provide support for the party. There remains, however, the attendant question of why parts of the electorate began to prove more receptive to the party's messaging in the second half of the 1960s; of why the SNP's critique of authoritarianism and the over-powerful central state, and commitment to decentralisation, proved more persuasive as the decade progressed. Here, it is worth returning to the contemporary commentary offered by John Mackintosh. Writing immediately after the Hamilton result, Mackintosh was keen to disabuse those among his Labour colleagues who wished to dismiss the result as no more than 'a protest vote, a by-election fluke'; rather, he was keen to set Hamilton within a wider Scottish context. While he accepted that there were specific failings within the Labour campaign in Hamilton that had aided the SNP's efforts, Mackintosh was adamant that 'even if there had been a proper organization, the ideal candidate and effective propaganda . . . there would still have been a huge SNP vote which would have to be explained.' Widening his lens to consider the broader rise in support for the SNP across Scotland, Mackintosh rejected the notion that this could be explained by any standard 'mid-term mood of disgruntlement'. Instead, he asserted that a perception had arisen that Scotland was suffering, both economically and culturally, as a result of being governed from London. While as a Labour MP he felt compelled to state that such claims were, in the main, 'complete rubbish', he still, nonetheless, accepted the political potency of the 'widespread, but elusive feeling that modern government' had become 'too complex, too remote'.[101] It is that intangible yet compelling sentiment that must now be explored.

LOSING FAITH IN THE STATE

Reconstructing, or even merely sketching, a political atmosphere is problematic. While election results and opinion polls might enable a degree of conjecture in relation to how the electorate viewed certain issues, the broader question of how voters felt about politics in a deeper sense, and how they believed their relationship with their political representatives to function, can feel troublingly vague, and difficult to answer with any certainty. Yet it remains possible to gain some indications of popular political feeling in Scotland in the late 1960s and to reach some conclusions about the context in which the SNP began to gain electoral momentum. Especially valuable here are the efforts made by the established political parties to understand why the SNP was experiencing such a rapid improvement in its fortunes. In particular, the Conservatives committed time and money to trying to understand Scottish public opinion in this period through the use of targeted constituency-level opinion polling and focus groups. The Conservatives had always been more comfortable using such methods than Labour; while attitudes had begun to change in the post-war era, for a section of the left politics continued to be a question of convincing the public of the merits of your policies, not simply finding out what the average voter believed and regurgitating those views.[102] There were also additional influences: by the late 1960s Scottish Conservatives had experienced almost a decade of declining popular support, and the emergence of the SNP was a particular threat to the party's position as the primary challenger to Labour in Scotland. Labour, in contrast, had retained its vote share in Scotland, and remained in office at Westminster. At a meeting of the Conservative leadership held in London a fortnight after Winnie Ewing's victory at Hamilton, it was concluded that the SNP vote was a protest 'against the present situation'. The task for Conservatives in Scotland was to show that they understood that voters had 'risen in dissent', and to demonstrate that they 'were the Party who was [sic] going to take note of this protest and meet the justifiable grievances of the Scots.' It was agreed that opinion polls in Labour-held constituencies would be commissioned to assist efforts to prevent the SNP supplanting the Conservatives as the second party in Scotland. 'The ultimate intention', it was resolved, was 'to show potential SNP voters that if they wanted to get rid of the unpopular Labour Government it was the Conservatives and not the SNP who would achieve this'.[103]

There are, of course, dangers in utilising such opinion surveys, and the argument that follows is unavoidably speculative. The surveys are, for the most part, small-scale and provide only a brief glimpse of public opinion. Further, they were relatively unsophisticated and suffer, unsurprisingly given the client, from biases in construction and presentation. Yet despite these weaknesses, the surveys do reveal the pervasiveness of a degree of political disillusionment among Scottish voters, and especially those inclined towards the SNP. This was, as will be seen, often portrayed as something akin to cynicism or political nihilism, a blanket distrust of government and politicians that came close to a form of anti-politics. But there was also something more, a sense of loss, of betrayal, of distance; a belief that the link between the people and their representatives had been severed, and now required renewal. Such attitudes were, to be sure, not unique to Scotland; they were evident, with shifts in emphasis, across the UK. Nevertheless, it appears that, in a Scottish context, they worked to reshape political debate in a way that created openings for the SNP.

Early indications of the unfolding of this process were visible in a survey of attitudes in Scotland, Wales and the West Country conducted for the Conservative Party in November 1966 by the polling company Opinion Research Centre (ORC). A response to the rising support for the SNP, Plaid Cymru and the Liberals respectively, the survey reported that in each area there was a common feeling of alienation and neglect, a sense that the two main parties were unsympathetic to the position of those outside London and the south of England. In Scotland, there was found to be an especially strong conviction that the Conservatives had little interest in Scottish issues, as well as a 'widely held . . . belief', dismissed as 'mistaken' by the report's authors given the ostensible generosity of the current administration's regional policy, that the government took out 'more than it puts' in. Notably, in Scotland support for a devolved parliament extended well beyond declared SNP supporters, with almost seventy per cent of those surveyed agreeing that Scotland's position would be improved if home rule were implemented.[104]

Polling conducted by ORC in the Glasgow Pollok constituency prior to the March 1967 by-election disclosed a similar strand of popular opinion. Drawing on interviews with more than 250 voters, the researchers found that 'cynicism' towards both 'the main parties' was 'widespread', with forty-three per cent of those questioned agreeing that they were 'fed up' with Labour and the Conservatives. Around half of those surveyed thought 'it would be a good thing' for either the Liberals or the SNP to do well in the forthcoming by-election. It was felt in Pollok that, while apathy was widespread, Labour voters were more likely to switch to a third party, a prediction proved correct by the eventual result. However, the report emphasised that the SNP's attacks on Westminster were 'widely accepted' by voters, with sixty per cent of respondents feeling that the UK government, whether administered by Labour or the Conservatives, had 'failed to do enough for Scotland' and, again, had taken 'out more wealth' than it had given back. There was a strong sense too that government had become too isolated and distant from voters: two-thirds of interviewees expressed a wish that their MP would 'give more attention to local problems than to national policy'.[105]

The Conservative focus on Scotland increased, for obvious reasons, following the result at Hamilton, which confirmed that the party was failing to benefit from the popular discontent with the Labour government that had arisen after the deflationary budget of July 1966, and the devaluation of sterling the following year.[106] In early 1968, as British politics adjusted to the SNP victory at Hamilton, ORC conducted a major survey of political opinion in Scotland for the Conservative Party, focusing on discussion groups that incorporated a range of 'strong' and 'weak' supporters of the SNP. As Ewen Cameron has observed, the results of this survey were profoundly dispiriting for Scottish Conservatives.[107] The party was deemed to have 'an exceedingly bad image' in Scotland, considered to be 'out of touch, a bastion of "Foreign" (English) privilege, Westminster oriented' and 'associated with recalcitrant landowners'; unlike the Labour Party, which retained some credibility with Scottish voters, the Conservatives were 'the only Scottish Party' that 'elicited mirthful or mirthless laughter' when mentioned.[108]

The insights revealed by the survey were not, however, limited to perceptions of the Conservative Party; rather, the participants expressed a deeper disenchantment with the wider political process. The authors of the report warned that support for the SNP should not be dismissed merely as a protest vote; instead, it needed to be understood as evidence of 'an extremely deep and powerful disillusionment with the existing situation' among voters 'who . . . felt that the bases of their political orientations' were turning 'to sand.' There was, it seemed, 'a very dangerous political vacuum in Scotland', fuelled by 'socio-political anxieties' that cut across the normal "Left-Right" political polarities'. The quasi-academic methodology and political assumptions that informed the discussion groups might, for contemporary readers, provoke a degree of scepticism – strong supporters of Scottish independence were, for example, alleged to be suffering from a 'loss of ego-identity' and were described as 'politically unsophisticated and naïve', while Conservative voters were apparently 'quite well informed' – but behind the psychological affectations lay important insights. Central to Scottish politics, the interviewers found, was a sense 'of political alienation' and 'socio-economic malaise', of 'sheer psychological and geographic distance from the centres of UK power' that encouraged an impression of Scotland as 'provincial, dull and grey'. This was compounded by a perception that Scotland lacked a political voice, with 'Whitehall' believed to be indifferent to Scottish issues and Scottish MPs perceived as having been 'corrupted by the blandishments of Westminster life'. A deep-rooted opposition to what was felt to be excessive government intervention in economic matters was evident across the political spectrum: there was 'too much centralist power lodged in Whitehall to too little effect'. There were 'almost obsessional' references to the level of personal taxation, considered to be 'too high', and the proceeds too often 'misspent', which contributed to a wider feeling that Scotland was being 'milked' for revenue by the government. This instinctive economic liberalism coexisted with an openly authoritarian position on crime. Support for the SNP, it was concluded, was not a protest vote in the traditional sense: these were 'not "floating voters"', but individuals 'mesmerized' by Scotland's political and economic marginalisation, and who 'felt at a loss. Their disaffection with traditional political parties very often appeared complete'.[109]

The report ended by imploring Conservatives to recognise the severity of the situation, and to renew their image in Scotland. Steps in this direction arrived almost immediately, with Ted Heath's so-called 'Declaration of Perth' at the Scottish Conservative conference in May 1968 committing the party to supporting the principle of devolution for Scotland.[110] The group established to consider potential schemes for devolution issued a report later that year, the findings of which suggested that Conservatives were at last beginning to understand the issues they faced in Scotland. The report stressed that the popular disenchantment that was driving support for the SNP was not unique to Scotland: the vital theme, evident across the UK, was 'a feeling that decisions are taken by people far away from the objects of these decisions, a sense of impotence in the face of governmental acts and policies', which resulted in 'a loss of faith in government'. These sentiments were, the authors concluded, the result of the growth of 'an increasingly complex and technical society', in which 'the buck can be passed, often regretfully and politely, but seemingly endlessly, with an apparent indifference and even contempt for the individual, who feels impotent and frustrated'.

While this feeling was 'intensified in Scotland and Wales because these are identifiable entities with their own culture and history', it was not simply a question of 'countering nationalist fervour': the 'malaise' was 'more fundamental and widespread'.[111]

This was an important conclusion. The late 1960s saw the advance of a portrayal of central government not as the straightforward representative or, even more optimistically, as the servant of the people, but rather as their opponent. For both Bill Schwarz and Camilla Schofield, the critical moment in the popularisation of this outlook was the infamous anti-immigration 'rivers of blood' speech delivered by Enoch Powell, the Conservative MP for Wolverhampton South West, in April 1968.[112] Both Schwarz and Schofield suggest that the speech, and the widespread popular support for Powell's position that surfaced in the years that followed, fractured the assumptions and deferential culture that had underpinned the post-war political settlement, and which had maintained the two-party system. Popular frustration with the welfare state in practice blended here with issues of morality, race and national identity to produce a discontent that viewed the government as dishonest, and as having betrayed the confidence of the people.[113] Powell pushed this outlook further during the 1970 general election campaign, when he accused the government and civil service of lying to the public about the true scale of immigration.[114] In Schwarz's words, Powell's interventions captured a 'crisis . . . a decisive moment in the protracted shattering of the post-war social-democratic settlement, a crisis, moreover, which turned on race.' What emerged was a 'populism which sought to claim back the nation from the politicians'.[115] Similarly, for Schofield, Powell's 'populist patriotism' positioned the 'white working class . . . as *victims* of a traitorous state', unsettling 'the fusion within Social Democracy of state and people.'[116]

To be clear, no moral or ethical equivalence is being drawn here between Powell's appeal to racist and anti-immigrant opinion and the SNP's version of Scottish nationalism. Both phenomena occurred, nevertheless, in the context of a broader loss of faith in representative democracy, a belief that the relationship between government and the people had broken down, and that political decision-making needed to be brought closer to the people. In England, Powell gathered such sentiments as part of a radical right-wing populism that, in the words of Richard Crossman, then a member of the Labour government, sought to speak for a 'mass opinion [that had] no respect for parliament' and which 'detests the bloody things that so-called educated people are doing to ordinary, decent mortals'.[117] In Scotland, however, it was the SNP that was best placed to channel this powerful, if vague, sense that government had become simultaneously too powerful and too remote, imposing not just onerous levels of taxation and regulation but also social reforms that took little account of public opinion. A Conservative observer at the SNP's 1968 party conference noted that the delegates shared 'one dominant phobia – a hatred of centralised bureaucracy' and an accompanying 'distrust of central government authoritarianism'.[118] Alongside this libertarian attitude was an ostensibly contradictory desire for the government to take a firmer stance on issues of law and order. A survey conducted prior to the October 1969 Glasgow Gorbals by-election, for example, found that SNP supporters were disproportionately in favour of the reinstatement of both capital and corporal punishment and wished to see lengthier prison sentences.[119]

The blend of instinctive individualism and moral populism that shaped nationalist rhetoric was evident as the 1970 general election approached. Hamish Watt, a former Conservative candidate now contesting Banffshire for the SNP, complained that the growing dominance of central government since 1945 had 'sapped' Scotland's 'energy and resources'. The SNP candidate in Moray and Nairn, Tom Howe, asserted that it did not matter whether Labour or the Conservatives were in power: both had been equally guilty of imposing centralising policies that harmed Scotland.[120] Elizabeth Whitley, standing for the SNP against Alec Douglas-Home in Kinross and West Perthshire, bemoaned what she described as the 'sense of helplessness [that] afflicts us all'. The individual, she suggested, 'no longer counts . . . he [sic] can no longer make his voice heard'; the feeling of impotence this generated was heightened by the fact that 'he still pays – more than ever – for the vast superstructure of state that he carries on his back'.[121] The SNP also demanded longer prison sentences for violent criminals, new 'military-style "glasshouses"' for young offenders, and a referendum on the restoration of capital punishment.[122] Donald Stewart, who would deliver the sole SNP victory in 1970 in the Western Isles, complained that the previous decade had witnessed a 'disastrous deterioration of the moral welfare of the country', and 'a frightening increase in the crime statistics', resulting in the creation of a 'climate repugnant to Christian and civilised standards'.[123]

The confidence with which the SNP could voice the growing popular disillusionment with central government was demonstrated by William Wolfe, the party Chairman. Speaking at a rally in April 1970, held to commemorate the 650th anniversary of the Declaration of Arbroath, Wolfe positioned the SNP as the only party committed to democracy and opposed to centralisation. Labour and the Conservatives were, he claimed, 'provincial parties', representing the 'force of suffocation, of death, of centralism' and committed to removing 'the last vestiges of self-determination which the people of Scotland still enjoy.' Nationalism, in contrast, was a 'radical force . . . of democratic and exciting national life' that offered 'the people of Scotland' a chance to take control of 'their responsibilities and opportunities as a nation', and 'to move again out of the stagnant waters of English provincialism'.[124] This ability to depict the SNP as representative of a modernising tendency within Scottish politics was vital, and ensured that the party's critique of centralisation and bureaucracy was, unlike Powellism in an English context, capable of encompassing more radical and left-leaning strands of opinion, concerned with questions of political representation and democratic participation as opposed to a focus on racial conceptions of national identity.

Here, the SNP began to find itself in sympathy with wider trends. During the 1940s and 1950s, distrust of central government and denunciations of aloof bureaucracy had been features of a right-wing rhetoric used to condemn socialism. By the late 1960s, however, such tropes were increasingly common on the political left.[125] While the Labour Party in Scotland remained deeply sceptical of constitutional reform, preferring to continue to point to the benefits that flowed to Scotland from being part of a planned UK-wide economy, among the trades unions and the wider left, a broader range of opinion was evident.[126] Frustration with the perceived failure of the economic policies of the Labour government during the late 1960s was superimposed upon a pre-existing concern within the Scottish labour movement regarding falling levels of employment in traditional industries such as coalmining, steel and shipbuilding, and a wider sense that Scotland was suffering from relative economic decline. Influenced, at least in part, by the socialist humanism of the early New Left, and the associated critique of the post-war welfare state and nationalised industries as excessively bureaucratic and lacking in scope for popular participation, trade unionists increasingly attributed these difficulties to the neglect of Scottish issues at Westminster, contributing to growing support within the trade union movement for some form of devolution as a means of returning a degree of political and economic autonomy to Scotland.[127] Both the Communist Party and the Scottish Area of the National Union of Mineworkers (NUM), in which individual Communists enjoyed considerable influence, had advocated the establishment of a devolved parliament since the early 1960s; by the close of the decade, this stance was attracting wider support, notably from the Scottish Trades Union Congress (STUC).[128] Speaking at the annual conference of the STUC in April 1969, at which a pro-devolution policy had been adopted, Mick McGahey, the Communist President of the Scottish Area of the NUM, backed a devolved assembly on the basis that it would address the widespread belief among the 'Scottish people . . . that they were alienated in terms of political decisions of the highest importance'.[129] This focus on participation and democracy was repeated the following year, when delegates from the STUC gave evidence to the Royal Commission on the Constitution established by the Labour government as a response to the SNP victory at Hamilton. James Jack, the General Secretary of the STUC, identified a need to 'bring the people as a whole closer to decision-making' and called for constitutional reforms that would 'improve the quality of democratic involvement in government administration.'[130] A similar perspective was offered by the Scottish Committee of the Communist Party, whose members asked the Commission to recognise the 'general trend of reaction among wide sections of the British people against an over-centralised governmental apparatus, and control by almost faceless men'. The party called for 'changes to the machinery of government' that would 'give the people greater control' over the decisions that affected their lives.[131] By 1970, then, a sense of political disaffection, and a belief that the UK government had become too distant, bureaucratic and unresponsive, was no longer to be found only among convinced supporters of Scottish independence, or the heirs to the libertarian analyses of the post-war years.

CONCLUSION

The 1970 general election was, in narrow terms, a disappointment for the SNP; the party returned just a single MP to Westminster and the expectations generated by the victory at Hamilton dissolved as Labour comfortably reclaimed the seat from Winnie Ewing. Yet in retrospect it is clear that the result represented a significant advance: for the first time, the SNP contested the vast majority of Scottish seats and the party's vote share more than doubled in comparison to the previous election, and was comfortably ahead of that achieved by the Liberals.[132] Particular areas of SNP strength were also now visible. Weak performances in urban and industrial Scotland were offset by the second-place finishes achieved by SNP candidates in rural seats such as Argyllshire, Banffshire, East Aberdeenshire, Galloway, Moray and Nairn, and South Angus. These results provided the necessary foundation for the more decisive electoral breakthrough that would occur in 1974. But of greater consequence was the growing prevalence, present now on the left as well as the right, of political assessments that concentrated on perceptions that government had become too remote from the people, and that the remedy to this lay in some form of constitutional reform. This dragged political debate on to territory more advantageous to the SNP.

This development was recognised in a post-election assessment authored by Isobel Lindsay, a sociology lecturer at the University of Strathclyde who had contested Motherwell for the SNP in 1970. Lindsay, a prominent figure in the campaign for nuclear disarmament and onetime Labour Party member who had joined the SNP in 1967, was identified with the younger, more radical wing of the nationalist movement; she would subsequently serve as a Vice-Chair of the party with responsibility for publicity and then policy.[133] Writing in the *Glasgow Herald*, she outlined what she believed to be the SNP's unique contribution to Scottish political debate. Lindsay rejected accusations that nationalism was an archaic political doctrine; instead, she portrayed the SNP, and Plaid Cymru in Wales, as movements that were forward-looking and concerned with the challenges created by contemporary society rather than remaining attached to outmoded, 'old and safe' ideologies. The nationalist parties had, she argued, 'tried to change the agenda . . . away from the issues which were quite rightly relevant in the first half of this century towards issues which will become of even greater fundamental importance in the second half.' For Lindsay, the most urgent political challenge was that posed by the growth of bureaucracy since 1945, which had displaced traditional economic understandings of class divisions by creating new tensions 'between those who make the decisions and those always on the receiving end.' While this was understandable given the extent to which the 'role of government had greatly expanded', it had not been matched by any equivalent modernisation of the political system; this, she believed, posed serious a 'threat . . . to democracy'. Lindsay was clear that she was not arguing for any reduction in the social responsibilities of government: 'the modern state with its extensive economic and welfare functions', was, she asserted, 'here to stay.' Her concern was with ensuring that individuals were able to retain a sense 'of community and identity' in an age when they were forced 'to operate within a scale which is larger and more impersonal than at any previous time in history'. Lindsay's favoured solution was smaller governing units that would bring the state 'closer to those it governs', making government more flexible and responsive. Scotland, as a source of a 'longstanding and ready-made sense of identity' that continued to be 'meaningful to people', presented an ideal 'social and political unit' of this scale.[134]

Lindsay advocated what she termed 'a radical decentralisation' and 'redistribution of power and initiative'. In doing so, she reflected what one near-contemporary study of the SNP recognised as 'the influence of the "small is beautiful" philosophy', with its 'emphasis on de-alienation of the individual through decentralisation and personal participation', that had become increasingly influential 'among radical non-Marxist groups' in the late 1960s.[135] Yet she was at pains to avoid being categorised as being straightforwardly on the political left, and careful to make sure that she offered equal condemnation of both Labour and the Conservatives. 'The gross over-centralisation' that she believed to be so dangerous had, she claimed, 'been pushed relentlessly forward by both Right and Left in this country'. Indeed, at times her criticisms resembled the anti-socialist warnings of the 1940s and 1950s: there had been, she felt, 'an alarming failure to appreciate the social and political dangers of concentrating power in fewer hands.' The 'task' of the SNP was, she concluded, to declare 'that bigness is not necessarily best, that diversity has virtues over uniformity, and that the dead hand of centralism is in danger of reducing us to a nation of battery hens.'[136]

Lindsay's desire to indicate that the SNP was not concerned with old-fashioned ideological divisions was shared, in perhaps a slightly more cynical fashion, by others within the party hierarchy. In an internal strategy paper examining how the party should respond to the Conservative Party's return to power after the 1970 contest, it was accepted that there continued to be opportunities to position the party to the left of Labour, especially on issues such as nuclear disarmament, and thereby win the loyalties of younger, more radical voters. The central conclusion was, however, that any conventional 'left-right frame of reference' should be 'avoided'. It was decided that, instead of simply repeating 'conventional' left-wing criticisms of unpopular Conservative governments, the SNP 'must attempt to cash in on the general discontent and give it an anti-centralist, anti-Westminster rationale.' The report also highlighted potential issues that would provide opportunities for such an approach, noting in particular that the SNP could 'hope to do well in by-elections against Tories by focusing attention on the Common Market', an issue where questions of bureaucracy and remote administration were to the fore.[137]

NOTES

1. On Hamilton's significance, see, for example: Devine, 'The Challenge of Nationalism'; Mitchell, *Hamilton 1967*.
2. NLS Acc. 10090/81: *Report of SNP National Organiser*, 25 April 1967; Hanham, *Scottish Nationalism*, p. 204.

3. Finlay, 'The Early Years: From the inter-war period to the mid-1960s'.
4. *Glasgow Herald*, 10 Mar. 1967.
5. Mackintosh, 'Scottish Nationalism', pp. 391, 394, 392–3.
6. See, for example: Finlay, 'Patriotism, Paternalism and Pragmatism'; Kendrick and McCrone, 'Politics in a Cold Climate'; Hutchison, *Scottish Politics in the Twentieth Century*, pp. 104–26; Lynch, *SNP*, pp. 93–122; Seawright and Curtice, 'The Decline of the Scottish Conservative and Unionist Party', pp. 319–42.
7. The literature on 'decline' is extensive. For excellent overviews, see: Tomlinson, 'Thrice Denied'; Edgerton, *The Rise and Fall of the British Nation*, Chapter 15.
8. McLean, 'The Rise and Fall of the SNP'.
9. NLS Acc. 11368/39: SUA WDC Minutes, 6 Nov. 1959; Acc. 10424/27: SUA WDC, *Annual Report 1959*, pp. 2–3.
10. Harvie, *No Gods and Precious Few Heroes*, p. 110; Finlay, 'Unionism and the Dependency Culture', p. 111; Mitchell, *The Scottish Question*, pp. 132–3.
11. Finlay, *A Partnership for Good*, pp. 138–9.
12. The Unionist vote in Glasgow totalled 34.4 per cent of the electorate in 1955, and 34.5 per cent in 1959. Figures taken from: Craig, *British Parliamentary Election Results, 1950–1973*.
13. *Glasgow Herald*, 9 Oct. 1959.
14. Liberal Party, *Liberalism Leads*.
15. Grimond, *The Liberal Future*, pp. 22, 63, 68, and 79. Capitalisation in original.
16. Morgan, *Britain since 1945*, pp. 199–238.
17. Finlay, Richard J. "Bannerman, John Macdonald, Baron Bannerman of Kildonan (1901–1969), politician and rugby player", *Oxford Dictionary of National Biography*, 23 Sep. 2004; accessed 2 Jun. 2021.
18. Bod. Lib. CPA SUMC 1/54: C. E. Bellairs to Thomas Moore MP, 5 Jul. 1962; *The Times*, 16 Jun. 1962.
19. On the organisational reforms of the 1960s and 1970s, see: Kellas, 'The Party in Scotland', pp. 688–9.
20. Bod. Lib. CPA CCO 20/11/1: Lord Aldington to R. A. Butler, 28 Apr. 1961.
21. Bod. Lib. CPA CCO 20/11/1: Lord Aldington to R. A. Butler, 16 Jun. 1961.
22. Bod. Lib. CPA SUMC 2/11: Minutes, 27 Nov. 1964.
23. Bod. Lib. CPA SUMC 2/13: Minutes, 9 Jun. 1964.
24. Morgan, *Britain since 1945*, pp. 209–15 and 223–8; Ramsden, *The Winds of Change*, pp. 158–64.
25. Cannadine, 'Apocalypse When?'; Edgerton, *The Rise and Fall of the British Nation*, Chapter 15
26. Pimlott, *Harold Wilson*, pp. 299–311.

27. Bod. Lib. CPA SUMC 2/13: Minutes, 9 Jun. 1964.
28. Levitt, 'The Origins of the Scottish Development Department'.
29. *Development and Growth in Central Scotland* (Cmnd 2188, 1963), p. 1.
30. Bod. Lib. CPA PUB: *The Campaign Guide 1959*, p. 389. Capitalisation in original.
31. Bod. Lib. CPA SUMC 1/54: *Suggested framework for Speeches*, 28 Sept. 1959. Capitalisation in original.
32. Bod. Lib. CPA PUB: *The Campaign Guide 1964*, pp. 362–5.
33. NLS Acc. 11368/90: *Sir Alec Douglas-Home: The Unionist Candidate* (Perth, 1964).
34. *Scotland with the Unionists* (Edinburgh, 1964).
35. NLS Acc. 11884/21: Lady Tweedsmuir Papers, Notes for Adoption Meeting, 24 Sept. 1964.
36. The Labour Party gained five seats in Scotland in 1964; the election resulted in a Labour majority in parliament of just three.
37. Bod. Lib. CPA SUMC 2/24: Minutes, 3 Nov. 1964.
38. NLS Acc. 11368/23: SUA EDC Minutes, 13 Nov. 1964.
39. NLS Acc. 11368/5: SUA CC Minutes, 13 Nov. 1964.
40. PKCA MS 152/6/1/3: Crieff Unionist Association Minutes, 17 Nov. 1964. Capitalisation in original.
41. NLS Acc. 11368/22: SUA EDC Minutes, 10 Jul. 1964. Capitalisation in original.
42. NLS Acc. 11368/5: SUA CC Minutes, 13 Nov. 1964. On resale price maintenance see: Findley, 'The Conservative Party and Defeat'.
43. Seawright, 'Scottish Unionist Party: What's in a Name?'.
44. Bod. Lib. CPA SUMC 2/24: Minutes, 24 Nov. 1964.
45. NLS Acc. 11368/40: SUA WDC Minutes, 4 Dec. 1964.
46. Campbell, *Edward Heath: A Biography*; Bale, *The Conservatives since 1945*, Chapter 4.
47. Bod. Lib. CPA PUB: *The Campaign Guide 1966*, pp. 13–14 and 267.
48. Taylor, 'The Record of the 1950s is irrelevant'.
49. Flores and Whitely, 'The "Beeching Axe" and Electoral Support in Britain'.
50. Bod. Lib. CPA SUMC 2/24: Minutes, 20 Jan. and 17 Feb. 1965.
51. McIntyre would return to the BBC in 1968, eventually becoming controller of Radio 4 and then Radio 3. See the obituary in: *The Scotsman*, 22 Apr. 2014.
52. NLS Acc. 13116/21 George Younger Papers: Ian McIntyre to George Younger, 1 May 1966.
53. Bod. Lib. CPA SUMC 2/25: Minutes, 11 May 1966.
54. *The Scotsman*, 12 May 1966.
55. Saleh, 'The Decline of the Scottish Conservatives in North-East Scotland'.
56. The nine constituencies were: Aberdeen North, Aberdeen South, Aberdeenshire East, Aberdeenshire West, Banffshire, Dundee East, Dundee West, North Angus and Mearns, South Angus.

57. NLS Acc. 11368/38: Scottish Conservative and Unionist Party: North-East Regional Council minutes, 11 Feb. and 22 Oct. 1966.
58. Saleh, 'The Decline of the Scottish Conservatives in North-East Scotland', p. 241.
59. *The Scotsman*, 22 Jan. 1962.
60. *Daily Telegraph*, 31 Dec. 1966.
61. NLS Acc. 7295/17: Arthur Donaldson, *SNP Chairman's Report*, 5 Sept. 1964.
62. NLS Acc. 7295/17: SNP, *Annual Report of the National Demonstrations Committee*, 1964 and 1965.
63. NLS Acc. 7295/17: SNP, *Report of Executive Vice-Chairman (Organisation)* and *Report of Executive Vice-Chairman (Publicity and Development)*, 28 Nov. 1964.
64. NLS Acc. 7295/17: Robert McIntyre, *SNP Election Committee Report*, 28 Nov. 1964
65. NLS Acc. 7295/17: Arthur Donaldson, *SNP Chairman's Report*, 30 Nov. 1965.
66. NLS Acc. 7295/17: Arthur Donaldson, *SNP Chairman's Report*, 3 Dec. 1966.
67. Webb, *The Growth of Nationalism in Scotland*, pp. 97–9; Brand, *The National Movement in Scotland*, p. 67.
68. Kemp, *The Hollow Drum*, pp. 94–5; Finlay, 'The Early Years: From the Inter-War Period to the Mid-1960s', pp. 28–30.
69. Brand, *The National Movement in Scotland*, p. 67; Finlay, 'The Early Years: From the Inter-War Period to the Mid-1960s', p. 28; MacDonald, *Whaur Extremes Meet*, p. 239.
70. Harvie, *No Gods and Precious Few Heroes*, p. 111; Kemp, *The Hollow Drum*, pp. 96–106; Lynch, *SNP*, pp. 93–122; Finlay, The Early Years: From the Inter-War Period to the Mid-1960s', p. 30; Mitchell, *The Scottish Question*, p. 119.
71. An exception is Ben Jackson's exploration of the political thought of Scottish nationalism. See: Jackson, 'The Political Thought of Scottish Nationalism', and *The Case for Scottish Independence*.
72. NLS Acc. 7295/17: Ian MacDonald, *Report of National Organiser*, 3 Dec. 1966.
73. Hanham, *Scottish Nationalism*, pp. 163–80.
74. Wilson, *SNP: The Turbulent Years*, p. 56.
75. *Aims and Policy of the SNP*, pp. 3–4.
76. *SNP & You*, p. 4. Following the Soviet intervention in Czechoslovakia in 1968, this claim was removed from subsequent editions.
77. NLS 10090/68: *Your Scottish National candidate is: Dr Robert McIntyre* (1966).
78. Scottish National Party, *The Scotland We Seek*, pp. 2–3. Capitalisation in original.

79. *Aims and Policy of the SNP*, p. 3.
80. Morton, *Unionist-Nationalism*.
81. NLS Acc. 10090/79: *The Scottish National Party: Election Fund Appeal* (1964).
82. NLS Acc. 10090/79: Arthur Donaldson, *Chairman's Speech to SNP Conference*, 22 May 1965.
83. NLS Acc. 10090/102: SNP Press Statement, 18 Sept. 1965.
84. *Daily Telegraph*, 31 Dec. 1966. Capitalisation in original.
85. Morgan, *Britain since 1945*, pp. 253–4.
86. *The Scotsman*, 6 Jun. 1966.
87. *Weekly Scotsman*, 26 May 1966.
88. Hill, 'Nations of Peace'.
89. Wilson, *Pirates of the Air*.
90. NLS Acc. 13687/1: *Radio Free Scotland: Opening statement of aims and ideals* (1960), pp. 3–4. Capitalisation in original.
91. Dyer, 'The Evolution of the Centre-Right and the State of Scottish Conservatism', p. 45; Hutchison, *Scottish Politics in the Twentieth Century*, pp. 119–21.
92. *Sunday Mail*, 18 Feb. 1968.
93. *Glasgow Herald*, 24 Apr. 1968.
94. NLS Acc. 11765/55: Scottish Liberal Party: General Council Minutes, 15 Dec. 1962.
95. NLS Acc. 11765/55: Scottish Liberal Party: General Council Minutes, 14 Dec. 1963.
96. NLS Acc. 13417/3: SNP: National Council Minutes, 7 Dec. 1963; National Executive Committee, 14 Feb., and 7 Mar. 1964.
97. NLS Acc. 6038/4: William Wolfe to Arthur Donaldson, 18 Aug. 1966.
98. *The Scotsman*, 22 Jan. 1969
99. Devine, 'The Challenge of Nationalism', p. 143.
100. Mitchell, *Hamilton*, p. 81.
101. Mackintosh, 'A Bed of Thistles', p. 12.
102. Beers, 'Whose Opinion? Changing Attitudes Towards Opinion Polling in British Politics'.
103. Bod. Lib. CPA CCO 20/11/3: 'Scottish Nationalism': Points of Action agreed at the Meeting held 16 Nov. 1967.
104. Bod. Lib. CPA CCO 180/29/1/1: Opinion Research Centre, *Special Attitudes in Scotland, Wales and the West Country* (Nov. 1966).
105. Bod. Lib. CCO 500/18/99: Opinion Research Centre, *A Survey on Pollok Constituency* (Jan. 1967), p. 4.
106. On these measures, see: Thorpe, *A History of the British Labour Party*, p. 166.
107. Cameron, *Impaled upon a Thistle*, pp. 282–3.
108. Bod Lib. CPA CCO 500/50/1: Opinion Research Centre, *The Motivations behind Scottish Nationalism* (Mar. 1968), p. 4.

109. Bod Lib. CPA CCO 500/50/1: Opinion Research Centre, *The Motivations behind Scottish Nationalism* (Mar. 1968), pp. 5, 16, 14, 8, 13, 11, 9, 17, and 10.

110. On the 'Declaration of Perth', see: Pentland, 'Edward Heath, the Declaration of Perth and the Scottish Conservative and Unionist Party'.

111. NLS Acc. 11368/79: Scottish Conservative and Unionist Association, *Government of Scotland Policy Group: First Report to the Constitutional Committee, August 1968*, pp. 3–4.

112. See: Schwarz, *The White Man's World*, pp. 33–52; Schofield, *Enoch Powell and the Making of Postcolonial Britain*, pp. 208–63.

113. On the public response to Powell, see: Ritscherle, 'Opting out of utopia', pp. 280–316; Whipple, 'Revisiting the "Rivers of Blood" Controversy', pp. 717–35.

114. Heffer, *Like the Roman*, pp. 553–65.

115. Schwarz, *The White Man's World*, pp. 37 and 399.

116. Schofield, *Enoch Powell and the Making of Postcolonial Britain*, p. 20. Emphasis and capitalisation in original.

117. Crossman, *The Crossman Diaries*, entry dated 28 Apr. 1968, p. 484.

118. Bod. Lib. Conservative Research Department 3/28/2: Keith Raffan, *The SNP: 34th Annual Conference, 10th June 1968*.

119. Bod. Lib. CPA CCO 500/18/125: Opinion Research Centre, *A Survey on Gorbals Constituency*.

120. NLS Acc. 7295/20(ii): *Nor 'East Symbol: The Independent Voice of the North East*, Jun.–Jul. 1969. Watt and Howe achieved second place finishes in 1970, and both seats would be won by the SNP in February 1974, with Watt elected in Banffshire and Moray and Nairn secured by Winnie Ewing.

121. *Scots Independent*, 7 Mar. 1970.

122. *Glasgow Herald*, 18 Mar. 1970.

123. NLS Acc. 13101/19: *Donald J. Stewart* (Stornoway, 1970).

124. *Scots Independent*, 11 Apr. 1970.

125. Panitch and Leys, *Searching for Socialism*, pp. 43–44.

126. See: Scottish Council of the Labour Party, *The Government of Scotland: Evidence of the Labour Party in Scotland to the Commission on the Constitution*.

127. See, for example: Lawrence Daly, 'Scotland on the Dole', *New Left Review* 17 (1962), pp. 17–23. On the New Left more generally, see: Kenny, *The First New Left*.

128. Aitken, *The Bairns o' Adam*, pp. 215–21.

129. Scottish Trades Union Congress, *72nd Annual Report* (Glasgow, 1969), p. 234.

130. Royal Commission on the Constitution, *Minutes of Evidence IV: Scotland* (London, 1971), p. 127. The evidence was given on 20 July 1970.

131. Royal Commission on the Constitution, *Minutes of Evidence IV: Scotland* (London, 1971), pp. 66 and 60. The evidence was given on 4–5 May 1970.

132. The SNP stood candidates in sixty-five of the seventy-one Scottish constituencies, up from twenty-three in 1966. The party polled 11.4 per cent of the total vote, the Liberals 5.5 per cent.

133. On Lindsay's career, see the interview in: Tom Freeman, 'Isobel Lindsay's Radical Road to Devolution', *Holyrood*, 1 Mar. 2019 https://www.holyrood.com/inside-politics/view,isobel-lindsays-radical-road-to-devolution_9959.htm, accessed 16 Jun. 2021.

134. *Glasgow Herald*, 22 Jun. 1970.

135. Webb, *The Growth of Nationalism in Scotland*, p. 111.

136. *Glasgow Herald*, 22 Jun. 1970. Capitalisation in original.

137. NLS Acc. 6038/Box 10: *SNP Research Department Memorandum: SNP Strategy* (Aug. 1970).

3

Combating Centralisation:
Europe, Local Government and the
Rise of the SNP, 1967–1975

IF THE 1960S WITNESSED the entry of the SNP into the Scottish political mainstream after more than three decades on the fringes, then it was in the early 1970s that the potential threat that the party could pose to the established political and constitutional order became fully apparent. As any account of twentieth-century Scotland will narrate, the advances achieved by the SNP at the two general elections of 1974, when the party had seven and then eleven MPs returned to Westminster and, perhaps more significantly, polled twenty-two and then thirty per cent of the vote, transformed Scottish politics permanently. At the October 1974 contest the SNP overtook the Conservatives to finish in second place in terms of popular support; beyond the eleven constituency victories, the party had finished second in an additional forty-two seats.[1] Scottish developments were granted further significance at Westminster as a result of the precarious parliamentary position faced by the Labour government after October 1974: the government's majority in the Commons was just three, and would evaporate by 1977, granting the new SNP contingent added weight and influence. And while support for the SNP would ebb in the late 1970s and 1980s, the party would never again return to the irrelevance it had previously endured.

The striking upsurge in support for the SNP evident in the early 1970s can perhaps be explained by the political atmosphere in which the 1974 elections were held. The Royal Commission on the Constitution established by the Labour government in 1968 as a response to the SNP victory at Hamilton, now led by Lord Kilbrandon after the death of the original Chair Lord Crowther, published its final reports in October 1973, with a majority of the Commissioners supporting legislative devolution for Scotland, returning questions of constitutional reform to political prominence.[2] Continued concerns over the state of the Scottish economy, and the initial rejection by the Heath administration of calls for government assistance for struggling industrial concerns, generated further discontent with the UK government among Scottish voters. Important here was the 'work-in' at Upper Clyde Shipbuilders (UCS) in 1971–2. UCS had been threatened with closure following the government's refusal of requests for financial support; the innovative industrial action undertaken by the workforce, with Jimmy Reid as its public figurehead, forced the government into a humiliating reversal and contributed to a broader debate over Scotland's economic future that deepened support for devolution among sections of the Scottish labour movement.[3] Contemporary economic uncertainties interacted with the more hopeful visions of the future enabled by the discovery of North Sea oil, the full extent of which was becoming clearer by the early 1970s. In the context of rising inflation, the global oil crisis of 1973, and the confrontations between the Conservative government and the National Union of Mineworkers that precipitated the February 1974 general election, the SNP's 'It's Scotland's Oil' campaign, launched in September 1972, held out the prospect of a wealthy, self-sufficient independent Scottish state no longer shackled to a Britain in seemingly irreversible economic and political decline.[4] As *The Economist* claimed in March 1974, for 'most Scots' oil was 'a way of winning back their economic self-respect after 50 years of industrial decline'.[5]

The debates over devolution, the economy and oil no doubt influenced the SNP's improved electoral performance in this period. But in each instance, there is some uncertainty as to precisely how, and to what extent, the issue in question benefited nationalist candidates. Although the SNP obviously supported constitutional change, devolution, particularly when advocated by the UK parties, posed intellectual and tactical challenges for the party; moreover, it was scarcely a first-order issue at the February 1974 election. Similarly, the SNP was restricted to a marginal role in the popular opposition to the economic policies of the Heath government. Lacking an established presence in the labour movement, the SNP had difficulty in adding a meaningful nationalist perspective to those offered by the STUC, the Labour Party, and, in certain industries, the Communist Party. Oil, meanwhile, was never a straightforward source of votes for the SNP, despite, as James Mitchell has noted, the image of an 'oil-fuelled Nationalism' becoming 'one of the central myths of modern Scottish politics'.[6] The oil campaign always risked making the case for self-government contingent on a favourable economic prognosis, leaving unanswered the question of whether an independent Scotland would remain viable without oil. More than this, it exposed the SNP to accusations of greed and selfishness that were, as opinion polling revealed, often off-putting to voters.[7]

The purpose of this chapter is not to argue that such questions played no part in the electoral realignment of the early 1970s; it is, however, to suggest that there were other determinants that were equally, if not more, significant. The SNP's political outlook was, by this time, well-established, and relatively consistent; as detailed in the previous chapter, the party's traditional distrust of bureaucracy and attacks on the centralising policies of successive UK governments, formed in the post-war era, had started to find a more receptive audience, and had been refreshed with newer left-wing perspectives. Until the late 1960s, however, Scottish nationalism's preference for decentralisation and localism remained a general critique of the alleged neglect of Scotland by a remote government at Westminster. But this would soon change as two issues emerged that provided specific targets for the SNP's rhetoric of anti-centralisation. The first was the question of the UK's membership of what was then the European Economic Community (EEC), more commonly referred to by contemporaries as the Common Market, eventually achieved in 1973; the second was the reform of Scottish local government, which resulted in the abolition of the ancient royal burghs and the creation of a two-tier system of districts and regions. Together, these questions granted the SNP's critique of remote and over-powerful bureaucracies a new coherence and electoral relevance. Crucially, the SNP was the only major party opposed both to Scotland joining the EEC as part of the UK and to the restructuring of local government, allowing the party to position itself at the 1974 general elections as the defender of Scottish interests in the face of an indifferent Westminster consensus.

SNP policy on the question of EEC membership has received some consideration from historians, as have nationalist attitudes during the 1975 referendum on continued UK membership of the EEC called by the Labour government.[8] In contrast, little has been written on the electoral consequences of local government reform.[9] While the European question was more charged, both cases nevertheless raised important concerns about Scotland's status within the United Kingdom and the potential impact of a further increase in the distance between political institutions and the voters they claimed to represent. Moreover, the issues of Europe and local government reform could, in different ways, be portrayed as infringing the Union settlement of 1707; together, they also appeared to threaten to impose new layers of expensive and unresponsive bureaucracy. Questions of representation, identity and popular consent appeared, then, in new ways in the early 1970s, shifting political debate away from economic concerns and towards the constitution. This was, it need hardly be said, ground upon which the SNP was far more comfortable than its opponents.

Concentrating on internal policy debates and the public rhetoric adopted by party figures, this chapter considers first the impact of the debate over UK entry to the EEC on nationalist policy and ideology. Beginning with a survey of the evolution of SNP policy towards Europe during the 1960s, the SNP response to the successful negotiations over UK membership of the EEC after 1970 is then explored; thereafter, the role the European question played in SNP electioneering in 1974 is assessed, before an analysis of the 1975 referendum on EEC membership in a Scottish context. The chapter then progresses to an examination of the SNP's response to the restructuring of Scottish local government.

THE SNP AND EUROPE, 1967–1970

The UK government had initially remained aloof from attempts to institutionalise economic integration in western Europe, staying outside the EEC upon its creation in 1957.[10] This decision has been criticised in retrospect as a strategic error that meant that British interests were not represented within the EEC from the outset, with long-term consequences. Yet, as Robert Saunders has suggested, such assessments underestimate the complexity of the choices facing senior UK politicians given the position of sterling and the extent to which the Commonwealth remained a key destination for UK manufacturing exports during the 1950s.[11] By the early 1960s, however, the sustained economic growth experienced in the EEC member states combined with a growing sense of Britain's relative economic decline to make a UK application to join the Common Market appear inevitable. EEC membership came to be viewed as a means of forcing the British economy to undergo a period of much-needed modernisation: as Jim Tomlinson has noted, 'the perceived superior economic performance' of the member states 'provided one major impetus' for a British 'application to join the EEC.'[12] A first attempt at membership was made by the Conservative government in 1961; a second UK application was submitted in May 1967, undertaken by a Labour Party that had reversed its previous opposition to membership once in office. While both applications failed as a result of French opposition, by the close of the 1960s there was an overwhelming domestic cross-party consensus in favour of membership: the Labour government's application was supported by the largest Commons majority recorded on any issue in more than two decades.[13]

The SNP had, in the immediate post-war period, been broadly sympathetic towards European integration. By the time of the 1967 application, however, the nationalist stance had begun to shift. At the Pollok by-election in March 1967 the SNP candidate George Leslie had backed calls for a referendum on the issue.[14] Two months later Gordon Wilson, then the National Secretary of the SNP, circulated a policy document urging opposition to membership of the EEC on the basis that, unless endorsed in a referendum by a majority of Scots, such a step would not only signify a breach of the Treaty of Union, but would also 'spell the beginning of the destruction of our national identity'. Advocating a 'wholehearted and intelligent' campaign against entry and a 'hard intransigent' attitude, Wilson, who expressed a preference for closer links with the Scandinavian nations, which then remained outside the EEC, suggested emphasising the dangers posed by the potential loss of sovereignty and the likely influx of cheap labour.[15] With the exception of his concerns regarding immigration, Wilson's suggestions were accepted, and the SNP's National Executive agreed to launch an anti-EEC campaign, with the emphasis to be placed upon the constitutional implications of membership.[16] Thereafter opposition to Scotland joining the Common Market, at least as part of the UK, began to feature more conspicuously in SNP literature. At this stage there was still a certain ambiguity regarding the party's position, which focused on concerns that Scotland would be relegated to a peripheral role within the EEC, denied the separate voice enjoyed even by Luxembourg. Party policy was most often summarised in the slogan 'no voice, no entry', a formulation that did not necessarily preclude the possibility of EEC membership for a future, independent Scotland. As a 1967 SNP pamphlet argued, there needed to be 'A voice – and a vote – for Scotland in the Common Market'; membership as a mere region of the UK would mean that 'Scotland's economic future' would 'be in danger'.[17]

This nuance was, however, difficult to maintain, and nationalist opposition to the Common Market was increasingly expressed in more absolute terms that at least gestured towards a rejection of membership in principle. At the Hamilton by-election in November 1967, held just weeks prior to the announcement that France would veto the second UK application, Common Market membership was described as 'national suicide' for Scotland.[18] Indeed, as Andrew Devenney has recognised, the SNP's criticism of the EEC became more 'vitriolic' by the end of the decade, as 'dire warnings of disaster . . . replaced the more cautious and tempered positions of the mid-1960s.'[19] Yet the extent of the shift in the party's rhetoric should not be overstated, and needs to be placed in context. SNP attitudes towards the EEC certainly hardened after 1967, but the underlying perspective was consistent with the party's general stance in the post-war decades. As UK membership of the Common Market became a serious prospect, so the issue became one to which the SNP could apply a pre-existing rhetoric that centred upon opposition to centralisation. Indeed, European integration offered nationalists a compelling illustration of the trends which they had long claimed to oppose. During an unsuccessful attempt to build links with the STUC on the basis of shared hostility towards EEC membership, Gordon Wilson informed James Jack, General Secretary of the STUC, that the SNP was committed to a campaign to prevent Scotland being 'dragged into the Common Market in its present bureaucratic form on the coat-tails of England'. But he also went further, arguing that the EEC 'now seems to be set irrevocably on the road to political unity and bureaucratic centralism', with the current level of integration representing just the 'tip of a much more sinister iceberg'.[20]

Europe assumed an increasingly pronounced place within SNP messaging prior to the June 1970 general election. A statement rejecting membership of the EEC as 'presently constituted' was issued in January 1970, and the following month it was agreed that Europe would be the 'main theme' of the party's campaign efforts.[21] And despite the South Ayrshire by-election, held the following month, producing a disappointing result for the SNP, the party's director of communications, and future MP, Douglas Crawford, reported that the Common Market had proved 'a very live and valuable issue in the campaign' and urged 'its use wherever possible and practicable'.[22] That month, the SNP, rather presumptively, sent a delegation to Brussels, which included Crawford and Winnie Ewing, with the intention of making senior figures within the Community aware of Scotland's distinctive interests and, as they saw it, unique constitutional position: they alleged that EEC representatives 'showed an almost religious determination to end national awareness'.[23] The delegation was deemed a success, having allowed the SNP to take the 'initiative' on the issue and garnering 'useful publicity' for the party.[24] This was followed by the drafting of a statement for dissemination by constituency parties entitled 'The Kingdom of Scotland: A Constitutional Crisis', which offered a concise summary of the constitutional basis of the SNP's opposition to entering the Common Market. The Treaty of Union had, the text asserted, offered Scotland a 'guarantee of formal equality of partnership' with England, as well as a series of 'guarantees' designed to protect Scotland's legal, educational and ecclesiastical traditions: EEC membership would upend this settlement, leaving Scotland without meaningful representation in European institutions, relegated to the 'status of a subject province'.[25]

The SNP's instincts on Europe were, in electoral terms, sound: polling conducted on behalf of the Conservative Party prior to the March 1970 South Ayrshire by-election found that more than half of the voters questioned were firmly opposed to joining the Common Market, with fewer than one in four in favour.[26] Similarly, a Scotland-wide poll undertaken by the University of Strathclyde found that sixty per cent of respondents were against EEC membership.[27] The pro-European consensus that prevailed amongst the leadership of the Conservatives, Labour and the Liberals therefore offered a clear example of the way in which Scottish opinion was being neglected at Westminster. It also provided the SNP with an opportunity to argue that they were the only party willing to speak on behalf of what appeared to be the majority of Scottish voters, and to take control of the anti-centralising rhetoric that had once been the preserve of Unionism. It was, then, little surprise that senior figures within the party were willing to offer increasingly unequivocal rejections of membership that went far beyond merely calling for separate Scottish representation within European institutions. At a nationalist rally in Paisley in April 1970, the party Chairman, William Wolfe, depicted the EEC as a dangerous manifestation of the force of 'political centralism', one that threatened to 'destroy . . . the principles of participating democracy [sic] and modern nationhood'. Wolfe went on to suggest that supporters of the Common Market were 'as much doctrinaire centralists as their opposite numbers in the Kremlin . . . Their political philosophy is insidious to those who are steeped in the democratic tradition. They say "To be big is to be good; to be bigger is to be better; to be biggest is to be supreme".'[28]

Similar criticisms of European integration, coupled with reminders that the SNP was the only major political party in Scotland opposed to EEC membership, could be found across the literature produced by the SNP during the 1970 general election campaign. At times the party returned to the earlier slogan of 'no voice, no entry', and an emphasis on the danger that 'Scotland would be totally unrepresented' if it were to be 'dragged into the Common Market on the coat tails of England'. In this reading, entry to the Common Market would require the explicit consent of the Scottish people: 'Scotland's voice' had, the SNP argued, to 'be heard'.[29] More often, however, party literature and statements issued by SNP candidates tended to express opposition to membership of the EEC in starker, less qualified terms. As James Kellas noted in the Nuffield review of the 1970 general election, during the campaign the SNP recognised that opposition to the Common Market was stronger amongst 'the Scottish electorate (especially in rural areas)', and offered the party 'a way of winning votes from outside the devolutionist sector'.[30] The SNP manifesto declared that the 'blind determination of the London Parties to enter the Common Market' was 'one of the crucial issues of our time'; moreover, the prospect of Scotland becoming 'a mere region of a member country' raised 'fundamental questions of constitutional law as well as of political morality'. The Common Market was, it was concluded, a 'dangerous experiment in gross overcentralisation', membership of which threatened to deal 'a death blow' to Scotland's 'very existence as a nation'. Voting for the SNP was 'the only way in which Scots' could 'vote against the Common Market'.[31] Contesting Motherwell, Isobel Lindsay echoed these sentiments, warning voters that 'a vote for the Labour, Conservative and Liberal Parties' was 'a vote for joining the Common Market': only the SNP reflected 'the wishes of the Scottish people', who realised 'that the Common Market' was 'against their interests'.[32] In Dundee, where the SNP was contesting the city's East and West divisions for the first time at a general election, Europe emerged as key theme of the campaign. This was especially true in Dundee East, where the sitting Labour MP, George Thomson, had, as Chancellor of the Duchy of Lancaster, played a key role in the negotiations surrounding EEC membership; here even the Conservative candidate, Allan Stewart, disowned his party's national policy and adopted an anti-Common Market stance.[33] Thomson's SNP opponent, Ian MacAulay, argued that Scotland should follow the example of Switzerland, and remain outside the EEC: he could, he stated, 'see no possibility of the conditions ever being right for Scotland to join the Common Market'.[34] In Dundee West, the SNP candidate James Shepherd stated that Common Market membership would be 'economic suicide' for Scotland.[35]

SNP condemnations of the Common Market were particularly pronounced in rural and semi-rural constituencies. In these areas, where fishing and agriculture remained important sources of both employment and local identity, opposition to membership of the EEC was especially strong. Here, where the Liberals might have been expected to gain from any rise in third-party support, Europe appeared to have introduced a new, constitutional dividing line into Scottish electoral politics: the SNP, as, to take the phrase used by Donald Stewart in his successful campaign in the Western Isles, the 'only major political party opposed to entry', were the beneficiaries.[36] In the two Perthshire constituencies, it was reported that the SNP hoped to take advantage of anti-EEC sentiments.[37]

In Argyllshire, Iain MacCormick, the son of John MacCormick, was running for the SNP against Michael Noble, the former Conservative Secretary of State for Scotland. At a rally in Oban, MacCormick rejected EEC membership and reminded those present 'that both the Tories and the Socialists [i.e. Labour] were intent on joining the Common Market'; this he attributed to 'the lust for power' and preference for a 'centralised form of government' that was 'shared by the leaders of both parties.' 'A vote for the SNP was', he suggested, 'the only way in which the Scottish electorate could register its opposition to the Common Market'.[38] MacCormick would eventually finish in second place, ahead of the Labour candidate, having polled thirty per cent of the vote in a seat the party had not contested since a by-election in April 1940.

As one contemporary academic observer noted, in the rural north-east of Scotland the SNP had, at the 1970 general election, become in effect the 'anti-Common Market party' rather than advocates 'of national liberation', a shift in emphasis that was especially damaging to the local Liberals.[39] Jim McGugan, the SNP candidate in North Angus and Mearns, warned against the 'craze for centralisation' that he believed underlay the desire to join the Common Market.[40] McGugan failed to make a significant impact against the Conservative incumbent Alick Buchanan-Smith, who wisely opted to simply avoid discussing the question of Europe during the campaign.[41] In Aberdeenshire East, Banffshire, Moray and Nairn, and South Angus, in contrast, SNP candidates were able to establish footholds that would help enable the victories eventually achieved in 1974. Tom Howe, the SNP nominee in Moray and Nairn and a local Councillor, maintained that the prospect of EEC membership was 'the greatest single issue facing the people of Scotland since 1707', and stressed once more that 'his party' was 'the only one opposed to Britain entering the Common Market'.[42] Alex Farquhar, standing for the SNP in Aberdeenshire East, accorded similar prominence to his opposition to the Common Market.[43]

While they were relatively modest, the inroads made by the SNP at the 1970 contest, especially in the north-east, where, unlike in Perthshire and Stirlingshire, the party had little prior track record of contesting parliamentary elections, should encourage a reassessment of the reasons for nationalist success in this period. Prior to the 1970 election, Scottish Liberals had condemned the SNP for its failure to join the other major parties in recognising the benefits of EEC membership. In a pamphlet authored by Christopher Scott, a former treasurer of the Scottish Liberals and close ally of David Steel, the Liberal MP for Roxburghshire, it was noted with some bemusement that while all the major parties in Scotland were committed to delivering economic growth and improved public services, differing only 'in how these highly desirable objectives [were] to be obtained', on Europe there was a 'great divergence', with the SNP arguing that 'Scotland's destiny is better away from the EEC'. It was, Scott concluded, disappointing that the SNP appeared to be 'lagging so far behind the thinking of all the other major parties', particularly when it was simply 'political good sense' that the UK should join the EEC.[44] It was, all the same, the SNP's rejection of political 'good sense' and consensus that allowed the party to establish a tentative electoral presence in parts of Scotland. The SNP had long proffered a critique of centralisation, and of remote government, that positioned the party as the defender of individual freedom; equally, it had long been largely ignored by Scottish voters, who found other parties better able to satisfy such sentiments. It was the issue of Europe that granted that critique a more immediate relevance and generated an audience more receptive to the SNP's message, providing a focus for what had in the past been a hazy mix of individualism and constitutional grievance. More than this, as the only party officially opposed to EEC membership, the SNP could, for the first time, claim plausibly to speak for popular opinion in Scotland. In an initial review of the 1970 election campaign, Douglas Crawford concluded that 'our opposition to the Common Market' had played an important role in garnering press coverage for the SNP.[45] Moreover, the surprise election of a Conservative government committed to pursuing UK membership of the Common Market ensured that Europe would continue to be central to SNP propaganda in the early 1970s.

REJECTING 'REMOTE CONTROL': THE SNP AND THE ANTI-MARKET CAMPAIGN, 1970–1973

The period after 1970 can appear as one in which support for the SNP ebbed, before reviving from late 1971 onwards, as the Conservative government's economic policy ran aground, and the nationalists' oil campaign began to garner public attention. In this reading, the critical electoral milestones are the 1973 by-elections in Dundee East and Glasgow Govan, held in March and November respectively. With Gordon Wilson achieving a strong second place in the former contest before Margo MacDonald recorded a surprise victory in the latter, these contests disclosed growing support for the SNP, and pointed towards the party's impressive performances at the 1974 general elections.[46] But if the SNP's performance in 1970 had felt underwhelming, especially given the expectations created by Ewing's victory in Hamilton, the ongoing importance of Europe provided a significant element of continuity within the party's campaigning efforts, and contributed to the improved results achieved in 1974. As the efforts of the Conservative government to take the UK into the EEC progressed during 1971 and 1972, Europe remained a key political question. With a few notable exceptions such as Enoch Powell, the Conservatives were, like the Liberals, relatively enthusiastic pro-Marketeers. The Labour Party, in contrast, was deeply divided. While a Labour government had been responsible for the 1967 application, there was a strong strand of principled opposition to the Common Market within the party, particularly on the left. After 1970, those hostile to Common Market entry began to more frequently raise the question of whether the Conservative government had a mandate to approve such a profound constitutional change given the perceived implications for parliamentary sovereignty. Similar arguments had been aired during the 1960s; however, the pre-election statement made by Ted Heath that UK membership would require the 'full-hearted consent of the peoples and parliaments' was misinterpreted – largely knowingly – by his opponents to suggest that the terms of entry would need to be endorsed by the electorate via a referendum.[47] In particular, some claimed that the cross-party consensus in favour of EEC membership that had existed at the 1970 general election, at least among the leadership of the Conservative, Labour and Liberal parties, meant that voters had been denied the chance to express their views on the European question. These calls were made most vocally by sections of the Labour Party. Tony Benn, Minister of Technology in the outgoing Labour government and now moving steadily leftwards, argued in December 1970 that Europe presented a 'unique and historic' political issue, and therefore required popular consent beyond a Commons majority.[48] Benn's argument, which itself drew upon the case made by Douglas Jay in his 1968 Penguin Special *After the Common Market*, began to gain credibility, both on its merits and as a way of by-passing, or at least displacing, the tensions that Europe had created within the Labour Party.[49] By March 1972, the Labour Party was committed to renegotiating British membership of the EEC and submitting the new agreement to the public for approval.[50]

These debates over representation and sovereignty were embraced enthusiastically by the SNP since they created further space for consideration of Scotland's constitutional position. As a result, the party continued to condemn the UK's entry to the Common Market throughout the early 1970s; indeed, nationalist hostility towards the EEC was reinforced as the question of UK membership, achieved in January 1973, became real rather than hypothetical. In late 1970, the SNP National Council passed a resolution stating that, without popular consent being obtained via a referendum, 'no government' had 'the right to negotiate for Scotland's entry into the EEC'. Firmer stances were also evident: a resolution submitted to the SNP National Executive by the Banffshire constituency association demanded a pre-emptive commitment that 'an independent Scotland' would 'not be a signatory to the Treaty of Rome'.[51] By the spring of 1971, the party was arranging anti-Market meetings across Scotland, as well as petitions and unofficial referendums in selected constituencies, once again most notably in the north east of Scotland.[52] In Moray and Nairn, then represented by the newly appointed Conservative Secretary of State for Scotland Gordon Campbell, but where the SNP had finished second at the 1970 general election, the survey, which was organised by the local SNP constituency association and which received almost 600 responses, found that a quarter of those asked placed Europe either in first or second place when asked to rank current political issues by importance. Only fourteen per cent of respondents were in favour of joining the Common Market; seventy-five per cent were against (although, significantly, a large majority assumed that membership was inevitable in any event). Two thirds of those asked wanted separate Scottish representation within the EEC in the event of UK membership, while more than seventy-five per cent backed a referendum on the issue, including one in three of those who favoured joining.[53]

Evidence of popular discontent with the government's pursuit of EEC membership, especially in the rural periphery, encouraged the SNP to publicise its anti-EEC stance further. Donald Stewart, now the MP for the Western Isles, participated in the 'Get Britain Out' organisation.[54] The party joined the north-east Scotland anti-Common Market campaign, which also featured figures from the Labour Party. Prompted by the presence of the Conservative Party's Scottish conference in Aberdeen in May 1971, the anti-Market campaign organised a series of demonstrations in the city, where complaints were voiced that 'The Treaty of Rome requires [the] surrender of our sovereignty'; given the cross-party nature of the campaign it was, however, unclear whether it was Scottish or British sovereignty that was being championed here. There were protests too that 'the bureaucrats in Brussels will have the power to override the authority of our Parliament'.[55] There was a degree of logic underlying the nationalist defence of Westminster's constitutional supremacy: the party's position appeared to be based on a belief that, once admitted, there was no provision for a member state to leave the EEC, a prospect that would essentially trap Scotland within the UK indefinitely. Still, the enthusiasm with which the SNP participated in the campaign against Common Market entry did, at times, prompt discomfort. In mid-1971, an internal party assessment warned that nationalist participation in heterogeneous anti-Common Market campaigns risked detracting from what was meant to be the party's main concern, constitutional reform. 'At times', it was felt, 'there has been a distinct impression that SNP members are prepared to make greater sacrifices, expend more energy and reserve more passion for opposing Market entry than they were ever prepared to give to the cause of Scottish independence.' This had led to party members appearing alongside 'very strange bed-fellows', including those whose distrust of the EEC was rooted in 'little Britisher' attitudes.[56]

That Europe had become the predominant theme in SNP campaigning by the early 1970s was evident at the September 1971 Stirling and Falkirk Burghs by-election, held immediately prior to the Commons vote on the principle of UK membership of the EEC, and which was contested by the SNP's President, Robert McIntyre. While McIntyre certainly raised other issues, including oil, during the election, distrust of the Common Market was a central element within his campaign.[57] McIntyre was keen to frame Europe as a confirmation of the government's inability – or refusal – to listen to public opinion: 'people' were 'sick and fed-up with politicians', and felt 'that they [had] no say in what [was] happening'. Europe, for McIntyre, provided 'a frightening example of how we are being sold down the river': the Conservative government feigned a desire for a 'great public debate', but was clearly determined to enter the Common Market whatever the attitude of the public. McIntyre concluded by drawing a parallel that would become a staple of nationalist rhetoric in the years ahead: the 'remote control from London' that Scots had endured as part of the UK had, he argued, been 'bad enough – even more remote control from the Brussels bureaucracy' would 'be a disaster'.[58] A conversation between McIntyre and Winnie Ewing, drafted as part of the materials distributed during the election, reiterated these arguments. Ewing again compared the Common Market with the 'Common Market with England' Scotland had joined 'in 1707'. Both agreed that UK membership of the EEC would see Scotland relegated to the 'fringe of the fringe', governed by a 'Brussels bureaucracy' that would be 'even farther away than the London bureaucracy' that had, in a revealing chronology, been so unresponsive 'in the last 30 years'.[59]

Stirling and Falkirk was a constituency in which the SNP and its candidate were relatively well-established: the party had contested the seat at every general election from 1959 onwards, and McIntyre had been Provost of Stirling since 1967. But McIntyre's performance was still impressive, as he secured thirty-five per cent of the vote, up sharply from the fifteen per cent recorded by the party in 1970. Although Harry Ewing comfortably defended a seat that the Labour Party had held since 1935, McIntyre relegated the Conservative candidate, David Anderson, to a distant third place. This was significant, as during the campaign Anderson had been vocal in his support of his party's pro-European policy, repeatedly stressing his belief in the merits of Common Market membership. Anderson asserted that the European issue presented voters with a fundamental choice regarding the future: 'in one direction', he stated, lay 'decay and decline, a pathetic little Britain' mired 'in mean and petty internal squabbling and bickering'; in the other, was 'the great promise of a future filled with peace, prosperity, security and happiness'. Anderson asked voters to back him as 'the only pro-Common Market candidate'; indeed, he went as far as to advise those opposed to entry to vote for the SNP, since, unlike the 'completely divided' Labour Party, the nationalists at least had the courage to hold a coherent position on Europe.[60] On the eve of the poll, Anderson again argued that EEC membership was 'the one subject overriding all others', and urged voters to 'vote for a dazzling future' inside the Common Market.[61] Anderson's pro-European attitude clearly backfired, as the Conservative vote collapsed to the benefit of the SNP. In contrast, and despite the undoubted splits within the Labour Party on the issue, Ewing stood as a 'confirmed anti-Marketeer', thereby nullifying McIntyre's potential appeal to Labour voters.[62] For both Ewing and McIntyre, the result was a 'rejection' of the Conservative government's policy of Common Market entry; this was, in McIntyre's view, 'clearly . . . not acceptable to the Scottish people'.[63]

The result in Stirling and Falkirk confirmed the continued electoral relevance of the SNP while simultaneously indicating the limitations of the party's appeal. The hostility of much of the Labour movement in Scotland towards the EEC restricted the ability of the SNP to exploit the European issue in constituencies held by the Labour Party. Here Labour figures, since 1970 relieved of the responsibility of defending government policy, could freely adopt anti-Common Market positions, closing off a potential source of support for the SNP. Rather, it was the Conservatives who were exposed by their support for EEC membership, and who were most vulnerable to SNP attacks. By the autumn of 1971 it was clear that the SNP's most likely route to electoral success would be as an alternative to the Conservatives in constituencies where the Labour tradition was weak: in such seats the SNP could aim to supplant

Toryism by posing as the best vehicle for opposition to the Common Market.

This potential appeal was enhanced following the Commons vote in favour of UK membership of the EEC at the end of October 1971. The Conservative government secured a comfortable overall majority in support of entry of 356 votes to 244. Scottish MPs, however, voted against entry by a margin of thirty-six to thirty-two: thirty-two Scottish Labour MPs voted against membership, with just eleven in favour; Scottish Conservative MPs supported entry by eighteen votes to three.[64] The outcome prompted the SNP to issue a 'Declaration of Rights', signed by William Wolfe as party Chairman and accompanied by a 'roll of dishonour' naming the Scottish MPs who had voted in favour of entry. The Declaration stated that:

> The decision of the Westminster Parliament to take Scotland into the Common Market against the opposition [sic] of the majority of her people is a flagrant negation of that basic principle of political democracy that government is by the consent of the people.

> The will of the Scottish people has been given no consideration in this grave constitutional decision. Yet it has been shown at every opportunity as overwhelmingly opposed to entry into the Common Market . . . The decision of the Westminster Parliament may take Scotland into the Common Market but does not commit the Scottish people therefore to obey the edicts of the European Economic Community.

The statement concluded with an assertion that 'an action taken so blatantly in defiance of democratic principle' could enjoy no 'constitutional authority in Scotland'.[65] As the UK's formal entry into the EEC approached, the SNP continued to assert that the decision lacked constitutional legitimacy in Scotland. A further delegation, this time composed of Wolfe and Stewart, was sent to Brussels in January 1972, with the intention of notifying the European Commission and the various member states 'that a self-governing Scotland would not be bound by any terms agreed' by the 'Westminster Government'. Wolfe had also issued an accompanying memorandum that summarised 'the relevant conditions of the Act of Union of 1707' and 'made it clear that [the SNP] were speaking as the only body competent to speak for the Scottish nation'.[66]

There was, to be sure, a certain Pooterish air to the flurry of declarations, deputations and memorandums produced by the SNP; certainly, it was difficult to imagine references to the 1707 Union carrying much weight in Brussels. But to merely note that the SNP exercised little meaningful political influence in this period would be to misjudge the purpose and impact of the party's attitude on Europe. At an ideological and intellectual level, Europe granted the traditional nationalist distrust of centralised, bureaucratic administration an immediate political relevance. And from a more cynical viewpoint, the overwhelming support for EEC membership within the Conservative and Liberal parties, and the rifts that the issue had generated within the Labour Party, created space for a party comfortable adopting a more straightforwardly critical stance towards the Common Market.

That the SNP's antipathy towards the EEC would remain politically worthwhile even after the UK had joined was demonstrated at the March 1973 Dundee East by-election, held two months after the UK officially entered the Common Market. Superficially, the strong second place finish attained by Gordon Wilson, who polled thirty per cent of the vote, up dramatically from the nine per cent secured by the party in 1970, might seem to contradict some of the preceding analysis: this was an urban constituency, held by Labour since its creation in 1950. Nevertheless, local peculiarities assisted the SNP in making Europe a fruitful issue. The election had been triggered by the appointment of the pro-Market Labour incumbent, George Thomson, as one of the first UK members of the European Commission. Unlike in Stirling and Falkirk, therefore, the incoming Labour candidate, George Machin, an Amalgamated Engineering Union member from Yorkshire who was personally opposed to EEC membership, struggled to pose credibly as an anti-Market candidate. Wilson was thus able to assume the role of principal critic of Common Market membership: during the campaign he authored an open letter to the President of the European Commission, Francois-Xavier Ortoli, informing him that Scotland was:

> . . . not, as an outside observer might suppose, incorporated within the English state. Scotland remains a distinct constitutional entity, linked to England by international treaty . . . Historically, sovereignty in Scotland resides with the people rather than, as in England, with Parliament. The constitutional powers of any elected Scottish legislature are limited by popular consent rather than by delegation from the UK parliament.[67]

The accuracy of Wilson's constitutional and historical analysis might be disputed; it suggested, nonetheless, that issues of sovereignty and representation, as provoked by the debate over the Common Market, retained their importance for the SNP. In Dundee East, local perceptions of Labour as a pro-Market party allowed the SNP to take votes from both major parties, and come within a little over 1,000 votes of victory in what had been a Labour-Conservative marginal in 1970. Again, the SNP's ability to channel anti-Market sentiments created particular difficulties for the Conservative Party, which was, at a UK level, obviously more enthusiastic about EEC membership than the bulk of the Labour Party: predictions in the press that the Conservatives were poised to capture Dundee East from Labour had proved to be woefully ill-judged.[68]

For Scottish Conservatives, who had, at least in their Unionist guise, spent much of the post-war era railing against the threat posed to Scotland by remote bureaucracies this was a jarring shift in emphasis; if socialist planning was suspect because it removed control of Scottish affairs to Whitehall, it was difficult to see why Brussels ought to be treated with any greater forbearance. Here, then, was an opportunity for the SNP to provide a home for voters already convinced that government from London was too distant and remote, and for whom being administered from Brussels promised to be even worse. Indeed, for nationalists, the EEC could serve as the ultimate embodiment of the centralising, uniformity-imposing, identity-eroding bureaucracy that had long haunted the party's rhetoric; for the SNP, in this period the EEC was a kind of distended Westminster-plus, even more distant, uncaring and corrupt than the London regimes that had so misgoverned Scotland for much of the twentieth century. In the aftermath of the Dundee East contest, one political correspondent observed that the 'old assumption that the SNP vote is a Labour protest and not a Conservative one' that had been created by Hamilton now appeared 'rather weak'.[69] The Scottish Young Conservatives saw the result in Dundee East in more existential terms, commenting that although Conservatives had 'become used to Tory voters in Labour strongholds like West Lothian, Hamilton and Stirling voting SNP as the only way to defeat Labour in these seats', the fact that the party had been 'beaten by the SNP in a marginal seat where we have a good record' was an indication of 'how rapidly' Conservatism was 'losing credibility in Scotland'.[70] These trends, glimpsed intermittently in the early 1970s, would come to the fore at the 1974 general elections.

THE 1974 GENERAL ELECTIONS

The decision of Ted Heath to contest an election in February 1974 was, notoriously, a response to the confrontation between the Conservative government and the National Union of Mineworkers, itself a symbol of the failure of the government's efforts to impose its incomes policy.

Contested against a backdrop of an energy crisis, industrial action and growing concerns over inflation, the election campaign was, at a British level, concerned primarily with economic policy, and the related question of how best to approach the relationship between the government and the trades unions. Although the Labour Party was committed to renegotiating the UK's membership of the Common Market, and then seeking public consent for the new terms either in an election or a referendum, Europe was a second-tier issue, overtaken by more immediate economic anxieties. The SNP's continued emphasis on Europe during the campaign was, then, conspicuous: while the party undoubtedly engaged with economic questions, and nationalist campaigning on North Sea oil was clearly forceful in this regard, the perceived negative consequences of EEC membership for Scotland remained a recurring theme. The SNP manifesto reiterated that the EEC was 'highly bureaucratic, centralist and undemocratic', and too 'remote from the control of ordinary people'; the party therefore continued to reject membership 'for political and economic reasons.'[71] As William Wolfe stated at a campaign press conference, the SNP was the only party that had 'consistently and unitedly opposed joining' the EEC, and was the only party that remained committed to leaving.[72]

As in 1970, this messaging on Europe was pursued especially vigorously in rural and semi-rural constituencies. Here rising prices were attributed to EEC membership; so too were the difficulties faced by the agricultural and fishing sectors. Standing once again in the rechristened Stirling, Falkirk and Grangemouth constituency, Robert McIntyre attributed 'price increases' to 'entry to the Common Market against our wishes'.[73] Donald Stewart, defending his Western Isles seat, pointed towards a perceived democratic deficit, arguing that membership had been imposed 'by Tory, Labour and Liberal MPs without reference to the wishes of the people', and despite the fact that a 'majority of Scots MPs voted against entry'.[74] In North Angus and Mearns, the SNP candidate Harry Rankin warned of a widespread 'disillusionment with the Common Market', a sense that voters had 'not had the deal' they had been 'promised'.[75] Contesting Perth and East Perthshire for the SNP, Douglas Crawford demanded at the very least a renegotiation of the membership terms and a referendum that would allow Scottish voters to make their voice heard.[76] For Iain MacCormick, running again in Argyllshire, Common Market membership had been a disaster, responsible for inflation and rising food prices.[77] In Inverness-shire, the SNP's Rob Gibson hoped to use popular 'support for the SNP's outright opposition to membership' to unseat the Liberal incumbent Russell Johnston.[78]

It was, however, in Moray and Nairn, held since 1959 by Gordon Campbell, the Conservative Secretary of State for Scotland during the Heath administration, that the SNP was able to exploit popular hostility towards the Conservative government's decision to join the EEC most fully. With a sizeable fishing community concerned about the impact of EEC membership, the constituency had been identified by the SNP as a key target years earlier; alongside Aberdeenshire East and Banffshire, Moray and Nairn formed part of the so-called 'North-east clean up' that nationalists hoped to deliver at the election.[79] Following her defeat at Hamilton in 1970, Winnie Ewing had accepted an invitation to contest the constituency, and had invested time and effort in cultivating local support in the year leading up to the election. Ewing brought the modern campaigning style she had deployed at Hamilton to the northeast. Although it was perhaps 'gaudy' by 'traditional local standards', it was undoubtedly effective, and made the Conservative campaign appear dull and old-fashioned: if Ewing was, in the words of one correspondent, 'waspish and witty', and popular with younger voters, Campbell appeared to offer as much excitement as 'the chrysanthemum awards at a village fete.'[80] Her official adoption meeting reportedly attracted an audience of 400, with another 200 supporters left waiting outside. Here Ewing described the Treaty of Rome as a 'monstrosity', and demanded a referendum that would give Scottish voters a chance to leave the Common Market.[81] Throughout her campaign, Ewing accused the Conservative government of having sold local 'fishermen . . . down the European river', and stated that the SNP was 'determined' that Scotland 'should get right out of European fishing policy' since 'the inshore fishermen will get nothing in return from the Europeans'.[82] In her memoirs, Ewing, who would become the first SNP Member of the European Parliament in 1975, and thereafter embraced the persona of 'Madame Écosse', claimed that she had always been enthusiastic about European integration so long as Scotland was 'able to negotiate' distinctive 'terms of entry'.[83] If true, that was a nuanced perspective that she chose to keep well-concealed in 1974. At an election meeting in Grantown, for example, Ewing told an audience of 120 that she was 'bitterly opposed to the Common Market and all its works', and warned that unless Scots found a way to leave the EEC, they would be reduced to 'powerless, helpless pawns', set to work in 'the great mills of the rich men of Europe'.[84]

Scottish Conservatives had claimed during the campaign that the Common Market was a 'dead issue' that would have little impact on the election result.[85] The outcome in the north-east suggested otherwise. Ewing defeated Campbell in Moray and Nairn while Douglas Henderson and Hamish Watt triumphed in Aberdeenshire East and Banffshire respectively. For Watt, there was no doubt that anger amongst voters regarding the Common Market had been the central factor in his success.[86] Europe played a similarly important role in the SNP victories in Argyllshire and the Western Isles. Assessments of the SNP's fortunes in the 1970s have noted that the party's success in seats that had been in Unionist and then Conservative hands since the 1920s generated a misleading impression that there had been a direct transfer of support from the Conservatives to the SNP. This, of course, may have happened to a degree; decisive, however, was increased turnout and the emergence of anti-Conservative tactical voting on the part of former Liberal and Labour voters.[87] Still, it should be recognised that nationalist candidates were only in a position to benefit from such patterns as a result of the second places achieved in 1970, when the SNP had emerged as the most enthusiastic advocate for anti-Market opinion and support for the pro-European Liberals had declined. Given the importance of Europe to the SNP's appeal in February 1974, the party was also in a stronger position in Conservative-held seats since, with only a handful of exceptions, this allowed the party to campaign against a pro-Market incumbent.[88] The same point can be made in reverse by looking at the two Labour seats that the SNP gained at the election. In Dundee East, where Gordon Wilson was elected for the party, Europe had been an issue locally due to the appointment of the former Labour MP George Thomson as European Commissioner, as witnessed during the by-election the previous year. In Clackmannan and East Stirlingshire, the Labour incumbent Dick Douglas had been one of the minority of Labour MPs in Scotland to vote in support of Common Market entry. His SNP opponent, the journalist George Reid, presented a 'very anti-Common Market' image to the electors, and took sufficient votes from both major parties to overcome a Labour majority of more than 10,000.[89] Oil and the renewed debate over devolution prompted by the Kilbrandon Report were, of course, important in granting the SNP greater prominence, and contributed to the general increase in support enjoyed by the party across Scotland. But in those crucial constituencies where Labour could not claim to speak for anti-Market voters, whether due to historic weaknesses in support or the pro-EEC attitude of the local MP, Europe was critical in providing Scottish nationalism with a distinctive election platform.

The return of Labour to office after February 1974 presented some challenges for the SNP, given that Labour's policy of renegotiating the terms of the UK's membership of the EEC, and offering the public a final say on the issue, appeared to address many of the nationalist criticisms.[90]

Nevertheless, the minority nature of the Labour government meant that a further election would inevitably be held before that policy could be delivered; this took place in October 1974, and the SNP continued to offer a focus for anti-Market opinion. The SNP's autumn manifesto repeated the established criticisms of the EEC as excessively 'centralist' and once more reminded voters that a majority of Scottish MPs had voted against entry.[91] Robert McIntyre dismissed Labour's referendum policy, predicting, not unfairly, that it was inevitable that the Labour government would 'recommend . . . that the voters say "Yes" to their renegotiated terms', and that anti-Market Labour MPs in Scotland would find themselves marginalised.[92]

In the three north-east constituencies captured in February, and in Argyllshire, the SNP had to fend off a Conservative Party that now real-ised the extent of the challenge that nationalism posed: as the *Aberdeen Press and Journal* reported, Scottish Conservatives, who had taken 'the hardest hammering from the SNP in February with the loss of four "safe" true-blue Highland seats' had 'at last set about . . . putting new zip into their machine'.[93] But SNP candidates continued to rely upon Europe to retain support. The SNP campaign in Moray and Nairn was blunt, stating simply that 'a vote for the Conservative Party' was 'a vote for the Common Market', and even accusing the Conservatives of supporting the eventual introduction of a single European currency.[94] In Banffshire, Hamish Watt criticised the continued Conservative commitment to the EEC, and pledged to protect 'Scottish fisheries' from incursions from 'Common Market fishermen'.[95] Douglas Henderson, defend-ing Aberdeenshire East, told voters that 'day by day' it was becoming 'clear that entry to the EEC was a colossal blunder' and bemoaned the fact that 'Scottish taxpayers' money' was 'being fed into the Common Market till to subsidise inefficient French farmers.'[96] Henderson laid the blame for rising inflation at the door of the EEC, which, he claimed, had driven up food prices. This was a point echoed in Argyllshire by Iain MacCormick, who asserted that the challenges facing the agricultural sector 'could only be ascribed to the fact that Britain had joined the Common Market', which had forced Britain 'to accept the agricultural policies of the EEC'. The result was that consumers were being asked to 'pay far higher prices than they had previously been paying.'[97]

Disillusionment with the Common Market was not limited to con-sumers: the farming community, faced with falling prices and rising costs, blamed the constraints imposed by EEC membership for the failure of the UK government to provide sufficient support, especially to struggling livestock producers. While the three UK parties professed their desire to renegotiate aspects of the EEC's Common Agricultural Policy, only the SNP advocated simply leaving the Common Market. As contemporary election coverage recorded, this stance was crucial in allowing the SNP to 'emerge as the most potent . . . vote-catchers' in farming communities.[98] To be sure, SNP candidates continued to benefit from anti-Tory tactical voting in central, eastern and south-west Scotland. But by October 1974 there were also indications that Conservative support was falling sharply in rural seats, a development that local commentators attributed to 'anti-EEC feeling among the farmers'.[99] This further weakening of Conservative support transformed more rural constituencies into potential SNP gains. In South Angus, the Conservative Jock Bruce-Gardyne, a vocal supporter of EEC membership as a means of modernising the British economy, saw his majority, which had remained above 5,000 at the February 1974 election, disappear as the Conservative vote fell by a quarter and the SNP's Andrew Welsh seized the seat. The fall in Conservative support in Galloway was not quite as dramatic, but was still sufficient to allow George Thompson to secure victory for the SNP with a majority of just thirty votes. Likewise, in the heartland Tory constituencies of Perthshire, the Conservatives struggled to retain support as the SNP continued to advance.[100] In Kinross and West Perthshire, where Nicholas Fairbairn had replaced Alec Douglas-Home as the Conservative candidate, the SNP nominee Derek Cameron was hopeful of receiving 'quite a few protest votes' from farmers 'disenchanted by the effect of EEC membership on the industry'.[101] Fairbairn polled almost 3,500 fewer votes than Douglas-Home had in February, most of which appeared to go directly to Cameron, who came within fifty-three votes of victory. In Perth and East Perthshire, the result was even more dramatic. Here Ian MacArthur, another Conservative supporter of EEC membership, shed more than 4,500 votes between February and October 1974, again to the benefit of the nationalist candidate; this time, the swing was sufficient to allow Douglas Crawford to take the seat for the SNP.[102] In the aftermath of the election, at which the SNP had replaced the Conservatives as the second largest party in Scotland in terms of vote share, the Conservative campaign manager in Scotland, James Anderson, accepted that the party could no longer depend upon being the default voice of rural and provincial Scotland. 'The days of the knights of the shires' were, he concluded, 'over'; Scottish Conservatives needed to shape 'a grass-roots party, a people's party . . . a Scottish party'.[103] But that more demotic, popular form of politics was, at least for the time being, now voiced far more convincingly by the SNP, which could more easily provide a home for dissatisfied and frustrated Scottish voters.

THE 1975 EEC REFERENDUM

The October 1974 election had been intended to provide the Labour government with a working Commons majority, an objective that was only barely delivered. Nevertheless, the government was able to honour its commitment to a referendum on the question of Europe; in January 1975, with renegotiations on the terms UK membership of the EEC approaching completion, the government announced that a referendum would be held later that year. The referendum presented the SNP with a genuine political opening: if the Conservatives and Liberals were over-whelmingly pro-Market, then Labour appeared hopelessly divided, with a majority of the Cabinet advocating continued EEC membership while a special party conference voted to reject the revised terms by a margin of two to one.[104] The SNP was, then, the only party in Scotland fully committed to supporting a vote against EEC membership, a stance that, according to opinion polls, continued to place the party on the same side of the debate as a majority of the Scottish electorate. Further, while there was little belief that a Scottish majority rejecting continued participation in the EEC would be enough to counter the weight of pro-EEC opinion in England, the SNP could also hope to use any discrepancy between the verdict of Scottish and English voters to highlight Scotland's periph-eral constitutional position within the UK.[105] In early 1975, Stephen Maxwell, the SNP's chief press officer and one of the party's leading intellectuals, noted with some optimism that the referendum was 'a tre-mendous opportunity' for the party to widen its appeal. A referendum campaign was, Maxwell felt, ideally suited 'to grass-roots campaigning of the sort at which the SNP . . . excels.' For Maxwell, the SNP would, moreover, be in a 'position to appeal to both the gut anti-EEC vote in Scotland and to that section of opinion which, while broadly sympa-thetic to the "European" idea, is sensitive to Scotland's lack of political status in European affairs'.[106]

The referendum campaign, once underway, undoubtedly gave the SNP a target at which to direct the party's by now well-rehearsed gen-eral condemnations of bureaucracy and centralisation; it also presented an opportunity to argue that Scottish opinion on the European question had been marginalised by successive UK governments. As in the election campaigns of the early 1970s, this anti-Market rhetoric was expressed, in the main, as opposition to the Common Market in principle, leavened on occasion by a focus on the particular iniquities raised by Scotland being, from the perspective of the EEC, merely a region of the UK rather than a partner nation. Speaking in December 1974 as the Labour government's renegotiations continued, Donald Stewart and Winnie Ewing declared that the SNP opposed continued EEC membership since the ultimate goal of the EEC was to 'establish a large power bloc controlled by a highly concentrated bureaucracy' that would see 'political authority removed from the ordinary citizen'. This, they claimed, ran 'counter to the philosophy of the SNP', which supported the 'diffusion of power'.[107] At a speech in Coldstream in April 1975, William Wolfe disparaged the EEC as 'highly bureaucratic, centralist and undemocratic', and 'remote from the control of ordinary people'. For Wolfe, the SNP's distrust of European integration was 'not unique'; rather, it was indicative of a global 'trend' that wanted less bureaucracy, not more.[108] Donald Stewart provided a similar assessment the following month, lamenting that, 'when the cry everywhere' was 'for more participation, more local control, more democracy', supporters of EEC membership offered only 'a retreat towards a "dark age" of bureaucracy and remote control'.[109] Douglas Henderson used near-identical language, stating his wish to see Scots able 'to govern themselves under a democratic system', free from 'the bureaucratic and remote system of Brussels control'.[110]

There were, of course, moments where the SNP's criticisms of the EEC were phrased in more prosaic terms. In Argyllshire, for example, adverts placed in the press by the local SNP constituency association focused on the financial costs of membership, and the alleged inflationary impact of Common Market entry: voters were encouraged to consider whether they could 'afford the Market prices'.[111] But the preference was for more dramatic assessments. As one nationalist pamphlet explained, the SNP existed 'to bring power to the Scottish people' while the EEC put 'power in the hands of small groups of politicians, bureaucrats and big businessmen': membership meant Scots were being 'denied the right to control their own country.'[112] The notion that the SNP was divided on the European question, and that there was a substantial strand of pro-EEC opinion within the party that needed to be appeased by a policy of 'no voice, no entry', which would postpone a decision on the merits of EEC membership until after independence had been achieved, overstates matters.[113] Even if true behind the scenes, from the public's perspective the SNP presented an unambiguously anti-Market image; retrospective assessments authored by senior SNP figures after their party's embrace of a pro-European outlook in the 1980s should be treated with a certain scepticism. There was, for example, little nuance in Winnie Ewing's contention that 'Euro-fanatics' within the EEC were keen to see the advent of a nuclear-armed 'Federal Western Europe'.[114] Likewise, Robert McIntyre gave no encouragement to the idea that an independent Scotland might one day join the EEC when he told a pre-referendum rally in Falkirk that the SNP was 'in its relation to the Common Market . . . concerned with human values', and did 'not believe that "bigness is best"'; 'We', he stated, 'do not want a new super-power'. For McIntyre, the economic case for membership was irrelevant: the key concerns were democratic accountability and ensuring that 'communities' were 'able to make their own decisions for their own future'.[115]

The clearest enunciation of the principled case against the EEC was given by William Wolfe in his address as Chairman to the SNP annual conference, held less than a week before the referendum. Deploying the chronology that had shaped nationalist thinking since the early 1960s, Wolfe bemoaned the expansion of 'government influence . . . in the economy' that had taken place since the First World War; he then reiterated his party's opposition to both 'economic' and 'political centralism'. In relation to the question of EEC membership, Wolfe made it clear that, under his leadership, nationalism's worldview 'did not include support for the centralised homogenous continental state', which, he claimed, had 'more potential for tyranny that any other concept the world has known'. Echoing Ewing's fears over the potential military ambitions of a federal Europe, Wolfe warned that 'continental rivalries' had 'the potential to be far more ferocious and destructive than those of small nation states.' Wolfe concluded his speech with a provocative comparison, suggesting that it was possible that coming generations would 'regard the creation of the EEC as a tragic blunder, comparable in its effects with the unification of the German States a century ago'.[116]

Subtler assessments, which left room for those sympathetic to the idea of EEC membership on the condition that Scotland enjoyed separate representation, were, to be sure, attempted. Writing in *The Scotsman*, George Reid maintained that the referendum was a 'charade', with the result a foregone conclusion: even 'if a narrow English "yes" vote were invalidated by a substantial Scottish "no"', he argued, there was no chance that the UK 'would leave the Common Market'. Rather, Reid encouraged voters to cast a 'tactical "no"' vote, one that would 'at least register our protest at the way in which we have been disfranchised.' This 'solid gesture of dissent', he asserted, could provide 'a tangible bargaining counter' in efforts to ensure that Scotland was able to 'decide her own links with the EEC' in the future.[117] Yet even analyses of EEC membership that concentrated on the effect of Scotland's subordinate position within the UK more often ended with a blunt warning that the Common Market risked replicating all the deleterious impacts that the Union had had for Scotland, only on an even larger scale. At the outset of the campaign Donald Stewart announced that he would oppose membership on the basis that it was a threat to sovereignty, and the Scots were 'a people who know what it means to have lost our sovereignty'.[118] Douglas Henderson reiterated the same point at an event in Aberdeen as the campaign moved towards its conclusion, where he claimed that voting to leave the EEC was a chance to reject more of the damaging 'centralisation' that Scotland had already suffered as part of 'the United Kingdom Common Market'.[119] An anti-Market pamphlet issued by the party reminded voters that the they had 'been in a Common Market with England since 1707', during which time 'power [had] become too centralised in London': how, then, could it be 'logical to hand over power to be centralised even further away?'[120] This argument was restated in unambiguous terms by Gordon Wilson in an open letter to George Thomson, his predecessor as MP for Dundee East and now one of the UK's representatives on the European Commission. Wilson ridiculed Thomson's contention that the European question was irrelevant when it came to debates over Scotland's constitutional status: for Wilson, the 'emergence of the SNP' was 'a reaction to the damaging processes of centralisation which the British Common Market' had inflicted upon Scotland, 'particularly during the last 60 years', and which EEC membership had accentuated. Wilson further dismissed attempts to justify Common Market entry on economic grounds. In Scotland, he argued, the principal concern was with the impact 'of even more centralisation' on a 'part of the United Kingdom' that had 'virtually no say in what the EEC decides except through the distorted looking glass of Whitehall and Downing Street'.[121]

In early 1975, it appeared that the SNP's dual approach of criticising the EEC as a further manifestation of centralisation while also highlighting the absence of a Scottish voice within European institutions would chime with a substantial section of the Scottish public. Indeed, in his letter to Thomson, Wilson enclosed the result of a survey he had undertaken in Dundee East that purported to show that forty-nine per cent of respondents wished to leave the EEC, compared to forty per cent in favour of the status quo.[122] Opinion polling undertaken for the *Glasgow Herald* in February 1975 detailed a similar picture across Scotland: forty-five per cent of those questioned were against continued participation in the Common Market, with just twenty-nine per cent in favour, in contrast to the broadly pro-Market tone in England. Immediately prior to the referendum, however, opinion in Scotland appeared to be shifting, with the *Herald* recording that there was now a forty-five to thirty-two per cent margin in favour of remaining within the EEC. This change was,

it seemed, being driven by Labour supporters abandoning their previous scepticism and swinging behind the renegotiated membership
terms promoted by the majority of the party leadership: the *Herald* poll
found that, in the month preceding the referendum, support for EEC
membership amongst Labour voters rose from thirty-seven to forty-six
per cent, while opposition within the same group fell from forty-four to
thirty-two per cent.[123] The Scottish institutions of the Labour movement
had been a powerful source of anti-Market opinion, but the campaign
to leave the EEC had fractured along party lines, with little cross-party
co-operation beyond the curious triumvirate of Labour's Jim Sillars, the
SNP's Margo MacDonald and the populist Conservative Teddy Taylor,
who toured Scotland together in support of a 'No' vote.[124] The identification of the anti-Market campaign with the SNP appeared to alienate
Labour supporters, who were also no doubt motivated by a desire to
ensure the survival of the Labour government. Polling conducted for the
Conservative Party further demonstrated that the key shift in opinion
took place amongst Labour voters. An ORC survey conducted in May
1975 found that views on the question of EEC membership remained
largely static amongst SNP and Conservative supporters: it was reported
that more than two-thirds of SNP voters planned to vote to leave the
EEC, compared to just one in five Conservatives, figures which had
held steady when compared to polling undertaken a year earlier. SNP
supporters, the researchers noted, were especially firm in their hostility
towards the EEC, believing that entry had been 'one of the major causes
of price inflation' and fearing that 'the institutions of Government in
Scotland' would 'become even more remote and unresponsive to the
wishes of the public' if membership continued. In contrast, opposition to
the Common Market among Labour voters had declined from sixty-one
to thirty-eight per cent in the same period.[125]

Labour voters' growing support for continued participation in the
Common Market, even if lukewarm, proved crucial in ensuring that
Scotland, like the rest of the constituent nations of the UK, returned
a majority in favour of EEC membership. Although Scots were, like
Northern Irish voters, less enthusiastic in their endorsement of membership than English and Welsh voters, with fifty-eight per cent backing
membership compared to sixty-nine per cent in England and sixty-five
per cent in Wales, the issue had undoubtedly been settled, and the constitutional and political tensions that the SNP had hoped would arise from
divergent verdicts were avoided. Given the outcome, it is tempting to
suggest that the SNP erred in committing so firmly to an anti-EEC position. The most authoritative contemporary account of the referendum

described the SNP's campaign in 1975 as an 'opportunistic gamble' that had 'signally failed'.[126] In a more recent assessment, Robert Saunders concluded that 'the result marked a rebuff not only for the SNP campaign, but for its analysis of Scottish political culture.'[127] Yet this supposition can be overemphasised. Most obviously, the results did demonstrate that Scots had a less enthusiastic view of European integration than the UK as a whole; further, the Western Isles and Shetland were the only counting areas to return majority 'No' votes. Given that the SNP had polled thirty per cent of the Scottish vote the previous autumn, and the substantial overlap that existed between support for the SNP and opposition to the Common Market, it might be concluded that nationalists were relatively successful in ensuring that their supporters' views were represented in the debate over Europe, while also managing to engage with other sections of the electorate. But even a more nuanced examination of the referendum results overlooks the large number of Scots who elected simply not to vote. In Scotland, turnout at the referendum fell sharply in comparison to the October 1974 general election, slipping from seventy-five to sixty-two per cent of the electorate; the comparative fall in England was from seventy-two to sixty-five per cent. The slump in voter participation was especially marked in areas where distrust of the Common Market, and, often, but not always, support for the SNP, had been highest. Turnout fell below fifty per cent in Orkney and Shetland, and was scarcely above that mark in the Western Isles; fewer than six in ten electors cast their vote in Grampian, Tayside and the Highlands. Turnout proved more robust in the central belt, most likely a reflection of the move towards a more pro-European position among Labour voters. Even in Dumfries and Galloway, which, alongside the Borders produced the most decisive 'Yes' vote, turnout fell from seventy-seven to sixty-one per cent between October 1974 and June 1975 [see Table 3.1].

The relatively weak turnout in much of rural and provincial Scotland suggests the presence of a degree of cynicism and apathy regarding the referendum: only Dumfries and Galloway and the Borders returned 'Yes' votes greater than forty per cent of the total electorate. It might, then, be hazarded that the more pessimistic opinions voiced by the SNP, to the effect that a majority Scottish vote in favour of leaving the EEC would, even if numerically decisive, simply be dismissed by Westminster, had been too effective. The belief that the result of the referendum was a foregone conclusion, and that Scottish opinion would, in any case, be ignored, may have played a role in depressing engagement among anti-Market voters, with the effect that the official results understated popular opposition to the Common Market in Scotland. Senior SNP figures

Table 3.1 Scottish results of the 1975 EEC referendum by counting area (ordered by turnout)[129]

Counting Area	Turnout (%)	Yes vote (%)	No vote (%)	Yes vote as % of electorate
Shetland	47.1	43.7	56.3	20.6
Orkney	48.2	61.8	38.2	29.8
Western Isles	50.1	29.5	70.5	14.8
Grampian	57.4	58.2	41.8	33.4
Highlands	58.7	54.6	45.4	32.1
Dumfries & Galloway	61.5	68.2	31.8	41.9
Strathclyde	61.7	57.7	42.3	35.6
Borders	63.2	72.3	27.7	45.7
Fife	63.3	56.3	43.7	35.6
Lothian	63.6	59.5	40.5	37.8
Tayside	63.8	58.6	41.4	37.3
Central	64.1	59.7	40.3	38.3

were aware of this possibility: Donald Stewart noted that the 'Yes' vote in Scotland was smaller than the number of non-voters, while Winnie Ewing highlighted the narrower margin in favour of membership north of the border.[128] Yet, whatever their validity, such arguments plainly sounded pitiful when made in the days after the referendum.

The shrewder response for the SNP was to adjust and accept the verdict of the referendum. At a meeting of the SNP National Council a week after the result, a majority of those present agreed to abandon the campaign to leave the EEC, and instead focus on continuing to make the case for separate Scottish representation within EEC institutions. Those committed to maintaining a firmer position, which would have seen the party call for a further referendum on Europe once Scotland had gained independence, were rebuffed.[130] For some former critics of the EEC, it should be said, this transition appeared to be remarkably straightforward. As early as January 1976, Gordon Wilson could be found arguing that membership of the EEC in fact made the case for independence stronger: the EEC, he asserted, made 'devolution a blind alley at the same time as making self-government both logical and gradualist'. He called for a campaign that would 'start underlining the effect of EEC membership in removing the imagined consequences of "separatism".'[131] For others, the logic was less clear. Stephen Maxwell responded to Wilson's suggestion by warning that he was conceding 'too much to the separatist charge'; moreover, Wilson was, Maxwell warned, making an argument that 'implies an admission that an independent Scotland would be isolated or "separate" outside the Common Market'. Were, Maxwell wondered, Norway or Switzerland 'isolated'? He concluded by contending that UK membership of the EEC had in fact created an extra hurdle for the independence movement. Maxwell quoted Schelto Patijn, a Dutch Labour Member of the European Parliament, who had warned that allowing Scotland to join the EEC as an independent state was not simply a matter of increasing the number of member states from the then nine to ten; rather, the choice was 'between nine and thirty or forty, bringing in Scotland, Jutland, Corsica, Bavaria, Sicily'. Maxwell stressed that the 'Council of Ministers' would 'want to keep the lid of that Pandora's Box firmly shut, with Scotland inside'.[132]

In the long-term, Wilson's newfound enthusiasm for the EEC would win out, and the SNP would move towards a pro-European policy under his leadership during the 1980s.[133] But the perception that took hold after June 1975 that the European question had been settled was damaging for the SNP since it abruptly removed one of the central contributing factors in the party's growth in the preceding decade. Still, as will be seen in the following chapter, there were aspects of the referendum debate that would, in the longer term, bolster the position of those who sought constitutional change.

DEFENDING DEMOCRACY? THE SNP AND LOCAL GOVERNMENT REFORM

The June 1975 European referendum campaign overlapped with another constitutional development that appeared to vindicate the criticisms of centralisation voiced by the SNP. Three weeks prior to the referendum a comprehensive reform of Scottish local government was finally implemented. The advent of the new two-tier administrative structure of districts and regions heralded the end for a patchwork of local authorities that could, in the case of the royal burghs, lay claim to a lineage that reached back to the twelfth century. Across Scotland, the occasion was marked by ceremonies that celebrated the passing of the old. A commemorative tapestry was unveiled in Edinburgh, while in Aberdeen there was a fireworks display.[134] In Dundee, the final meeting of the Town Council was a solemn occasion, as 'mourners' gathered 'in the public gallery . . . to hear the last rites'; the 'Councillors . . . wore their good suits and the atmosphere was heavy with emotion.'[135] In Culross, one of the oldest royal burghs in Scotland, there was a slow march through the village led by two pipers. In Glasgow, the atmosphere was more celebratory, with a feast of roasted ox followed by fireworks; on the Western Isles, there were dances.[136] Everywhere, though, proceedings were infused with a sense of loss as local institutions disappeared: as the *Glasgow Herald* reported, 'loyal local tears were wept as loyal local places had their names wiped from the map.'[137] There were fears too that the new system would prove 'less democratic' and 'less sensitive to grass-roots feeling'.[138]

A potential restructuring of Scottish local government on a two-tier model had been mooted for more than a decade before being implemented. In 1963, the Conservative government had issued a White Paper that determined that the structure established by the previous round of reforms in 1929 had been overtaken by demographic shifts and that future economic growth would be increasingly focused on urban centres. Existing local authorities were, it was concluded, 'too small' to be able to deliver the necessary services and were restricted by 'increasingly artificial' boundaries that no longer reflected social and economic realities. The White Paper envisaged what was described as 'a simple two-tier system' of expanded 'county councils responsible for major services' and enlarged burghs that would deliver 'essentially local services'.[139] These proposals were terminated by the defeat of the Conservative government at the 1964 general election. The desire for reform survived the change in administration, however, and in 1966 the Labour government appointed a Royal Commission to examine the question of Scottish local government, under the direction of Lord Wheatley, the former Labour MP for Edinburgh East who had subsequently served as Solicitor-General and Lord Advocate. The Commission, which eventually issued its report in September 1969, reiterated the previous conclusions that the existing authorities were too small, and were restricted by obsolete boundaries. Again, the remedy proposed was a two-tier system of discrete directly elected authorities, although in this arrangement there were to be seven regional councils, which would handle planning, education, social work and housing, and thirty-seven district councils that would, among other functions, oversee leisure and recreation, museums and libraries, and refuse collection.[140]

The Wheatley commissioners had shown an awareness of the risks inherent in any restructuring of local government. Although the final report had opened with the abrupt declaration that 'Something is seriously wrong with local government in Scotland', there was a recognition that any reform needed to produce councils that were 'independent', 'viable' and 'community-based': it was accepted that local government units had to correspond to 'a genuine community', otherwise the 'people' would 'not think of it as *their* authority'. Indeed, the Commissioners saw the creation of larger regional authorities as, in effect, a form of devolution, a step that would bring political power closer to the people by allowing decision-making powers that currently resided with central government to be devolved to the proposed regions. As the final report noted, 'many' might wonder what the impact on 'local democracy' would be 'if authorities' were to become 'so much larger and councillors less numerous'. The response was that stronger, larger councils would 'be able to take a bigger part in the life of the nation', and that 'things that are now determined centrally' would, 'in future', be able to 'be settled regionally or locally.' Crucially, however, the commissioners were aware that this would require a transformation in the attitude of central government towards local authorities, and an acceptance that councils needed greater financial autonomy. Community councils were also recommended as a means of ensuring that local opinion would continue to find an outlet for expression.[141]

Despite the sensitivities displayed by the commissioners, however, the Wheatley proposals received an overwhelmingly negative reaction, at least from those who stood to be most affected by any change in structure. *The Economist* could, for example, declare airily from a distance 'that nearly all Scots would be better off with the greater administrative efficiencies of Wheatley', while the *Glasgow Herald* editorialised that the reforms would 'alter the character, efficiency, and relevance of Scottish local government' in ways that would mostly 'be very much for the better'.[142] In contrast, and perhaps unsurprisingly, the local authorities that faced abolition were almost unanimously opposed; this was especially true of the ancient royal burghs.[143] Further hostility was generated by the proposed boundaries of the seven regions, which were intended to reflect contemporary economic realities rather than historic identities and, in consequence, had used urban centres and their area of economic influence as a basic framework. These outlined a 'West' region, centred on Glasgow but also encompassing Ayrshire and parts of Argyllshire alongside the counties of Dunbarton, Lanark and Renfrew, that, with over 2.5 million residents, would be responsible for more than half the total population of Scotland. It was also recommended that the county of Fife be broken up, with the north-east portion allocated to the 'East' region together with Dundee, Angus, Kincardine and parts of Perthshire. Central and western Fife was to be included in a 'South-East' region that would have Edinburgh at its heart, but would, in another controversial proposal, also include the Border counties. A further small area in west Fife would fall within the proposed boundaries of the

'Central' region.[144] Immediately after the release of the Wheatley Report, it was reported that local authorities across Scotland were organising a campaign to oppose the suggested reforms, and 'to retain their identities'. The Scottish political editor at the *Daily Express*, Charles Graham, offered vocal support, calling for a campaign against 'a faceless takeover' of 'Scotland's counties, cities and burghs' by 'nameless regions ruled by faceless men'. Graham had no time for claims that restructuring would lead to 'efficiency', arguing that there was no guarantee that the 'bureaucratic paradise' of the commissioners would prove 'any more efficient than the current happy shambles'; in any case, he defended the right of the public to opt for a system that was 'wrong, inefficient and stupid' if they so wished.[145]

Opponents of Wheatley faced, though, a challenge to find parliamentary support. The shared preference of both the 1963 White Paper and the subsequent Royal Commission for a new two-tier local government structure ensured that leading Conservative and Labour figures were broadly supportive of the scheme.[146] Indeed, Scottish Conservatives were happy to claim the Wheatley report as 'a remarkable vindication' of their earlier proposals. Likewise, the Scottish Liberals, who had been represented on the Commission by Russell Johnston, the MP for Inverness, were largely in favour of the reforms, although they wished to see around 100 districts, as opposed to the thirty-seven suggested by the majority of the Commission, and had concerns about the size of the 'Highland' region, in line with the dissenting notes signed by Johnston. Only the SNP criticised the Wheatley scheme from the outset, dismissing the proposals as a 'bureaucratic design to destroy local democracy'. George Leslie, a party Vice-Chair and Councillor in Glasgow, warned that 'the Wheatley bulldozer' would only exacerbate the 'current disillusion [sic] with politics' by undermining local 'involvement and participation' and enabling 'remote control by desk-bound bureaucrats and second-rate technocrats'. The SNP Provost of Cumbernauld, Gordon Murray, labelled the report an 'Orwellian Planner's Fantasy'.[147] A detailed rejection of the recommendations was issued by the SNP in January 1970.[148]

As was the case in the context of the debate over EEC entry, therefore, in the late 1960s the Scottish nationalists found themselves the only declared opponents of a policy for which there was a consensus at Westminster, but that appeared, initially at least, to enjoy scant support from the wider public. The SNP's rejection of the Wheatley report was, again, like the party's scepticism towards Common Market membership, inspired by a longstanding opposition to unnecessary administrative centralisation, and a conviction that bureaucracy was inherently undemocratic and unaccountable. This was accompanied by a more straightforwardly nationalist interpretation of the 1707 Treaty of Union, Article 21 of which had protected the rights and privileges of the royal burghs. The party's basic position was therefore to defend the royal burgh as the foundation of Scottish local government on both democratic and constitutional grounds. Writing in response to the 1963 White Paper, Arthur Donaldson, the then Chairman of the SNP, rejected what he saw as the prevailing 'tendencies . . . toward larger and more remote units over which the voter's influence becomes ever less effective.' 'Regionalisation', Donaldson warned, was 'not acceptable': Scots did 'not need or want a new system in which a top tier of large authorities would have all the real power and the second and only truly democratic tier would be relegated to parish pump affairs'.[149] During the 1966 general election campaign, SNP literature accepted that some reform of local government may be valuable, but suggested that 'traditional local authorities' should be maintained as far as possible, as considerations of scale and 'efficiency' had always to be balanced with the right of people 'to belong to real communities'.[150]

This outlook shaped the SNP's submission to the Wheatley Commission in October 1966, which opened with a declaration that 'local democracy' rested upon 'the individual's personal identification with his local community', and cautioned against any measures that would 'create large units of administrative convenience' that risked 'destroying the feelings of local pride and community awareness that are so valuable in protecting the individual from the social and cultural sterility of an increasingly conformist society.' The party wished for the royal burghs to continue as the 'basic unit' of administration, with regional commissions to assess extensions of specific boundaries, subject to a local plebiscitary veto. Burghs would then cooperate with their neighbours to form joint bodies to administer services that required economies of scale, such as housing and roads; these bodies would be composed of delegates and would be temporary and tied to specific projects. Finally, the SNP was willing to tolerate regional authorities responsible for planning, emergency services and education. These were, though, again to be comprised of delegates, rather than being directly elected, ensuring that ultimate authority and accountability remained at the burgh level. It would be, the submission concluded, 'a system that seeks to use rather than destroy the patterns of tradition and local identity that are so closely woven into the fabric of our national spirit'.[151] It was also precisely the kind of informal system of administration that the Wheatley Commission aimed to bring to an end. The SNP's negative reaction to the scheme eventually proposed

by the Commission was, then, to be expected. The party welcomed the
Wheatley report as a recognition of the need for reform of some kind,
but bemoaned what was perceived as an understanding of local government as 'the administration of power rather than as the administration
of government by people effectively representing their area'. The suggested regions and districts were both criticised as being far too large.
In particular, the party rejected the projected three-way division of Fife,
and called for the size of the 'West' region to be revised.[152]

The question of local government reform was largely absent from
the 1970 general election campaign, provoking nationalist protesta-
tions at the lack of debate from 'the London parties', who supported
reforms that represented a 'sentence of death on democratic local government.'[153] The SNP alleged that 'the Tory/Labour establishment' had
colluded to avoid a public debate over either 'the C[ommon] M[arket] or
far-reaching local government reform', which, William Wolfe declared,
were the 'main issues' facing Scottish voters.[154] No matter the lack of
debate on the subject, the new Conservative government moved swiftly
to provide an outline of its planned local government reforms.[155] A new
White Paper was published in February 1971, which in general adhered
to the Wheatley recommendations, but with some amendments, the
most significant of which were the creation of an additional region in
the Borders, and the awarding of a distinctive all-purpose status to the
Orkney and Shetland isles; the number of district authorities was also
increased to forty-nine. The government intended that this scheme would
provide a firm basis for legislation, rather than simply triggering another
round of consultation.[156] Yet the revised structure addressed few of the
criticisms voiced previously, and instead appeared only to have created
precedents that could be used by communities to dispute the intended
boundaries. Most obviously, the decision to grant regional status to the
Borders, an area with just 96,000 residents and no single urban focal
point, meant that the principles that were alleged to have underpinned
the Wheatley report were no longer being applied consistently. This
example was immediately pounced upon by those determined to ensure
that Fife survived as a single authority. Similarly, the residents of the
Western Isles demanded that they be given the same status as Orkney
and Shetland. Lastly, the colossal region proposed in the West remained
a source of unease, with demands soon emerging for this to broken up
into smaller sub-divisions. It was also unclear how the regional authorities would function were the Royal Commission on the Constitution,
which would not issue its report until October 1973, to recommend a
devolved Scottish assembly.[157]

An all-purpose authority for the Western Isles was conceded even before legislation came before the Commons in December 1972, but at this stage the Conservative government remained committed to the regional structure outlined in the White Paper. In February 1973 regional status for Fife was secured following a sustained local campaign supported, in the end, by a parliamentary alliance between Labour critics of the government's proposals and Conservative rebels marshalled by Sir John Gilmour, the Conservative MP for East Fife.[158] On the issue of the West region, now labelled Strathclyde, the government refused to compromise, despite widespread local opposition and the efforts of the Labour peer Lord Hughes of Hawkhill, a former Lord Provost of Dundee and Scottish Office Minister, who orchestrated a vote in the Lords in favour of his plan to replace Strathclyde with four smaller regions.[159] The legislation was eventually passed with the Strathclyde region intact.

Local government reform was, from a national perspective, a less momentous issue than EEC membership; for the SNP, though, as the only party opposed absolutely to the new structure, it provided similar opportunities. Most significantly, it allowed nationalists to claim that they were the chief defenders of democracy and local identity in Scotland at a moment when concerns that government was becoming too remote were increasingly widespread. Once the Conservative government produced its White Paper, the SNP abandoned any nuance in relation to local government, switching instead to a full-hearted defence of the royal burghs. The party's 1972 conference denounced the proposals, declaring them to be in breach of the Treaty of Union, and the SNP encouraged royal burghs to seek legal advice as part of their efforts to resist abolition.[160] In its opposition to the reforms, the SNP found itself in sympathy with a broad swathe of Scottish society. Predictably, there was significant unease in rural and provincial areas at the prospect of being included within regions that would be administered from relatively distant cities. But sections of the political left were also troubled by the proposals. The proposed Strathclyde region, while welcomed by many Labour representatives in Glasgow, generated passionate opposition in Ayrshire, with the local Labour MPs, Willie Ross, Jim Sillars and David Lambie, all speaking out against plans for a single region in the west of Scotland.[161] The Ayrshire region of the NUM also declared its opposition to the reforms, with the full support of Mick McGahey, President of the Scottish Area of the NUM.[162] It should be remembered too that Jimmy Reid, like McGahey a prominent member of the Communist Party of Great Britain and then in the midst of the successful work-in at UCS, took time during his famous 'Alienation' address following his installation as Rector of the University of Glasgow in April 1972 to criticise the failure of the Conservative government to ensure that the planned reforms would return 'power . . . to local communities'. 'Instead', Reid lamented, 'the proposals' for local government reform were 'a blue-print for bureaucracy, not democracy.' Reid, then still a local Councillor in Clydebank, took specific aim at the scale of the projected regions. If the reforms were implemented, Reid noted,

> . . . in a few years, when asked, 'Where do you come from?' I can reply: 'The Western Region' . . . It stretches from Oban to Girvan and eastwards to include most of the Glasgow conurbation . . . I must ask the politicians who favour these proposals – where and how in your calculations did you quantify the value of a community? Of community life? Of a sense of belonging? Of the feeling of identification? These are rhetorical questions. I know the answers. Such human considerations do not feature in their thought process . . .[163]

At the February 1974 general election, with the first elections to the new councils due to be held in May 1974 prior to the new structure coming into effect the following year, the SNP continued to be critical of the reforms, reasoning that both the regions and districts were 'too large' and did not reflect any sense of 'natural community'.[164] In South Angus, the party's candidate, Malcolm Slesser, warned that Scots were living 'in an era of Government by stealth', as evidenced by 'the imposition of local government reform on an unwilling . . . public'. 'In just a few weeks', Slesser stressed, the royal burghs would fade 'away into the pages of the history books . . . Your rights and privileges guaranteed under Clause 21 of the Treaty of Union will be in default.' Linking local government reform to the question of Europe, Slesser claimed that these 'honoured institutions were to be replaced by regions designed to facilitate the administration of the faceless men of the Common Market.'[165] This opposition was repeated at the October 1974 election, where the reforms were attacked for having 'destroyed democratic community government for the sake of bureaucratic convenience', leaving the public 'more remote' from their 'elected representatives'.[166] Iain Murray, the SNP candidate in North Angus and Mearns, called for the regions to be pre-emptively abolished before they could do any serious damage.[167] In Argyllshire, Iain MacCormick repeated his opposition to the county being forced to become part of Strathclyde.[168]

Identifying a direct electoral dividend for the SNP as a result of the party's opposition to the new local government structure in the early

1970s is difficult. If it might be suggested credibly that a critical stance towards the plans did the SNP some good in areas such as Argyllshire and Galloway, it remains a speculative conclusion. Yet to aim for precision would be misguided. Alongside Europe, local government reform mattered first because it allowed the SNP to claim to speak for Scotland in the face of an apparent consensus at Westminster: popular antipathy towards the proposals and the determination of the government to press ahead with the scheme could easily be framed as evidence that the Union settlement was no longer being respected by the UK government. As William Wolfe phrased it immediately prior to the 1970 general election, in opposing both the Wheatley report and the Common Market, the SNP spoke 'for the majority of the people of Scotland'. Further, the revised structure, and especially the regions, offered clear targets for the SNP's by now customary condemnations of remote government and centralisation, offering another complement to the campaign against EEC entry. Indeed, Wolfe was willing to make the link directly, arguing that 'If Wheatley is bureaucracy writ small, the Common Market is bureaucracy writ large'.[169] That both policies were ultimately carried forward by a Conservative administration was also likely a factor in that party's loss of support at the 1974 elections, and the ability of the SNP to make inroads in parts of rural Scotland.

But the nationalist campaign against the reforms failed, with the new two-tier system arriving as planned in May 1975. The new authorities, and especially the regions, proved unpopular from the outset, not least because their advent was accompanied by a sharp increase in local rates that, while largely a consequence of wider inflationary pressures, was attributed to the restructuring.[170] Leading figures in the SNP were, of course, more than willing to endorse such conclusions. A statement issued in July 1975 by Robert McIntyre blamed the 'shock increase in rates' on the recent 'administrative changes' promoted by successive Labour and Conservative governments.[171] The following month, Andrew Welsh, the SNP MP for South Angus, alleged that the 'chaos' in the two-tier system had 'made a laughing stock' of the Labour and Conservative 'establishment'.[172] Still, public hostility towards the new regions presented challenges for those who favoured an alteration in Scotland's constitutional status. By the close of 1975, political debate in Scotland was beginning to focus on the Labour's government commitment to establishing a devolved Scottish Assembly.[173] And while a majority of Scots appeared to support devolution, local government reform had encouraged a belief that Scotland was now over governed, with too many competing administrative tiers. Polling undertaken by the Conservative Party revealed that a clear majority wanted a devolved assembly with significant autonomy; equally, though, a majority felt that, if an assembly was instituted, another level of government should be removed, with the regions the preferred candidate for abolition.[174] There was, however, no prospect of the government agreeing to such a step, which left the proposals for a devolved assembly vulnerable to the same complaints of excessive centralisation and bureaucratisation that had been levelled at the regions. The concerns expressed previously regarding the compatibility of a devolved assembly with the new regional authorities remained unresolved.

CONCLUSION

In April 1975, a dinner was held in Edinburgh to commemorate the thirtieth anniversary of Robert McIntyre's election as the first SNP Member of Parliament. In his address to those in attendance, McIntyre was keen to assert the consistency of his party's appeal during the preceding decades. Recounting the frequent jeremiads he had issued during the 1940s regarding the growing power of the state, McIntyre claimed that these warnings had, regrettably, been vindicated. There had been, he asserted, a 'steady increase of central control', while 'the State' was becoming 'more and more authoritarian every day'. Alluding to the ongoing debates over Europe and local government, McIntyre concluded that the 'drive to centralism' was increasingly 'destructive', and had led to a widespread sense of 'anonymity' and 'the depersonalisation of society' and government. 'Where', McIntyre asked, 'does the buck stop now?' After recommending E. F. Schumacher's *Small is Beautiful*, published two years earlier, McIntyre asked his audience to reject 'the worship of bigness', and to remain committed to the pairing of 'national freedom with individual freedom' that he believed was at the core of the SNP's outlook.[175]

McIntyre's emphasis on the continuity of nationalist thinking in the post-war period might provoke scepticism, a suspicion that he was choosing to overlook the important role of New Left and other socialist influences on the thinking of a new generation of nationalists politicised during the 1960s and early 1970s.[176] Perhaps, but ideological evolution has to be balanced with an understanding of the influence exercised by political context and electoral opportunity. McIntyre's retrospective assessment revealed the ongoing importance to Scottish nationalism of an anti-bureaucratic and anti-centralist rhetoric, formed in the 1940s: Europe and local government reform offered concrete examples against which this rhetoric could be deployed. They were, moreover, issues which transcended generational and ideological divides, and united those who might take very different stances on economic questions. The coherence of the early 1970s would, nonetheless, prove fleeting. However unpopular Common Market membership and the new regional authorities had been among Scottish voters, by mid-1975 it was clear that these issues had been settled for the foreseeable future. Further, the SNP would struggle to apply a critique of centralisation to the debate over devolution that came to dominate Scottish politics in the second half of the 1970s. McIntyre might, in late 1975, try to portray a Scottish assembly as signifying a 'revival of democracy' and a 'chance of piercing the curtain of bureaucratic secrecy' that had arisen since the Second World War; but devolution could just as easily be dismissed as yet another unnecessary and expensive layer of bureaucracy.[177] All the same, devolution, and the failed referendum on the issue that took place in March 1979, did assist in the creation of new political languages that could be used by supporters of constitutional reform. In particular, the acceptance by Westminster, whatever the intentions of individual MPs, that Scotland's constitutional status was, in the end, a decision for the Scottish people, represented a profound shift in understandings of sovereignty.

NOTES

1. Cameron, *Impaled upon a Thistle*, pp. 291–2.
2. Mitchell, *Devolution in the United Kingdom*, pp. 113–15.
3. Phillips, *The Industrial Politics of Devolution*, Chapter 3; Foster, 'Upper Clyde Shipbuilders 1971–2 and Edward Heath's U-Turn'; Knox and McKinlay, *Jimmy Reid*, Chapter 4; Gibbs, *Coal Country*, Chapter 6.
4. Lynch, *SNP*, pp. 124–8.
5. *The Economist*, 9 Mar. 1974, p. 32.
6. Mitchell, 'From Breakthrough to Mainstream', p. 36. For one such interpretation, see: Levy, *Scottish Nationalism at the Crossroads*, Chapter 3.
7. See: Miller, Brand and Jordan, *Oil and the Scottish Voter*.
8. Devenney, 'Regional Resistance to European Integration', and 'Joining Europe: Ireland, Scotland and the Celtic response to European integration'; Saunders, *Yes to Europe*, Chapter 13.
9. For a brief discussion, see: Cameron, *Impaled upon a Thistle*, pp. 303–5.
10. The initial membership of the EEC was limited to the so-called 'six': Belgium, France, Germany, Italy, Luxembourg, and the Netherlands.
11. Saunders, *Yes to Europe*, pp. 41–2.
12. Jim Tomlinson, 'Inventing "Decline"', p. 754.
13. The Commons endorsed the application by 488 votes to 62. See: *Glasgow Herald*, 11 May 1967.

14. NLS Acc. 13687/11: SNP, *Pollok Looks to Leslie* (Glasgow, 1967).
15. NLS Acc. 10090/92: Gordon Wilson, *Foreign Affairs: EEC*, 10 May 1967.
16. NLS Acc. 10090/92: SNP National Executive Minutes, 12 May and 18 Aug. 1967.
17. NLS Acc. 10090/176: SNP, *21 Wasted Years* (West Calder, 1967).
18. NLS Acc. 10090/176: SNP, *Face the Facts: The Brutal Failure* (Hamilton, 1967).
19. Devenney, 'Regional Resistance to European Integration', p. 337.
20. NLS Acc. 13099/2: Gordon Wilson to James Jack, 23 Feb. and 28 Mar. 1970.
21. *Scots Independent*, 24 Jan. 1970.
22. NLS Acc. 10090/130: *Report from Douglas Crawford to SNP NEC* and SNP NEC minutes, 13 Feb. 1970.
23. NLS Acc. 10090/130: *Memorandum from William Wolfe: EEC – Visit to Brussels*, 2 Apr. 1970.
24. NLS Acc. 10090/121: *36th Annual Conference of the SNP, 29–31 May 1970: Reports of National Office-Bearers*, pp. 8–9; *Scots Independent*, 28 Feb. and 28. Mar. 1970.
25. NLS Acc. 10090/130: *The Kingdom of Scotland: A Constitutional Crisis*.
26. Bod. Lib. CPA CCO 500/18/33: Opinion Research Centre, *A Survey on South Ayrshire Constituency* (1970), p. 3.
27. NLS 13099/95: *SNP Research Bulletin*, Apr. 1970, p. 5.
28. Wolfe, *Scotland Lives*, pp. 138–9.
29. NLS Acc. 10090/147: SNP, *Scottish Viewpoint No. 8: The Common Market* (1970).
30. Kellas, 'Scottish Nationalism', p. 458.
31. Scottish National Party, *The New Scotland*, p. 6.
32. NLS Acc. 10090/147: *Vote SNP, Vote Lindsay* (Wishaw, 1970).
33. *Dundee Courier and Advertiser*, 6 Jun. 1970.
34. *Dundee Courier and Advertiser*, 26 May and 11 Jun. 1970.
35. *Dundee Courier and Advertiser*, 4 Jun. 1970.
36. NLS Acc. 13101/19: *Donald J. Stewart* (Stornoway, 1970).
37. *Perthshire Advertiser*, 30 May 1970.
38. *Argyllshire Advertiser*, 2 Jun. 1970.
39. Dyer, 'The Politics of Kincardineshire', p. 324.
40. *Dundee Courier and Advertiser*, 6 Jun. 1970.
41. Dyer, 'Politics of Kincardineshire', pp. 331–2.
42. *The Northern Scot*, 6 Jun. 1970.
43. NLS Acc. 10090/147: *Vote SNP: Vote Farquhar* (Peterhead, 1970).
44. Scott, *The Liberals, the Common Market and the SNP*, pp. 8–9.
45. NLS Acc. 10090/147: Douglas Crawford, *Press and Radio Coverage during the Campaign and the Future*, 22 Jun. 1970.
46. Lynch, *SNP*, pp. 124–8.

47. Saunders, *Yes to Europe*, p. 56.
48. *The Times*, 13 Dec. 1970.
49. Jay, *After the Common Market*.
50. Butler and Kitzinger, *The 1975 Referendum*, Chapter 1.
51. NLS Acc. 10090/130: SNP National Executive Committee minutes, 7 Dec. 1970.
52. *Scots Independent*, 27 Feb. 1971.
53. NLS Acc. 10090/130: SNP National Executive Committee minutes, 9 Apr. 1971; NLS Acc. 13099/95: SNP Research Bulletin: May 1971, pp. 2–3.
54. Saunders, *Yes to Europe*, p. 353.
55. NLS Acc. 10090/118: *North-East Joint Anti-Common Market Campaign: Common Market: Keep Britain Out* (Aberdeen, 1971), pp. 1–3.
56. NLS Acc. 13099/95: *SNP Research Bulletin*, Jul. 1971.
57. *Falkirk Herald*, 4 Sept. 1971.
58. NLS Acc. 10090/124: *It's the opportunity of a lifetime . . . give your vote impact: vote . . . Dr Robert McIntyre* (Falkirk, 1971).
59. NLS Acc. 10090/161: *Draft Q&A between Winnie Ewing and Robert McIntyre, Stirling and Falkirk Burghs by-election, September 1971*
60. *Stirling Observer*, 7 Sept. 1971.
61. *Grangemouth Advertiser and Eastern District Chronicle*, 15 Sept. 1971.
62. *The Guardian*, 3 Sept. 1971.
63. *Stirling Observer*, 21 Sept. 1971; *Falkirk Herald*, 18 Sept. 1971.
64. *Glasgow Herald*, 29 Oct. 1971.
65. *Scots Independent*, Nov./Dec. 1971, p. 9.
66. NLS Acc. 10090/122: *38th Annual Conference of the SNP, 26–28 May 1972: Reports of National Office-Bearers*, p. 16.
67. University of Dundee Archives MS 315/3/1: *Press Release 21 Feb. 1973: SNP candidate writes to Common Market President (Francois-Xavier Ortoli)*.
68. *Glasgow Herald*, 27 Dec. 1972.
69. *Glasgow Herald*, 5 Mar. 1973.
70. NLS Acc. 11987/110: *SNP Research Bulletin*, Apr. 1973.
71. *SNP and You: Aims and Policy of the Scottish National Party* 4th ed. (Edinburgh, 1974), p. 6.
72. *Aberdeen Press and Journal*, 22 Feb. 1974.
73. *Stirling Observer*, 20 Feb. 1974.
74. *Aberdeen Press and Journal*, 14 Feb. 1974.
75. *Aberdeen Press and Journal*, 18 Feb. 1974.
76. *The Scotsman*, 14 Feb. 1974.
77. *Argyllshire Advertiser*, 26 Feb. 1974.
78. *Aberdeen Press and Journal*, 20 Feb. 1974.
79. Ewing, *Stop the World*, pp. 128–38.
80. *Glasgow Herald*, 25 Feb. 1974.
81. *The Northern Scot*, 16 Feb. 1974.

82. *Aberdeen Press and Journal*, 14 and 19 Feb. 1974.
83. Ewing, *Stop the World*, p. 152.
84. *The Northern Scot*, 23 Feb. 1974.
85. *The Scotsman*, 26 Feb. 1974.
86. *The Scotsman*, 2 Mar. 1974.
87. Mitchell, *Strategies for Self-Government*, p. 209; Hutchison, *Scottish Politics in the Twentieth Century*, pp. 119–26; Lynch, *SNP*, p. 130.
88. The only Conservative MPs representing Scottish constituencies to vote against EEC membership in 1971 were: Michael Clark Hutchison (Edinburgh West); Colin Mitchell (Aberdeenshire West); and Teddy Taylor (Glasgow Cathcart). Patrick Wolrige-Gordon, the MP for Aberdeenshire East, abstained.
89. *The Scotsman*, 2 Mar. 1974.
90. Thorpe, *A History of the British Labour Party*, pp. 188–92.
91. Scottish National Party, *Scotland's Future: SNP Manifesto 1974*, p. 11.
92. NLS Acc. 10090/161: Robert McIntyre, 'Untitled Speech' (undated, autumn 1974).
93. *Aberdeen Press and Journal*, 27 Sept. 1974.
94. *The Northern Scot*, 14 Sept. 1974.
95. *Aberdeen Press and Journal*, 23 Sept. and 3 Oct. 1974.
96. *Aberdeen Press and Journal*, 8 Oct. 1974.
97. *Argyllshire Advertiser*, 8 Oct. 1974.
98. *The Scotsman*, 8 Oct. 1974.
99. *Aberdeen Press and Journal*, 3 Oct. 1974.
100. *Perthshire Advertiser*, 21 Sept. 1974.
101. *The Scotsman*, 4 Oct. 1974.
102. *Perthshire Advertiser*, 12 Oct. 1974.
103. *The Scotsman*, 12 Oct. 1974.
104. Thorpe, *A History of the British Labour Party*, p. 193.
105. See Chapter 4 for a more detailed discussion of the constitutional implications of the 1975 referendum.
106. NLS Acc. 10090/131: SNP National Executive Committee Papers, *Memorandum from Stephen Maxwell to NEC, MPs and research officers* (undated but Jan. or Feb. 1975).
107. NLS Acc. 10754/26: SNP Press Release, 5 Dec. 1974.
108. NLS Acc. 10754/26: SNP Press Release, 23 Apr. 1975.
109. NLS Acc. 10754/26: SNP Press Release, 16 May 1975.
110. NLS Acc. 10754/26: SNP Press Release, 3 Jun. 1975.
111. *Argyllshire Advertiser*, 20 May 1975.
112. NLS Acc. 10090/176: SNP, *No: Choose no, vote Scotland free* (West Calder, 1975).
113. Saunders, *Yes to Europe*, p. 352.
114. NLS Acc. 10754/26: SNP Press Release, 28 May 1975.
115. NLS Acc. 10754/26: SNP Press Release, 28 May 1975.

116. NLS Acc. 10090/125: *41st Annual Conference of the SNP: Address by William Wolfe, Chairman of the Party, Friday 30 May 1975*.
117. *The Scotsman*, 2 Jun. 1975.
118. *Aberdeen Press and Journal*, 19 Mar. 1975.
119. NLS Acc. 10754/26: SNP Press Release, 28 May 1975.
120. NLS Acc. 10090/176: SNP, *Scotland and the EEC: The Facts* (1975).
121. NLS Acc. 13099/4: Gordon Wilson to George Thomson, 27 May 1975.
122. NLS Acc. 13099/4: Gordon Wilson to George Thomson, 27 May 1975.
123. *Glasgow Herald*, 2 Jun. 1975.
124. Richard West, 'Scotland and the Market', *New Statesman*, 28 Mar. 1975, pp. 404–5. On the broader Scottish context of the campaign, see: Butler and Kitzinger, *The 1975 Referendum*, Chapter 6.
125. Bod. Lib. CPA CCO 180/29/1/4: Opinion Research Centre, *Survey on Scottish Attitudes to Devolution, Oil and the EEC* (Jun. 1975), pp. 5–6 and 11.
126. Butler and Kitzinger, *The 1975 Referendum*, p. 152.
127. Saunders, *Yes to Europe*, p. 363.
128. NLS Acc. 10754/26: SNP Press Release, 9 Jun. 1975; *Dundee Courier and Advertiser*, 7 Jun. 1975.
129. Figures taken from: *Glasgow Herald*, 7 Jun. 1975.
130. NLS Acc. 13099/6: Extracts from Minutes of SNP National Council Meeting, 14 Jun. 1975.
131. NLS Acc. 13099/4: Memorandum from Gordon Wilson to Margo MacDonald (Chair of SNP Strategy and Tactics Committee), 6 Jan. 1976.
132. NLS Acc. 13099/4: Memorandum from Stephen Maxwell to MPs and other senior SNP figures, 8 Jan. 1976.
133. Important here was the influence of Jim Sillars, the former Labour MP for South Ayrshire who joined the SNP in 1980 following the collapse of the Scottish Labour Party, the pro-home rule breakaway party he had founded in 1976. Sillars, like Wilson, had been an anti-Marketeer in 1975, but soon changed his mind. Sillars was an important architect of the SNP's pro-Europe stance in the late 1980s. See: Sillars, *Independence in Europe*.
134. *The Scotsman*, 16 May 1975.
135. *Dundee Courier and Advertiser*, 16 May 1975.
136. *Glasgow Herald*, 16 May 1975.
137. *Glasgow Herald*, 16 May 1975.
138. *The Scotsman*, 16 May 1975.
139. Scottish Development Department, *The Modernisation of Local Government in Scotland* (Cmnd. 2067, 1963), pp. 3–6.
140. The Commissioners were unanimous in support for the two-tier principle, although there was some dissent as to the exact boundaries and total number of authorities in each tier. See: *Royal Commission on Local Government in Scotland, 1966–1969* (Cmnd. 4150, 1969).

141. *Scotland: Local Government Reform (Short Version of the Report of the Royal Commission on Local Government in Scotland)* (Cmnd. 4150-I, 1969), pp. 1, 8, 12 and 17. Italicisation in original.

142. *The Economist*, 27 Sept. 1969, 21; *Glasgow Herald*, 26 Sept. 1969.

143. *The Scotsman*, 26 Sept. 1969.

144. *Glasgow Herald*, 27 Sept. 1969; *The Scotsman*, 27 Sept. 1969.

145. *Daily Express*, 26 Sept. 1969.

146. *Glasgow Herald*, 22 Sept. 1969.

147. *The Guardian*, 26 Sept. 1969; *Scots Independent*, 4 Oct. 1969.

148. *Scots Independent*, 17 Jan. 1970.

149. NLS Acc. 10754/7: Arthur Donaldson, 'Notes on SNP Local Government Policy' (undated), pp. 1 and 3.

150. NLS Acc. 10090/99: *SNP Election Broadsheet No. 8* (Glasgow, 1966).

151. NLS Acc. 10090/99: Scottish National Party, *Memorandum on reorganisation of local government to be submitted to the Royal Commission on Local Government in Scotland*, October 1966.

152. NLS Acc. 10090/99: *The SNP: Report of the Royal Commission on Local Government in Scotland* (1969).

153. Scottish National Party, *The New Scotland* (Glasgow, 1970), p. 4.

154. NLS Acc. 11987/110: *SNP Research Bulletin, June 1970*; *Scots Independent*, 13 Jun. 1970.

155. The Scottish proposals were accompanied by measures to reform local government in England and Wales.

156. *Reform of Local Government in Scotland* (Cmnd. 4583, 1971).

157. See, e.g. NLS Acc. 10090/205: Convention of Royal Burghs of Scotland, *Observations on White Paper in relation to Reform of Local Government in Scotland*, 2 Jun. 1971.

158. *The Guardian*, 21 Feb. 1973.

159. *Glasgow Herald*, 16 and 23 Oct. 1973.

160. NLS Acc. 10754/8: Letter from Roxburgh, Selkirk and Peebles SNP Branch to Provost of Peebles (undated, 1972).

161. See the contributions during the parliamentary debate in: *Hansard* HC Deb. cols.909-1041, 4 Dec. 1972.

162. *Daily Express*, 17 Sept. 1973.

163. Reid, *Reflections of a Clyde-built Man*, p. 103.

164. *SNP and You: Aims and Policy of the Scottish National Party*, 1974.

165. *Aberdeen Press and Journal*, 19 Feb. 1974.

166. Scottish National Party, *Scotland's Future: SNP Manifesto 1974*, p. 8.

167. *Aberdeen Press and Journal*, 3 Oct. 1974.

168. *Argyllshire Advertiser*, 1 Oct. 1974.

169. *Scots Independent*, 13 Jun. 1970.

170. *The Scotsman*, 16 May 1975.

171. NLS Acc. 10754/26: SNP Press Release, 10 Jul. 1975.

172. NLS Acc. 10754/26: SNP Press Release, 23 Aug. 1975.

173. The government's White Paper on devolution was published in November 1975. See: *Our Changing Democracy: Devolution to Scotland and Wales* (Cmnd. 6348, 1975).

174. Bod. Lib. CPA CCO 180/29/1/7: Opinion Research Centre, *Attitudes to devolution in Scotland and Wales among English, Scottish and Welsh voters* (Nov. 1976), pp. 5–6.

175. *Scots Independent*, Jun. 1975, p. 9.

176. Gibbs and Scothorne, '"Origins of the Present Crisis": The Emergence of "Left-Wing" Scottish Nationalism'; Hames, *The Literary Politics of Scottish Devolution*, Chapters 1 and 2; Jackson, *The Case for Scottish Independence*, pp. 167–9.

177. NLS Acc. 10754/26: Testimonial Dinner for Arthur Donaldson in Montrose: Speech by Dr Robert McIntyre, 10 Oct. 1975.

4

Letting the People in?
Direct Democracy and Popular Sovereignty
in Post-war Scotland

UNTIL THE 1970S, METHODS of direct democracy remained outside the political and constitutional traditions of the United Kingdom. True, there had been limited local plebiscites on the question of prohibition earlier in the twentieth century. Equally, the Edwardian era witnessed attempts to introduce the referendum as a means of resolving controversial political and constitutional issues; most notably, opponents of Irish home rule advocated a referendum as a means of demonstrating the lack of popular support enjoyed by the Liberal government's proposed constitutional reforms.[1] Nevertheless, in general the referendum was viewed as being incompatible with Britain's parliamentary traditions. Moreover, from the initial creation of a mass electorate in the late nineteenth century until the 1960s, the authority of Parliament remained, with perhaps a few momentary exceptions, largely unquestioned, a popular consensus rooted in both the historic prestige enjoyed by the House of Commons, which transcended political divisions, as well as the central role that the battle for the franchise had played within the nineteenth-century radical tradition inherited by the Labour Party.[2] And while a progressive account of British political history might stress the measured expansion of the electorate, the dominant view remained that those returned to Parliament were elected to exercise their judgement, not take formal direction. In Vernon Bogdanor's phrase, beyond their participation in elections, in this period 'the British constitution knew nothing of the people'.[3] Britain was understood to be a representative, parliamentary democracy: famously, when rebuffing Winston Churchill's suggestion in May 1945 that a referendum be held to ascertain if the public wished the wartime coalition to continue until the final conclusion of the Second World War, the Labour leader and then Deputy Prime Minister, Clement Attlee, described the referendum as 'a device . . . alien to all our traditions', which had 'too often been the instrument of Nazism and Fascism.'[4]

During the 1970s, however, UK governments resorted repeatedly to the referendum as a method of answering constitutional questions that appeared to be impossible to resolve via traditional electoral politics. In March 1973, following the imposition of direct rule from Westminster, a border poll was organised in Northern Ireland in an ineffectual effort to legitimate the new constitutional settlement. Two years later, the first nationwide referendum was held to determine whether the UK should remain within the EEC. Finally, in March 1979 referendums on the Labour government's proposals for devolved assemblies took place in Scotland and Wales. That the 1970s saw the constitutional referendum become an indisputable part of the UK constitution, however unplanned and lacking in formal guidelines, has been confirmed by subsequent events.[5] Still, this transformation in constitutional practice has been treated primarily as the unintended legacy of short-term political manoeuvring and efforts at party management, especially by the Labour government that held office between 1974 and 1979.[6] Such judgements are, of course, understandable. After an unexpected defeat at the 1970 general election, the Labour leader Harold Wilson unenthusiastically adopted the policy of offering an essentially retrospective referendum on UK membership of the EEC as a way of alleviating the seemingly intractable divisions Europe had created within his party. Once Labour had been returned to office and the referendum had been held, Wilson was adamant that the innovation would not be repeated.[7] Even so, his successor, James Callaghan, was almost immediately forced to concede the polls on Scottish and Welsh devolution, once more to address the challenges posed by divisions within the parliamentary Labour Party. As such, the arrival of the referendum has been viewed as a consequence of the rise of constitutional issues that failed to align with established party identities.[8]

But to consider the referendums of the 1970s purely through the lens of parliamentary high politics and party management is to overlook their wider import, particularly in a Scottish context. Whatever the motivations and attendant qualifications, the decision to accord the electorate an explicit voice in constitutional matters was significant and appeared to confirm the existence of a growing distance between MPs and those they were meant to represent, and to vindicate the charge that Parliament had become too distant from the people. Further, it should be recognised that if Harold Wilson was able to use the referendum as a tool to resolve an intra-party conflict, this was a plausible option only because it had already been proposed by myriad voices from across the political spectrum. The 1975 European referendum should, then, be understood within the context of the wider loss of trust in parliamentary representation and party politics that had informed a range of contradictory political phenomena since the late 1960s, including the rise of Scottish and Welsh nationalism, the popularity of Enoch Powell, and the revival of Liberalism.

At a UK level, the referendums of the 1970s thus signalled a new-found willingness on the part of politicians to question the claim of Parliament to represent the people. In Scotland, where an assertion that there existed a unique tradition of popular sovereignty had been a strand within nationalist rhetoric since at least the 1950s, the impact was even more profound. As constitutional scholars have noted, when discussing referendums a distinction needs to be upheld between, on the one hand, relatively straightforward decision-making plebiscites, and, on the other, those instances where the people are able to assume a form of constituent power and confer legitimacy on new or revised constitutional settlements.[9] If the local polls on prohibition of the early twentieth century clearly belonged to the former category, the referendums of the 1970s held a deeper constitutional importance. As Stephen Tierney has argued persuasively, 'constitutional referendums' in effect substitute 'the people directly for the representative role traditionally played by the democratic constitution'; as a moment where the people are able to intercede directly on constitutional questions, such referendums can, Tierney maintains, be understood as 'real-world manifestations' of popular sovereignty.[10] Further, as Tierney recognises, the impact of constitutional referendums can go beyond offering a verdict on a specific proposal. Such polls necessarily require 'an anterior act of demotic border-drawing' that involves identifying and delimiting both a people and a territory.[11] For Tierney, the 'very act of staging a constitutional referendum is itself both a declaration that a people exists and a definition of that people.'[12] Understood from this perspective, the referendums of the 1970s did more than measure the opinion of Scottish voters on Europe or devolution; they also contributed to perceptions of Scotland as a distinctive political community, bolstering the belief that there was a sovereign popular voice that may, on certain issues, be in conflict with that of MPs in the House of Commons. While the referendum might have been adopted by the Labour government on certain issues as a makeshift solution to political challenges, in Scotland it prompted questions of national identity and constitutional legitimacy.

The political and constitutional consequences within Scottish politics of the growing prevalence of notions of popular sovereignty are the main concern of this chapter. The analysis traces a shift in understandings of the mechanism by which any change in Scotland's constitutional status would be achieved. In the middle decades of the twentieth century, even Scottish nationalists understood sovereignty in parliamentary terms, with the SNP convinced that a majority of Scottish MPs would provide the required mandate for independence; by the 1970s, this view no longer dominated, and the importance of a popular mandate was increasingly acknowledged. The chapter begins with an examination of understandings of sovereignty during the 1940s and 1950s, focusing on the failed attempts of the Scottish Plebiscite Society and the Covenant Association to use extra-parliamentary campaigning methods, such as local polls and mass petitions, to stimulate public support for a devolved Scottish parliament. The appearance of demands for a formal referendum on the question of Scotland's constitutional status during the second half of the 1960s is then considered. An important factor here was the example provided by the referendums arranged by the UK government in parts of the receding British Empire, including Newfoundland, Malta and Gibraltar, which offered pro-referendum voices precedents to which they could appeal. Also significant were the wider demands for direct democracy that emerged in the late 1960s. The impact in Scotland of the 1973 border poll in Northern Ireland and the 1975 EEC referendum is then assessed. In particular, the debate over how the latter poll should be counted is considered. The final section of the chapter focuses on the March 1979 devolution referendum. While the results of this vote, and the consequences of the imposition of the so-called forty per cent rule, are well known, the emphasis here is on the wider impact of the decision to hold a constitutional referendum in Scotland, and the extent to which this contributed to the emergence of a political rhetoric in Scotland – by no means confined solely to the SNP – that emphasised popular readings of sovereignty.[13]

'WHAT KIRRIEMUIR DOES TO-DAY, SCOTLAND DOES TO-MORROW': PLEBISCITES AND PETITIONS IN POST-WAR SCOTLAND[14]

In 1977, Peter Thomson became the first Sheriff to be removed from office in modern Scottish history. Thomson, first appointed as a Sheriff in 1955, had been found to be no longer fit for judicial office after an investigation into his alleged political activism by the Lord President and Lord Justice-Clerk, the two most senior members of the Scottish judiciary. Of particular concern was Thomson's continued advocacy of a plebiscite on the question of Scottish home rule, over which he had already received a formal warning in 1974 after a local poll he had organised in Rutherglen.[15] Although Thomson's removal was recommended following the judicial enquiry, it required political approval, which was granted by the Secretary of State for Scotland, Labour's Bruce Millan. The initial order was placed before Parliament in July 1977, with the final decision being confirmed, amid some controversy, following a Commons vote in December 1977.[16]

Thomson's support for a referendum predated both his judicial career and the devolution debate with which his removal ironically coincided; for more than three decades, he had been the driving force behind the Scottish Plebiscite Society. Founded in 1946 by Thomson and his brother, the Society planned to arrange a series of local plebiscites that would offer voters the chance to record their support for one of three options: independence, a devolved Scottish parliament on the model that then prevailed in Northern Ireland, or the status quo.[17] Thomson was keen to present the Society as an impartial arbiter, which would be able to remove the constitutional question from party politics and focus straightforwardly on establishing the true wishes of the Scottish public.[18] Yet it was clear that Thomson favoured a devolved parliament as a means of reversing the trend towards centralisation of authority in London that had been apparent during the 1940s; he was sure that these local polls would disclose overwhelming public support for devolution, and would put pressure on the Labour government to implement constitutional reform, or at least sanction a Scotland-wide referendum on the question.[19] Indeed, Thomson at times tended towards to what Colin Kidd has identified as the 'strict' construction of the Union settlement that was surprisingly common amongst mid-century Scottish nationalists.[20] In late 1946, for example, he complained that Scottish conscripts to the British army were subject to English law during their period of service; this, he asserted, was a breach of the 1707 Treaty of Union.[21]

The first notable intervention by the Plebiscite Society took place in early 1949 in the Angus burgh of Kirriemuir, where the Town Council gave consent for Thomson to undertake the first of his local plebiscites on the question of home rule.[22] The poll, which followed the three-option model and required the return of a postal ballot, secured an impressive level of engagement from the local electorate, with over eighty-five per cent of local voters participating. The result was a decisive endorsement of devolution: sixty-nine per cent backed a devolved Scottish parliament, with twenty-two per cent favouring independence and just five per cent backing the current constitutional arrangement.[23] Still, it was not always evident what the Kirriemuir poll was intended to achieve. At times, Thomson flirted with an embrace of a popular understanding of sovereignty, intimating that his ultimate aim was a national plebiscite that would allow the Scottish people to express their wishes: such a vote would reveal conclusively what 'the Scottish people wanted', and there was, he argued in 1947, 'no answer to the clearly expressed will of the majority.'[24] But Kirriemuir was also plainly intended to generate publicity that would highlight the shortcomings of the Labour government's policy towards Scotland; in this regard, it was relatively successful, even if the Labour Secretary of State for Scotland, Arthur Woodburn, felt able to ignore the result.[25] There was, then, an implicit tension within the Society's approach, with an appeal to popular sentiment functioning, in effect, as only a single element within a wider campaign to influence parliamentary opinion. Even proponents of constitutional reform, it appeared, continued to accept that ultimate authority was held by Westminster.

While the Kirriemuir plebiscite failed to convince the Labour government of the need for constitutional change, it did encourage others to attempt to find ways of demonstrating the true extent of popular support for some form of self-government for Scotland. Scottish Convention, the pressure group founded by John MacCormick following his departure from the SNP in 1942, foreswore direct intervention in electoral politics in favour of an immediate focus on attempting to build cross-party support for legislative devolution.[26] MacCormick had initially hoped that the Labour Party would use its substantial Commons majority to honour its commitment, reiterated at the 1945 election, to some form of Scottish home rule.[27] He soon realised, however, that the government had no interest in implementing any such reform.[28] As detailed in Chapter One, the initial consequence of this was to push MacCormick towards attempting to broker an alliance with the Unionists, National Liberals, and Liberals, efforts that would lead to him returning to the electoral field to contest the February 1948 Paisley by-election as a 'National' candidate.[29] In tandem with this engagement in party politics, from 1947 onwards Scottish Convention also organised a series of National Assemblies.[30] Initially, the Assemblies, intended to be representative of Scottish society, concentrated on producing a draft scheme for a devolved parliament that would then be presented to parliamentarians.[31] The result in Kirriemuir, however, offered encouragement to those

Assembly participants who favoured a shift towards seeking broader public support for self-government. The possibility of attempting to organise a plebiscite or petition had been mooted at the second Assembly meeting in 1948, but after Kirriemuir the Convention called on the government to hold a Scotland-wide referendum on self-government.[32] This was, once again, rejected by Arthur Woodburn, who, in response to a question in the Commons from the pro-Convention Unionist MP for Edinburgh South, Sir William Darling, stated that 'the issues involved' in any debate over self-government were 'much too complicated' to be settled by a referendum. 'Public opinion on such issues' was, Woodburn concluded, 'best made effective through the procedure of Parliamentary democracy.'[33] In response to Woodburn's refusal to countenance a referendum, Scottish Convention announced the launch of a mass petition, labelled the Covenant in allusion to Scottish (and, it should be said, Ulster) history, that would allow Scots to publicly pledge their support for a devolved parliament.[34] The Scottish Covenant was officially unveiled at the third National Assembly in October 1949; within a year, it had attracted an alleged 1,700,000 signatures.[35]

Despite the success of the Covenant in attracting public support, it was, in political terms, a disappointment. Unable to force a change in government policy, and with the Conservative victory at the 1951 general election making no appreciable difference, the campaign soon lost momentum; although the Covenant Association, as Scottish Convention became in 1951, staggered on for the remainder of the decade, it lacked any serious presence in Scottish politics, and disappeared following MacCormick's death in 1961.[36] The authors of the Covenant have been criticised for failing to include a 'sanction clause' that would have committed signatories to withdrawing their support from politicians who failed to take heed of public opinion on the constitutional question.[37] But while such an assessment has a certain validity, it overlooks more fundamental contradictions within the Covenant movement. First, the Covenant was an attempt to use popular support for devolution as a counterweight to parliamentary indifference. There was, though, little indication that in the immediate post-war period Scottish voters, even those who had signed the Covenant, viewed politics in this manner; rather, turnout at general elections, and the mass membership enjoyed by both the Unionist and Labour parties, suggested instead that the electorate remained convinced of the legitimacy of representative government. While the Covenant certainly revealed a generally favourable public attitude towards the prospect of a devolved Scottish parliament, there was still widespread acceptance that political sovereignty resided, in the end, at Westminster. Both Labour and their Unionist opponents were, then, on relatively sure ground in declining to alter course in response to the Covenant. Hector McNeil, who replaced Woodburn as Secretary of State for Scotland in 1950, rejected MacCormick's contention that the level of support enjoyed by the Covenant justified the holding of a referendum, arguing bluntly that 'constitutional change in this country is considered and settled by the normal process of Parliamentary democracy'. McNeil's Unionist shadow, James Stuart, reached a similar verdict, explaining patiently to MacCormick that his party did not believe 'that such extremely complex matters' could 'be properly determined either by plebiscite or by reference to the number of signatures affixed to any document.' Stuart concluded that 'the constitutional methods by which the people in our democracy can make their wishes known and effective are well understood, generally respected, in constant use, and available to all shades of opinion'.[38]

Second, and as had been the case at Kirriemuir, it was not clear that the organisers themselves really believed that they could oppose popular to parliamentary opinion in a fundamental way. From the outset, the ideal outcome for those involved in the Covenant campaign was to try to influence opinion within the two main parties, in the hope of inspiring greater political support for devolution. When the decision was made by the Convention's National Committee to prepare the Covenant, it was, to be sure, maintained that this would produce 'an impressive declaration of the will of the Scottish people'; all the same, the assumed purpose of the campaign was to provide 'an effective means of bringing pressure to bear on all political parties and upon the Government of the day.'[39] The declaration of support for self-government that the public were asked to sign featured, moreover, a preceding 'pledge' of 'loyalty to the Crown' and an acceptance of the established 'framework of the United Kingdom'.[40] Even allowing for the desire to gather a broad coalition around the Covenant, this was hardly a full-throated declaration of popular sovereignty; for all the publicity MacCormick and his allies generated, and the ostensible distinctiveness of their approach, the Covenant was, ultimately, as James Mitchell has recognised, little more than 'a pressure group', and not all that dissimilar from earlier organisations such as the Scottish Home Rule Association.[41]

As Ben Jackson has detailed, a conviction that in Scotland there prevailed a tradition of popular sovereignty, traceable to the 1320 Declaration of Arbroath and the right of resistance promulgated by the sixteenth-century humanist and political theorist George Buchanan, and which could be contrasted with the English model of parliamentary sovereignty, which in turn relied upon an absolutist understanding of monarchical authority, certainly circulated among nationalists during the 1940s and 1950s.[42] Nevertheless, the political implications of such a position were still to be fully developed. Some supporters of constitutional change may well have contended that Scotland enjoyed a more democratic and egalitarian political culture than the other nations within the UK, but there persisted a belief that constitutional change remained the prerogative of Parliament. Of course, the seventy-one MPs then sitting for Scottish constituencies could be construed as the bearers of a discrete, and potentially detachable, Scottish sovereignty, not yet completely subsumed within the English tradition of parliamentary sovereignty. Notably, that was a notion shared by certain strands of Unionist opinion, who seemed willing to treat Scottish MPs as a separate group when it came constitutional questions: the *Glasgow Herald*, unequivocally Unionist in its politics, stated that a devolved parliament would arrive only 'when 36 or more . . . Scottish MPs were . . . pledged to' support such a policy.[43] Perhaps more surprisingly, in the post-war era the SNP shared this belief in the centrality of parliamentary opinion. Individual members of the party surely participated in the activities surrounding the Covenant, but at an official level the party was dismissive of the campaign. Some of this scepticism was presumably motivated by lingering animosity towards MacCormick, and his conduct since leaving the SNP in 1942; there were, however, also more considered grounds for the party's decision to oppose the turn towards rousing popular opinion. The possibility of supporting any form of national plebiscite was overwhelmingly rejected by delegates at the 1949 SNP conference, held a week before the formal launch of the Covenant. The vast majority of those present dismissed the notion of moving away from the electoral route to independence as 'defeatist', and as 'a sign of weakness': the party continued to view the return of thirty-six SNP MPs as a mandate for independence.[44]

The idea that a referendum, rather than a majority of Scottish MPs, would provide a route to constitutional change would not gain widespread support for another two decades, even amongst independence supporters. The *obiter dicta* that MacCormick managed to elicit from Lord Cooper, the Lord President of the Court Session, during the unsuccessful legal action he raised in 1953 questioning the right of the new monarch to adopt the title of Queen Elizabeth II, since there had not been a Queen Elizabeth I of Great Britain, would in later decades provide a handy precedent for those seeking a legal basis for a Scottish tradition of popular sovereignty. In an oft-quoted passage, Cooper noted that parliamentary sovereignty was an English doctrine, and had no counterpart in Scottish constitutional law; he concluded by stressing that he did not comprehend why the British Parliament established in 1707 would have inherited 'all the peculiar characteristics of the English Parliament but none of the Scottish Parliament'.[45] Yet in the context of the 1950s, such comments, while perhaps of interest, had no practical political application. It would require a more sustained divergence between electoral loyalties in Scotland and England for Cooper's words to assume a greater significance.

Intermittent attempts to repeat the Kirriemuir poll, or to find a means to determine popular opinion on the constitutional question across Scotland, would resurface throughout the 1950s and early 1960s. A further local plebiscite was held to coincide with the Glasgow Scotstoun parliamentary by-election in October 1950. As in Kirriemuir, local participation was impressive and once more a large majority was recorded in support of devolution; again, though, the wider impact was minimal.[46] Thomson's Plebiscite Society continued to pursue local interventions in an attempt to maintain public interest in constitutional questions. Following polls in Banff and Lanark that produced majorities in favour of a devolved parliament, the Society arranged another plebiscite in Peebles in May 1959. Turnout in the burgh was seventy-five per cent, which compared favourably with the levels witnessed in municipal elections; sixty-six per cent of respondents supported a devolved parliament, with sixteen per cent in favour of outright independence; only twelve per cent of those who voted backed the existing constitutional arrangement.[47] Two years later, the Plebiscite Society launched an appeal to raise £100,000 to fund a Scotland-wide plebiscite on the question of home rule. Although there was some support from national political figures, including the Earl of Airlie, John Rankin, the Labour MP for Glasgow Govan, and John Bannerman, Chairman of the Scottish Liberals, the campaign misfired: only £3,000 was raised, and the effort was soon abandoned.[48] As had been true of the Covenant campaign, the Plebiscite Society was able to uncover general backing for the idea of some form of self-government. But such sentiments were still disconnected from electoral concerns. If voters were willing, when asked, to express support for the creation of a devolved parliament, the issue did not appear to influence who they voted for in a general election. More than this, there was no expectation amongst the public that popular methods such as petitions and plebiscites would have any direct political consequences. The belief that the Scottish people could find a political outlet outside of a general election, and that their views were distinct from, and perhaps even superior to, those of their parliamentary representatives, would not begin to take hold until the late 1960s, in part due to domestic pressures, but also as a result of the policy adopted by the UK government overseas.

EXTERNAL INFLUENCES: DEMANDS FOR REFERENDUMS IN THE 1960S

In late 1945, the Labour government announced that an elected National Convention would be established in Newfoundland, which would be charged with exploring 'possible forms of government to be put before the people at a national referendum.'[49] Until 1934 Newfoundland had enjoyed dominion status, but a financial crisis, exacerbated by the impact of the economic depression of the 1930s, saw self-government replaced by a UK-appointed Commission of Government. This had always been intended to be a temporary constitutional measure, and the conclusion of the Second World War enabled support for a more permanent solution to be canvassed. The Convention recommended that voters be asked to choose between establishing the Commission of Government on a permanent basis or returning to what was termed the 'responsible government' of the dominion era. The UK government, however, was keen to see Newfoundland become a province of Canada and ensured that this third option was included in the referendum.[50] The initial poll in June 1948 failed to deliver the required majority in favour of a single proposal, meaning that a second referendum was held the following month, and a majority in support of the Canadian route was eventually secured. On 31 March 1949, Newfoundland formally became a province of Canada.[51]

The decision of the UK government to deploy the referendum as a tool to manage constitutional change in Newfoundland attracted some attention from supporters of Scottish self-government. In early 1949, Sir William Darling, the Unionist MP for Edinburgh South who, given his links with Covenant campaign was more sympathetic towards legislative devolution than many of his colleagues, raised the issue in the House of Commons.[52] Darling asked the Labour Prime Minister, Clement Attlee, whether he would, after the experience in Newfoundland, 'consider setting up a committee to investigate the possibility of embodying this device in the British Constitution.'[53] A year later, in a letter to James Stuart, the Unionist Shadow Scottish Secretary, John MacCormick also tentatively highlighted the potential precedent that he believed the Newfoundland polls had created.[54] These early attempts to use British policy overseas in debates over Scotland's constitutional position were ineffective, with senior Labour and Unionist figures able to maintain that such a device was unnecessary in Britain, where Parliament remained best-placed to decide on such questions.

Yet while such arguments appeared convincing in the immediate post-war political context, by the 1960s the balance was beginning to shift, as a fresh round of referendums in British territories overseas triggered new debates over the potential for constitutional referendums to be held within the UK. One example was provided by the poll undertaken in Malta in May 1964, which produced a majority vote in favour of a new constitutional settlement that would see the island gain its independence after having been under British rule since the early nineteenth century.[55] Of greater significance within British domestic political debate was the referendum held in Gibraltar in September 1967, when Gibraltarians were asked whether they wished to continue as a British Overseas Territory, or to come under the jurisdiction of the Spanish state. Despite the examples offered by the polls in Newfoundland and Malta, the Labour government had initially been wary of resorting to a referendum in Gibraltar. Responding to questions in the Commons in early 1967, which had been prompted by a resolution passed in December 1966 by the United Nations General Assembly calling for negotiations between the UK and Spanish governments on the status of Gibraltar, Judith Hart, the Minister of State for Commonwealth Affairs, stated that she did not believe 'that a referendum would be helpful at present.'[56] Within months, however, the government's stance had altered, and a referendum was now being presented as a way of resolving the debate over Gibraltar's constitutional position. It was clear that the appeal of the referendum lay in the perceived legitimacy that any poll would be expected to grant British rule in Gibraltar. In June 1967, after planned talks between the UK and Spain had been abandoned, Hart announced that a referendum would now be held in Gibraltar. Hart justified this decision in terms that appeared to accept a popular understanding of sovereignty; any process of 'decolonisation', she informed MPs, could not be reduced to 'the transfer of one population, however small, to the rule of another country, without regard to their own opinions and interests.' Hart went further, suggesting that any referendum would settle the question only for as long as the people of Gibraltar wished: they retained, she stated, 'the right at any future time to express by a free and democratic choice the desire to modify their status by joining with Spain'. Nobody believed that this was a plausible prospect; nevertheless, Hart was clear that this was a question of 'the interests of the people of Gibraltar' and that they had to 'decide what they believe their interests to be and where they believe their interests to lie.' While the opinion of elected representatives in Gibraltar was a useful indicator of opinion, Hart maintained that it would be 'infinitely more meaningful if the people themselves' had an opportunity 'to express their views on where their interests lie by means of a referendum.'[57] The referendum would ultimately demonstrate near-unanimous support for Gibraltar to continue as an Overseas Territory, a popular mandate that, as *The Times* concluded, made 'it perfectly plain for all the world to see that the Gibraltarians do not want to become Spaniards'.[58]

That the arguments used in the case of the Gibraltar referendum might be applied to the Scottish context was obvious almost instantly. During the initial Commons debate on the referendum, David Steel, the Liberal MP for Roxburghshire, had asked Hart if she had considered 'extending this constitutional innovation to the people of Scotland'.[59] Thereafter, Gibraltar provided an important example that could be referenced by those seeking a referendum on the question of constitutional reform within the UK. In April 1968, James Davidson, the pro-devolution Liberal MP for Aberdeenshire West, asked the Labour Prime Minister, Harold Wilson, why it appeared that 'different criteria' governed 'the holding of referenda in Commonwealth and United Kingdom territories.' Specifically referencing the poll conducted in Gibraltar the previous autumn, Davidson encouraged Wilson to 'allow the Scottish people a referendum' that would enable them 'to express their wishes regarding the future government of Scotland'. Davidson was rebuffed by Wilson, who argued that the referendum had no place within domestic politics; nevertheless, Davidson continued to press the issue.[60] Later that year he introduced a Private Members' Bill that proposed consultative constitutional referendums in Scotland and Wales; these were to be multi-option, and would have allowed voters to choose between no change, greater administrative devolution, devolved legislative assemblies, and full independence.[61] Although he received favourable coverage in *The Scotsman*, in parliamentary terms, Davidson's Bill was a failure, being rejected at its second reading by eighty-one votes to thirteen.[62] Yet the debate his proposed referendum prompted amongst MPs was revealing. The majority of Labour and Conservative MPs who responded to Davidson continued to reject the notion of a referendum on principle. For Norman Wylie, the Conservative MP for Edinburgh Pentlands, 'direct democracy' was an authoritarian tool, one designed to erode the authority of representative government. Fitzroy Maclean, Wylie's Conservative colleague in Bute and North Ayrshire, rejected the notion that devolution was a question only for Scottish and Welsh voters as it would impact England too. Moreover, Maclean felt that a referendum on independence was unnecessary, arguing that, if the SNP returned a majority of Scottish MPs, then he would accept there was a sufficient mandate for self-government. Others pointed to the risks of allowing popular sentiments to dictate government policy. For George Lawson, the Labour MP for Motherwell, the adoption of the referendum might have unwelcome consequences on questions such as capital punishment. In a similar vein, Donald Dewar, then representing Aberdeen South for the Labour Party, warned Davidson that he was 'hopelessly confusing the respective roles of the Government and Dr Gallup.'[63]

A significant contribution was made by Winnie Ewing, then still the sole SNP representative in the Commons. Ewing acknowledged her party's formal position, which had, since the 1940s, been that the route to independence lay in securing a majority of Scottish MPs. But Ewing was clearly becoming conscious of the opportunity that any referendum might present for nationalists, and the potential potency of placing popular and parliamentary sovereignty in conflict. She alleged that Labour and Conservative opposition to Davidson's plans was driven not by constitutional propriety, but rather by cowardice, and a deliberate commitment to not finding out what the Scottish public thought on the question of the constitution. Ewing then noted the different attitude adopted by the government in the case of Gibraltar, when it had been clear that popular opinion would endorse the existing constitutional arrangements. Were, she wondered, referendums only to be granted if the government was 'sure of two things – first that it knows the answer and second that it knows that it will like it?'[64] By the late 1960s, the possible opportunity offered by a constitutional referendum was beginning to hold more appeal for nationalists.

If a commitment to constitutional change underlay Liberal and SNP support for a referendum in Scotland, on the political right there were other issues that remained more influential. The belief that liberalising social legislation did not reflect public opinion encouraged some MPs to promote the referendum as a means of preventing parliamentarians from imposing cultural change upon an unwilling population. This was an understanding of direct democracy that cleaved close to the notion, voiced first by Unionist opponents of the Liberal government's proposals for Irish home rule in the early twentieth century, of the referendum as the 'people's veto', a means of checking a government bent on using a majority in the House to Commons to pursue policies that had not received a popular mandate.[65] In July 1967, for example, Harold

Gurden, the Conservative MP for Birmingham Selly Oak and a member of the right-wing Monday Club, attempted to use a Private Members' Bill to call for the use of consultative referendums that would gauge public opinion on 'contentious' issues, such as capital punishment, same-sex relationships, and abortion. Gurden adopted an explicitly populist, majoritarian language in speaking in support of the referendum: the central question in any 'democracy', he suggested, was whether 'the will of the majority of the people' was being respected.[66]

Gurden's legislative efforts were unsuccessful, but the underlying sentiments were a significant element within the growing sense of political disillusionment prevalent by the late 1960s. As discussed in Chapter Two, the widespread popular support for Enoch Powell that was evident after his April 1968 'rivers of blood' speech was driven in part by a sense that parliamentarians were dismissing public opinion, and failing to represent the views of their constituents. This was a development understood most clearly by Tony Benn, then the Minister of Technology in the Labour government. In the wake of Powell's speech, and the confrontational public demonstrations of support that Powell's position had received, Benn delivered an address in late May 1968 in Llandudno to the Welsh Council of Labour. Here Benn identified what he saw as a 'wave of anxiety, disenchantment and discontent' that, although clearly influenced by economic concerns, also had important political determinants. For Benn, there was a risk that this widespread sense of frustration with the political process might, as Powell's conduct showed, be exploited by right-wing politicians; indeed, Benn raised the prospect of that 'discontent' and 'apathy' eventually resulting in 'violent protest' and 'bloodshed'. Central to Benn's proposals for counteracting such a possibility was a reinvigoration of the UK's political institutions, and the creation of 'a new popular democracy' that would allow the public a greater voice than the 'five-yearly cross on the ballot paper' emblematic of the parliamentary system. Benn speculated that technological advances might facilitate the holding of regular 'electronic referenda' as a means of 'sharing responsibility' between politicians and the public on aspects of 'public policy'.[67]

While Benn's willingness to confront the new challenges facing parliamentarians received some sympathy, his backing for the referendum as a method of renewing democracy was criticised.[68] His speech was also a source of some discomfort for his colleagues in the Labour government, since his comments could, without much effort, be read as suggesting that his own administration lacked popular legitimacy. Duncan Sandys, the senior Conservative backbencher and former Cabinet minister, took great pleasure in asking Harold Wilson if he shared Benn's view that the government was 'out of touch with the country', and, if so, if he had 'considered the idea of holding a General Election'. All the same, hostility towards the prospect of UK membership of the Common Market allowed some on the political right to respond more enthusiastically to Benn's suggestion that the referendum should be embraced as a way of increasing public engagement in the political process. Here a left-leaning concern for popular participation overlapped with more populist understandings of the referendum as means by which the views of voters might be invoked to oppose government policies perceived to be running counter to the weight of public opinion. Speaking immediately after Sandys, Robin Turton, the Conservative MP for Thirsk and Malton, called for a referendum to decide 'whether or not we should withdraw our application to join the Common Market'. This was rejected by Wilson, who declared that he refused to engage in 'government by referendum'.[69] But the issue refused to fade: in late 1969 Neil Marten, the Conservative MP for Banbury who would become one of the most dogged supporters of a referendum on the question of Common Market membership, once again raised the issue in the Commons. Citing the domestic precedent provided by the local referendums that had previously been held in Scotland and Wales regarding alcohol licencing, and pointing towards the referendums that had taken place in current EEC member states, Marten argued that the severity of the constitutional limitations that EEC membership would allegedly impose were sufficient to justify the innovation of a nationwide referendum. Such arguments were rebuffed by Wilson, who maintained that referendums were 'contrary' to Britain's political 'traditions'. Members of the Commons had, Wilson insisted, been elected by the public to debate and decide on such issues, and should exercise that mandate.[70] Marten, however, was undeterred, and would revisit the question in early 1970, changing tack this time by challenging Harold Wilson to explain his refusal to hold a referendum on EEC membership when a constitutional referendum had recently been sanctioned in Gibraltar. Wilson, for his part, still clung to the assertion that the UK, unlike Gibraltar, was blessed with a fully sovereign parliament and, as such, had no need to turn to the referendum to determine such constitutional questions.[71]

Still, Wilson's invocation of parliamentary sovereignty was double-edged, since the argument in favour of a referendum was precisely that EEC membership would constrain this sovereignty, perhaps irrevocably.

It was, ironically, Winnie Ewing who provided a clear summary of
the threat that Common Market entry posed to the traditional standing of the House of Commons. Intervening in a debate on the question in February 1970, Ewing began by reiterating the by now standard
economic and constitutional reasons for the SNP's opposition to EEC
membership. Thereafter, however, Ewing broadened her analysis, and
addressed the extent to which the EEC would, she felt, challenge the sovereignty of Parliament. Ewing argued that, even if she set aside her own
commitment to Scottish independence, she still could not 'understand
the advantage to Britain as a whole of going into the Common Market.'
The EEC was, Ewing stated, 'clearly an undemocratic community': it
might be 'a community of nations', but it was still 'controlled by bureaucrats.' While for Ewing the House of Commons undoubtedly had many
'faults', it remained 'a democratic forum . . . constantly trying to be democratic', and she cautioned against exchanging that 'for an unknown
arrangement.' Ewing further stressed the absence of a mandate from
the English electorate in favour of EEC membership. In Scotland anti-
Common Market voters could, she pointed out helpfully, give their support to the SNP: in England, where all the major parties were in favour
of membership, 'the people . . . will be denied the opportunity to vote for
a specific party with that point of view.' It was, Ewing concluded, difficult to see how any UK government, whether Labour or Conservative,
would be able to claim that there was a popular mandate for entry: the
'only way' that a mandate could delivered in such circumstances was
'by referendum.'[72]

The decision by successive UK governments to authorise referendums
in overseas territories thus merged with the debate over Europe to create
new demands for a constitutional referendum to be held on the question of EEC membership. There were certainly figures within the Labour
and Conservative parties willing to make the case for direct democracy.
Nevertheless, the blend of populist distrust of central government and
support for constitutional reform that informed calls for a referendum
was clearly one that was, in key respects, most conducive to the form
of politics then espoused by the SNP. While the party remained formally committed to its longstanding position that securing a majority
of Scotland's seventy-one MPs would provide a legitimate basis for the
commencement of negotiations over Scottish independence, by 1970 it
was apparent that, as Europe became a critical political issue, the referendum might provide an alternative means of pursuing constitutional
change.[73]

WHICH PEOPLE? THE ACCEPTANCE OF THE REFERENDUM AFTER 1970

The victory in June 1970 of a Conservative Party committed to EEC membership ensured that Europe became an increasingly significant political issue in the first half of the 1970s. While a sizeable minority within the Labour Party supported the Heath administration's policy on Europe, the return to opposition allowed Labour to criticise the terms of entry negotiated by the Conservative government while leaving open the possibility of supporting membership in principle. It was in this context that the prospect of a referendum on Europe began to garner support. Again, it was Benn who made the key intervention, arguing in a December 1970 article in *The Times* that a referendum was necessary due to the 'unique and historic' nature of the issue, which would see the sovereignty of parliament 'subordinated . . . to a supra-national authority'; a referendum would, he argued, also be a 'conscious extension of the idea of democratic decision making'.[74] While Benn's suggestion was initially rejected by his Labour colleagues, by early 1972, with the French government having announced that they would hold a referendum on the question of UK accession to the EEC, the position had changed, and a majority of the Labour Party's National Executive Committee now supported a referendum on the issue.[75]

If Europe was the principal driver behind demands for a referendum, other influences continued to play a role. In March 1972, as the Labour Party debated its position in relation to the EEC, the Conservative government announced that a so-called 'border poll' would be held in Northern Ireland the following year in an attempt to resolve the ongoing religious and political tensions within the province, which had erupted into open violence in the late 1960s. There was in theory a certain logic behind the decision to hold a constitutional referendum in Northern Ireland in order to determine whether a majority of the population preferred to remain within the UK or wished to become part of united Ireland: while formally part of the UK, Northern Ireland had, since its creation in 1921, been a constitutional anomaly, enjoying both a devolved parliament and a distinctive electoral politics in which British parties did not participate, at least formally. Nevertheless, the border poll did represent a fundamental change in how referendums were explained and justified by UK administrations. The polls in Malta and Gibraltar had been rationalised as being necessary because voters in those territories lacked the full portion of sovereignty that came with representation in the House of Commons; whatever the political realities, the same could not be said in relation to Northern Ireland, where electors could, at least if they wished, participate in Westminster elections. Inherent within the decision to sanction a border poll was, then, an admission – profound in many respects – that Commons representation might, in certain contexts, not be quite enough to ensure constitutional legitimacy.

The circumstances prevailing in Northern Ireland were clearly unique in many regards. Nevertheless, the border poll was seized upon by supporters of devolution as justifying a referendum on the question of Scotland's constitutional status within the UK. The day before the Northern Ireland border poll was held, William Baxter, the idiosyncratic Labour MP for West Stirlingshire, sought to introduce a Private Members' Bill in the House of Commons that would have approved a multi-option constitutional referendum in Scotland. Baxter acknowledged that referendums had not previously been part of British constitutional practice, but he asked MPs to recognise the changed landscape that had been created by the Conservative government's policy in Northern Ireland, and by the Labour Party's new position on Europe. Notably, Baxter also accepted that the standing of the House of Commons had declined, and that MPs no longer enjoyed the authority with the public that they once had. In an echo of a perspective more often heard from representatives from the SNP, Baxter suggested that the UK's membership of the EEC would lead to a further centralisation of economic decision-making, which would require a review of constitutional structures. A referendum on the issue of devolution was, he concluded, necessary at this juncture to allow Scottish voters to express their opinion on an issue that cut across traditional party divides and could not, therefore, be decided satisfactorily at a general election.[76]

While Baxter's parliamentary efforts were marginal, his arguments did receive sympathetic coverage in The Scotsman, which had, since the 1960s, adopted a pro-devolution perspective.[77] In an editorial published on the day of the border poll, and sarcastically entitled 'Westminster wisdom', it was remarked that at least a poll on Scottish devolution would not require the presence of soldiers to protect the ballot boxes. More seriously, for The Scotsman an important political lesson had been learned: while the Conservatives and Labour appeared willing to concede a referendum as a concession to 'violence in Ulster' or for reasons of political expediency, such a measure would never be granted if it threatened to come 'at the expense of Westminster's power'.[78] Two days later, following the declaration of the result of the referendum in Northern Ireland, which had, as expected, produced an overwhelming majority in favour of remaining part of the UK as a result of mass abstentions among the Catholic and Republican communities, *The Scotsman* again highlighted the insincerity and hypocrisy that appeared to lie behind the government's decision to hold a referendum in Northern Ireland, while refusing a similar poll on devolution for Scotland. Only in the latter case were voters subjected to vague platitudes about the need to defend 'Parliament's traditions and authority' and 'pious nonsense about referenda stirring up passions and prejudice'. Whereas in the case of Northern Ireland – and, indeed, in Gibraltar – the government had been sure that a referendum would deliver majority support for the constitutional status quo, in Scotland, *The Scotsman* argued, a referendum 'would almost certainly show a majority in . . . favour' of some form of devolution. The attitude of the 'main parties' was, it was concluded, 'so plainly a matter of expediency, of calculating votes, that it inevitably breeds disillusionment and frustration among Scots to whom the desire for responsibility in running their country is a matter of the first importance.' There was a marked need to recognise that 'people' were 'no longer content to mark a ballot form once every few years', and that they wished for 'more influence in making decisions that affect them vitally.'[79] Even the *Glasgow Herald*, traditionally far less sympathetic towards constitutional reform than *The Scotsman*, worried that the Northern Irish poll had merely highlighted 'the futility of referenda which governments in their minds only allow when they know that the result is a foregone conclusion'.[80]

As the debate over Europe continued even after the UK formally joined the EEC at the start of 1973, the poll in Northern Ireland also offered an important domestic precedent for advocates of a referendum on Common Market membership. This was especially significant after Labour's return to government in February 1974. By the time of the October 1974 general election it was clear that, if the party was able to secure a Commons majority, then Labour would seek to renegotiate the membership terms before returning the question to the people, most likely in a referendum. There were, to be sure, some within the Labour Party in Scotland who remained opposed to a referendum on Europe precisely because they understood that it might be used to justify a further plebiscite on the issue of devolution. John Mackintosh, a supporter of both EEC membership and devolution, saw referendums in fundamentally negative terms, as a cynical tool through which Commons majorities in support of what he believed were progressive reforms might be reversed. For Mackintosh, a referendum on Europe would be both 'unprecedented', as well as a 'serious attack . . . on our system of representative government.'[81] Despite these warnings, the Labour government pressed ahead with its proposals, officially confirming in January 1975 its plans for a renegotiation of the terms of the UK's membership of the EEC, with the revised terms to be put to the public in a referendum.

That the referendum might have implications for the UK's internal constitutional settlement as well as relations with the EEC was immediately understood. Given the SNP's electoral successes the previous year, and the degree to which the party's anti-Common Market stance appeared, in early 1975 at least, to resonate with the majority of Scottish voters, one of the government's principal concerns was how to manage the referendum count and declaration in the event that the result in Scotland conflicted with that recorded in the UK overall. The initial solution, as outlined in the White Paper published by the government in February 1975, was to come down in favour of a centralised national count that would be followed by 'a single declaration of the United Kingdom result'. It was even suggested that this national count would, 'in the interests of security and economy of organisation', be conducted at a single site in London, and in such a way as to ensure that the final totals could not be disaggregated. These arrangements were justified on the grounds that the referendum was to be a 'national poll on a national issue, organised to secure the verdict of the whole British [sic] people'; the relevant 'constituency', it was concluded, was therefore 'the whole of the United Kingdom'. The idea that the results should be made available on a constituency or regional basis was firmly rejected.[82] The problem facing the government was, nonetheless, that the motivations underlying this position were painfully transparent. There was a clear awareness within government and the civil service that the referendum, by giving political weight to a popular mandate, was capable of enhancing a sense of a distinctive Scottish sovereignty and identity. In a confidential report prepared for the Cabinet prior to the official announcement of the referendum, these fears were acknowledged explicitly. The argument for the 'publication of only a total United Kingdom result' was made on the basis that it would 'diminish' any 'tensions' that might be generated by the poll and reduce the ability of individual 'regions' to gain 'special influence' following the declaration. The authors of the report were, however, still forced to concede that, if efforts were made to prevent local constituency results from becoming known, it would be 'obvious' that this had been 'undertaken only with the intention of obscuring area differences'.[83]

For all the prior consideration given to the question, the government's plans for a single national count and declaration were condemned almost as soon as they were made public. Immediately prior to the publication of the White Paper, both the SNP and Plaid Cymru warned that, if, as was then being speculated, a central count was adopted, they would attempt to hold unofficial polls in order to ensure that there some avenue for the expression of distinctive Scottish and Welsh verdicts.[84] Nevertheless, the government remained committed to its original proposals in the months that followed, and expended substantial parliamentary time and political energy upholding the idea of a national count. Speaking in the Commons during an adjournment debate on the referendum in early March 1975, Ted Short, the Labour Leader of the Commons, defended the government's approach. Short began by restating the case for a referendum in principle, reminding MPs that, since both Labour and the Conservatives were divided on the European question, the issue could not be resolved in the standard way at a general election. Furthermore, he maintained that the final decision would still rest with parliamentarians, and that the sovereignty of Parliament would remain unaffected. Short then turned to the specific question of how the count and declaration were to be undertaken. Here he was unequivocal about the government's reasoning: in opting for a national count and result, which it had been stated would take place in London at Earls Court, the intention was 'to unite the country behind a decision', and to prevent any divergent results in the constituent parts of the UK being 'used . . . by those who wish to divide the United Kingdom.'[85]

Short's directness garnered little sympathy in the Commons, with MPs from all parties declaring their unhappiness at being denied the chance to discover their constituents' views on the Common Market. The sharpest criticisms were made by those, such as Roy Hughes, the anti-Common Market Welsh Labour MP, who pointed out that a central count would create ongoing political speculation and controversy that would be 'nothing short of a gift to the Nationalists'.[86] Hughes' argument was endorsed, mischievously or not, by Winnie Ewing, who by now sat as the SNP MP for Moray and Nairn. Ewing told MPs that if she and her fellow SNP members 'were political Machiavellis' they 'would say "This is a marvellous grievance, let us continue with the central count".' But her broader arguments in favour of a constituency-level count illustrated the extent to which the turn towards the referendum had reshaped nationalist thinking in relation to sovereignty and, by extension, the method by which Scottish independence might be realised.[87] If the SNP had traditionally persisted with the notion that a majority of Scottish MPs would provide a mandate for independence, that position had shifted by the early 1970s towards a tentative, if not complete, adoption of the referendum as a means of delivering constitutional change.[88] In Ewing's hands, however, this history was rewritten, and she now claimed that her party had 'always believed in the weapon of a referendum', and had considered it to be 'the most democratic of tools' long 'before the EEC was on anyone's agenda'. The SNP, she asserted, had 'always wanted . . . a referendum on Scottish self-government'.[89]

Ewing went on to reaffirm the SNP's commitment to ensuring that a separate Scottish verdict was made public whatever the government's position. To adhere to a single UK count would, she argued, represent a further insult to both Scottish opinion and to Scottish sovereignty. Given that a majority of Scottish MPs had voted against EEC membership, a central count that made no effort to establish the wishes of the Scottish electorate would mean that both Scotland's parliamentary and popular voices were being ignored. The context of the referendum pushed Ewing to grant more weight, though, to the latter, as she argued that in Scotland a different constitutional standard operated. For Ewing, 'the sovereignty of Parliament' was 'not the law of Scotland.' Rather, 'the sovereignty of the people' was 'above the sovereignty of Parliament according to . . . Scots constitutional law.' While it had been possible to discern something approaching this perspective in the debates prompted by the earlier activities of the Plebiscite Society and Covenant Association, and in the opinion of Lord Cooper in the 1953 Royal numerals case, this signalled a far more direct invocation of popular sovereignty. And notably, the SNP had remained aloof from those prior efforts, preferring a reading of Scottish sovereignty that focused on the Treaty of Union and Parliament: now the notion of a distinctive Scottish tradition of popular sovereignty began to move to the centre of nationalist rhetoric. Ewing also issued the government a warning, promising that:

> If we are cheated out of the truth about the facts, we shall find out by democratic methods. We shall take sample polls. In some constituencies we shall take total polls. We shall have tellers at the gates. We shall adopt all manner of methods to find out how people voted . . . If we are to find out, how much better it would be if the answers given to us were authoritative.[90]

There were signs too that these arguments over the nature of Scottish sovereignty were beginning to resonate beyond the Commons. A survey commissioned by the Conservative Party to test Scottish opinion during the debate over the referendum found that voters were largely positively disposed towards 'the constitutional novelty' of being able to interpose their views directly into the political process, with 'a majority' of respondents rejecting 'the idea of Parliament rather than the voting public having the final decision'. There were, though, significant partisan and class divides at play, with Conservative supporters, and those from middle- and upper-class backgrounds more broadly, seemingly far more uneasy about the prospect of the referendum. Notably, the greatest 'enthusiasm for participatory-style Government' was located amongst 'the most strongly anti-market elements of the population: SNP supporters and pro-independence voters'.[91] Unsurprisingly, SNP MPs sought to speak to such sentiments. During the Referendum Bill's second reading in early April, Douglas Henderson, the SNP MP for Aberdeenshire East, dismissed the idea of a single central count, and resumed the argument made by Ewing a month earlier that methods of direct democracy were especially well-suited to Scotland, where a popular, rather than parliamentary, understanding of sovereignty apparently prevailed. Henderson maintained that what he portrayed as the stronger tradition of 'constitutional freedom' that had resulted ensured that Scots were more at ease with allowing the people a direct political role; indeed, he criticised MPs opposed to the referendum for what he described as their 'smugness and complacency' in believing that only they, and not 'the people', could 'be trusted to take a decision on an issue'. Citing Lord Cooper's 1953 opinion, Henderson offered his support for the European referendum and assured the Commons that, from a Scottish perspective, 'in questions of constitutional change . . . the sovereignty of the people' was always 'the overriding consideration'. 'Constitutional law", Henderson concluded impishly, was 'perhaps, another branch of Scots law from which the House and lawyers in other parts of the kingdom may profitably learn and borrow.'[92]

In such a political climate, and with Scottish MPs having voted narrowly to reject the Labour government's renegotiated membership terms, the proposed national count, always impractical, was now increasingly unjustifiable.[93] As the *New Statesman* warned, the SNP 'would inevitably gain a huge propaganda weapon from any attempt to submerge Scottish votes in an amorphous national aggregate.'[94] The government's commitment to a single national count finally dissolved in late April, when, despite still offering half-hearted defences of the original proposals, a free vote on the question was conceded. A substantial majority emerged in favour of declarations at the regional and county level of local government rather than using parliamentary constituencies. This compromise allowed discrete national verdicts to be recorded, while simultaneously protecting individual MPs from being placed in a situation where they would be shown to have adopted the opposite position on Europe to that espoused by the majority of their constituents.[95] Bizarrely, the government still attempted to assert that these regional and county declarations would be undertaken at Earls Court, a stance that lasted barely twenty-four hours before it was accepted that the counts would also be handled at a local level.[96]

In the end, the debate over the declaration of the referendum result proved unnecessary, at least in narrow terms. Although Scottish voters were, as noted in the previous chapter, less enthusiastic towards the Common Market than their English counterparts, and despite the majorities in favour of leaving the EEC recorded in Shetland and the Western Isles, there was still a majority in each of the four nations of the UK for continued EEC membership. But, like the referendum itself, the questions that were raised should not be dismissed as having been motivated only by political expediency, or as having had only a fleeting impact on Scottish and British politics. In calling the referendum, the Labour government had been forced to confront the practicalities of the count, and the concerns over what might happen if Scotland was to return a divergent result. These anxieties represented, in effect, a concession, however grudging and implicit, that Scotland was not just an administrative unit, or a historic nation, but rather a distinct – and continuing – political community. The government's fear was not just that the referendum might play out to the immediate benefit of the SNP, but that allowing separate declarations, which might show that Scottish voters held a different position on the EEC from their counterparts in the rest of the UK, would further awaken and entrench this sense of political difference, with long-term constitutional consequences.

Further, the referendum exercised an important influence on the SNP, and nationalist rhetoric more broadly. In the spring of 1975, nationalists sensed a weakness in the government's position, a fear that, in offering the Scottish people a vote on the European question as part of a UK-wide referendum, a space might be left open that would allow deeper, more essential questions to be raised; to move, to use Stephen Tierney's framing, from first-order legislative questions to second-order considerations of the source of constitutional legitimacy and authority.[97] In response, the SNP adjusted the way in which it understood and argued about Scottish sovereignty in order to emphasise the need for popular consent. This approach operated in two directions. First, the SNP backed a referendum on Europe on the basis that it affected Scottish sovereignty, which had been deposited at Westminster in 1707, but, crucially, remained distinctive. As Douglas Henderson told the Commons in March 1975, 'the sovereignty of Scotland' was 'at present' located in Westminster, but any decision to transfer it 'to any third party' required the consent of 'the Scottish people'.[98] Second, and more profoundly, Scottish sovereignty was reinterpreted as having always been popular rather than parliamentary in nature. Margo MacDonald, then serving as a SNP Vice-Chair, declared during the referendum campaign that 'national sovereignty was the main referendum issue in Scotland'. This was, to an extent, a predictable claim from a senior SNP figure. But notable was the emphasis that MacDonald placed not just on the need for the Scottish nation to avoid being subsumed within the EEC as part of the UK, but also on the need for popular legitimacy. As MacDonald elaborated, the sovereignty to which she had referred was not that 'of a remote and ineffectual parliament, but the sovereign rights of the Scottish people'.[99] If the SNP accepted the result of the EEC referendum quickly, and abandoned its opposition to Common Market membership, this new emphasis on popular sovereignty would remain a more permanent feature of nationalist rhetoric.[100] It would, moreover, spread beyond the ranks of the SNP.

POPULAR SOVEREIGNTY, THE REFERENDUM AND DEVOLUTION

In the days that followed the European referendum, the political correspondent of the *Glasgow Herald*, John Warden, reasoned that the result, which had ostensibly shown public and parliamentary opinion to be in alignment, demonstrated that the 'assertion of a divide between Parliament and the people', a 'jibe' popular with 'trendy reformers', had been mistaken. He concluded that the referendum had, if anything, strengthened 'our occasionally wavering faith in parliamentary democracy', and that the country would 'have no more truck with referenda and their like for a long time.'[101] As the focus of constitutional debate shifted during the second half of 1975 from Europe to the Labour government's proposals for devolved assemblies in Scotland and Wales, such predictions proved to be ill-founded. This, of course, had always been the concern expressed by those opposed to the EEC referendum: that it would create a precedent that would be returned to by those who wished to block or reverse policies which they feared were able to command a Commons majority. William Hamilton, the Labour MP for Central Fife, had made the point during the Commons debates on the European referendum when he warned that it had been 'idle and irresponsible' for government ministers to claim that the Common Market was a unique issue, and that they were not making a fundamental change to the constitution. For Hamilton, once introduced, the referendum would become an 'accepted . . . principle', available in the future as a tool to resolve 'this, that or the other issue.'[102]

Even before the publication of the government's devolution proposals in late 1975, the prospect of a referendum on the issue was being
raised.[103] Initially, the government rejected such calls, with Ted Short
attempting to uphold a division between the European issue, which had
related to 'the constitutional relationship between this country and other
countries', and devolution, which was 'a domestic affair' that would not
affect the sovereignty of Parliament.[104] Short's interpretation was countered by Norman Buchan, the Labour MP for West Renfrewshire and a
former junior minister at the Scottish Office. In a lengthy article in *The
Times*, Buchan argued that while the government might seek to maintain
that devolution had no implications for sovereignty, Scots were, in reality, being asked to consider the most profound constitutional question:
'under what government they wish[ed] to live.' In such a context, and
with support for the SNP having reached unprecedented levels, it was,
Buchan argued, only 'proper' that steps were taken to determine 'the
basic will of the people'. Buchan's proposals were, it should be said,
peculiar: he advocated a referendum that would address the question of
independence, in the hope that a comprehensive 'no' verdict would prevent a new devolved assembly from being used by the SNP as a vehicle
for 'separatist arguments'.[105]

The government's efforts to prevent the European precedent being
used in the case of devolution did not last. A joint Scotland and Wales
Bill, detailing devolved settlements for both nations, had been introduced in November 1976; within weeks, in the face of widespread hostility, particularly from backbench Labour MPs, the government was
forced to concede a referendum on the proposals. The Bill collapsed
in February 1977 when a guillotine motion, designed to bring an end
to parliamentary debate and hasten the progress of the legislation, was
defeated by twenty-nine votes, with twenty-two Labour MPs voting
against the government, and an additional twenty-three electing to
abstain.[106] Nevertheless, the commitment to a referendum on devolution was retained, and survived the splitting of the legislation into separate Scottish and Welsh bills when it was once again brought before
Parliament in November 1977. There were ironies inherent in these
developments. The loudest voices arguing in favour of a referendum were
those who were also most firmly opposed to devolution, and who saw
an opportunity to use popular opposition, or at least apathy, to block
the government's constitutional reforms; there was scarcely any serious
intellectual commitment to popular sovereignty. It was, *The Scotsman*
noted in a caustic editorial criticising the granting of a referendum
on devolution, curious that it was those MPs who most professed

'to be attached' to 'the supremacy of Parliament' who were doing their best to undermine that status.[107]

There is a need, though, to be conscious of consequences, and not just intent. Once the principle of a referendum had been introduced into the devolution debate, it gave added impetus to the fundamentally national-ist argument that there was a unique Scottish tradition of popular sov-ereignty. As Margo MacDonald wrote perceptively in November 1976, a referendum on devolution had 'a number of implications favourable to the cause of independence', not least since it signalled 'Westminster's acceptance of the principle that the future of Scotland must be deter-mined by the people of Scotland – i.e. that sovereignty is popular rather than parliamentary.' Further, MacDonald noted, a devolution referen-dum would create 'a precedent' that any future Scottish Assembly could 'invoke to hold subsequent referenda on the extension of the Assembly's powers'. 'Resort to a referendum', MacDonald surmised, marked 'the final acceptance by English opinion' that there was 'a constitutional way to dissolve the Union.'[108] Speaking to Neal Ascherson, the influ-ential pro-devolution *Scotsman* journalist, MacDonald speculated that 'if, at some point in the future, the Scottish people were to organise a referendum through the Assembly, and voted for independence quite regardless of what Westminster or anybody else says – then presum-ably they will have exercised their sovereign vote to be independent.'[109] This was a supposition that Gordon Wilson was eager to pursue during the Commons debates on the Scotland and Wales Bill. For Wilson, the imprimatur of authority that a referendum would confer would enti-tle the proposed Assembly to refuse to recognise decisions emanating from Westminster where these appeared to run counter to 'the sover-eign will of the Scottish people'. Government spokespersons might try to refute such claims: John Smith, as the Minister of State responsible for steering Labour's devolution proposals through Parliament, dismissed Wilson's argument as 'absurd', and maintained that the new Assembly would enjoy only the 'detailed powers conferred on it by this sovereign Parliament at Westminster.'[110] Nonetheless, if that were true, then it was difficult to see why it was necessary for the devolution legislation to receive a popular mandate via a referendum.

More than this, the use of the referendum in the context of the gov-ernment's devolution proposals could, viewed from a certain perspec-tive, be seen as vindicating the sense of discontent with representative, parliamentary politics that had been rising since the late 1960s. This was, for John Mackintosh, the principal danger posed by the referen-dum. Speaking in December 1976, he warned that parliamentarians

had, in recent years, already demonstrated the limits of their authority on 'macro-economic questions'; indeed, he doubted if the Commons
could continue to claim that it was 'sovereign in that respect.'[111] Two
months later, Mackintosh reiterated his concerns, describing the decision to allow a referendum on devolution as 'disastrous'. The issue, for
Mackintosh, was that a referendum was being used to mask the fact
that the devolution legislation did not enjoy the support of a majority
of MPs; in effect, Labour MPs who opposed devolution were opting to
vote for the Bill in the hope that the public would reject the scheme in a
referendum. It was, Mackintosh concluded, a cowardly and dangerous
approach for MPs to take, 'to hand on the responsibility to the electorate' on the 'spurious' basis that devolution required a distinctive 'mandate' from the electorate.[112]

It was this notion of the mandate, and the way in which it was delin-
eated, that was especially important. The decision that Scottish devolution was a matter that required the input of only the Scottish electorate
also represented, at a basic level, an acceptance that Scotland's constitutional status was a matter to be decided by the Scottish people. Here
could be seen in practice the 'border-drawing' effects of referendums
theorised by Tierney: in the debates over devolution, Scotland was
being defined both as a territory and as a people, one imbued with the
authority to exercise the final decision over their collective constitutional
future.[113] Whatever the aims of those MPs who supported a referendum – and they were largely opponents of devolution – and no matter
that any poll would technically be advisory, the debate unfolded in a
way that granted a degree of agency to the Scottish electorate: they were
to be given the ultimate say on devolution. It was telling that few serious
attempts were made to argue that voters in England were entitled to
express their views on the question of devolution. This was, of course,
partly a question of political pragmatism: a UK-wide devolution poll
would raise, in more extreme form, the same fears regarding conflicting
results as had been evident during the EEC debates. But there was also
an acknowledgement that, at a moral level, the conclusive verdict must
rest with Scottish voters.

Equally significant in this regard were the debates that took place following the return of the devolution legislation to Parliament in late 1977
over the need for any vote in favour of a devolved assembly to achieve
a specific level of support from the electorate, rather than just a simple
majority. This would result in the notorious amendment, introduced in
January 1978 by the Labour MP for Islington, George Cunningham,
that required the pro-devolution vote to secure the backing of forty

per cent of registered voters; if this threshold was not met, the government was obliged to return to the Commons and give MPs the opportunity to repeal the legislation.[114] The forty per cent rule has been treated primarily as a spoiling tactic – and it was certainly that – but the underlying assumptions appeared to suggest that even opponents of devolution accepted that, when it came to Scotland's constitutional position, weight of support amongst the public carried greater authority than any manifesto pledge or Commons majority.[115] Indeed, if anything the Cunningham amendment strengthened the sense that the referendum result would be binding on parliamentarians, rather than advisory, further entrenching notions of popular sovereignty in a Scottish context. As Alick Buchanan-Smith, the MP for North Angus and Mearns and a lonely pro-devolution voice on the Conservative benches, noted, the 'moment' that 'certain percentages' were introduced into the referendum, it would 'strengthen the power of the referendum and move it into the area in which . . . [it] . . . might become mandatory.'[116] The other key amendment made to the Scotland Bill, which would have allowed the Orkney and Shetland isles to opt out of the devolution settlement should a referendum reveal that a majority of local residents were opposed to the creation of a devolved assembly, might also be said to have similarly privileged the need for popular consent.[117]

As is well known, when the devolution referendum was eventually held on 1 March 1979 the 'Yes' campaign failed to surmount the barrier of the forty per cent rule: although a narrow majority of those who voted supported devolution, turnout was disappointingly low, and the yes vote represented just under one-third of the total electorate.[118] Further, there were notable regional disparities in support, with backing for the devolution proposals strongest in the urban and industrial communities of the central belt, but weaker in rural areas, including those that had, perhaps paradoxically, returned SNP MPs five years earlier [see Table 4.1]. In practical terms, this was, at best, an unenthusiastic endorsement of the government's devolution scheme; indeed, it can be hazarded that, even if the forty per cent rule had not been in place, the future of the Assembly would have been in doubt given the lack of legitimacy it would have suffered from the outset. Yet, it was, nevertheless, notable that in the aftermath of the referendum many in the ranks of both the Labour Party and the SNP, and who had, for very different reasons, been unconvinced of the merits of devolution earlier in the decade, found themselves now adopting a majoritarian language. Responding to questions in the Commons a week after the referendum, the Labour Prime Minister James Callaghan was keen to reassert his government's commitment to devolution despite the regrettably narrow nature of the referendum result. Callaghan reminded MPs that 'consideration' had to be given to the fact that a pro-devolution verdict had been 'secured in Scotland.' Callaghan received conspicuous support from William Ross, the former Labour Secretary of State for Scotland, who, despite his prior record of scepticism towards devolution, asked Callaghan to remind those demanding the immediate repeal of the Scotland Act 'that the "Yes" side actually won'. Callaghan welcomed Ross's intervention, and argued that 'it would be irresponsible' to simply abandon the devolution legislation 'and to say that all the wishes of that majority are to be flouted.'[119]

These comments were, of course, motivated by the need of the Labour government, which had, since 1977, lacked a Commons majority, to retain the support of SNP MPs who were demanding that the devolution proposals be implemented despite the failure of the 'Yes' vote to clear the forty per cent hurdle. The government's efforts to buy time, perhaps through the vehicle of all-party talks on how the Scotland Act might be amended, were unsuccessful, culminating in the vote of no confidence on 28 March 1979, supported by the SNP and carried by a single vote, that brought down the Callaghan administration, and resulted, a little more than a month later, in the election of a Conservative government under the leadership of Margaret Thatcher that would prove to be entirely uninterested in devolution.[120] But although the Labour

Table 4.1 Results of the 1979 devolution referendum in Scotland[122]

Counting Area	Yes vote (%)	No vote (%)	Yes vote	No vote	Turnout (%)
Borders	40.3	59.7	20,746	30,780	67.3
Central	54.7	45.3	71,296	59,105	66.7
Dumfries & Galloway	40.3	59.7	27,162	40,239	64.9
Fife	53.7	46.3	86,252	74,436	66.1
Grampian	48.3	51.7	94,944	101,485	57.9
Highland	51.0	49.0	44,973	43,274	65.4
Lothian	50.1	49.9	187,221	186,421	66.6
Strathclyde	54.0	46.0	565,519	508,599	63.2
Tayside	49.5	50.5	91,482	93,325	63.8
Orkney	27.9	72.1	2,104	5,439	54.8
Shetland	27.1	72.9	2,020	5,466	51.0
Western Isles	55.8	44.2	6,218	4,933	50.5
TOTAL	51.6	48.4	1,230,937	1,153,502	63.6

government collapsed, taking the model of devolution contained within the Scotland Act with it, the devolution referendum hardened a rhetoric and a way of thinking present since the early 1970s, and which would become increasingly significant after the 1979 general election. As Neal Ascherson argued in his *Scotsman* column in the days following the referendum, to say that devolution had been rejected by Scottish voters required a prior acceptance of the legitimacy of the forty per cent rule. 'A sliver of a majority was', Ascherson maintained, 'still a majority. To deny it would be a crime against the common understanding of democracy.' Ascherson warned those keen to now see the rapid demise of the Scotland Act that they risked setting 'a fateful pattern for times to come' since, if the majority in favour of devolution was dismissed, 'a formidable part of the Scottish political community' would 'refuse to accept' the validity of that 'verdict.' Rather, he predicted with some accuracy, they would 'say and go on saying for the rest of their lives that Scotland was cheated.'[121] Popular opinion, and with it the notion of a mandate, however defined, had become central to Scottish politics, giving credence to those who promoted a popular reading of sovereignty. This was, perversely enough, now true even of those opposed to devolution, who rested their calls for the repeal of the Scotland Act upon the lack of popular enthusiasm for constitutional reform said to have been apparent at the 1979 referendum. This would be a shift with long-term political and constitutional consequences.

CONCLUSION

Following the May 1979 general election, the new Conservative government moved swiftly to unwind the devolution scheme outlined by its predecessor; the following month, MPs voted to repeal the Scotland Act by the comfortable margin of 301 to 206 votes.[123] In making the case for repeal, the incoming Conservative Secretary of State for Scotland, George Younger, relied upon what he portrayed as the at best inconclusive nature of the referendum result. Younger, who was clear that he was including non-voters in his assessment, determined that the 'only responsible and reasonable conclusion' that could 'be drawn from the referendum result' was 'that 67 per cent of the Scottish electorate' had been 'either positively opposed to the Scotland Act', or did 'not feel that they want it enough to bother to vote for it.'[124] Younger's argument was, on its own terms, logical, and, it could be said, at least respected the intention of MPs when they had backed the forty per cent rule, which had been designed to ensure that devolution would only be implemented

if there was sufficient positive desire on the part of the public to coun-
teract the scepticism of many parliamentarians. Nevertheless, Younger's
willingness to appeal to what he represented as the attitude of the majority of the Scottish electorate towards constitutional reform held certain
dangers for the Conservative Party in Scotland. Despite having recorded
an improved performance at the 1979 general election, regaining seven
seats from the SNP and recovering some, but by no means all, of the vote
share shed by the party in the early 1970s, the Scottish Conservatives
remained well adrift of the Labour Party in terms of both seats and
popular support.

This was a point made at length by Bruce Millan, now Labour's
Shadow Secretary of State for Scotland. Responding to Younger, Millan
began by noting that the forty per cent rule only required that an order
to repeal the Act come before Parliament: there was no obligation on
MPs to vote in support of repeal. Millan then offered his own majoritarian interpretation of the referendum results, maintaining that the
most 'important thing about the referendum result', which 'no amount
of logic chopping and argument' could 'set aside', was 'that a majority
of the people of Scotland who voted in the referendum voted "Yes".'
Millan further advised Younger to be wary of the implications of his
own case. If non-voters were to be taken into consideration, then the
new Conservative government enjoyed the support of just thirty-three
per cent of the UK electorate; in Scotland, the position of the government was even weaker, with fewer than one in four of the Scottish electorate having voted Conservative. The Conservatives, Millan stated, had
'no majority in Scotland' and 'no particular mandate from the people
of Scotland.' He concluded by suggesting that Younger 'might be just
a little less arrogant in describing the views of the people of Scotland,
in view of the miserable results that his party had at the last general
election in Scotland'.[125] Millan's arguments were echoed by another
figure from the right of the Labour Party, Donald Dewar, since 1978
the MP for Glasgow Garscadden, who protested that, if devolution was
abandoned, then in areas such as education, health and housing, policy
in Scotland would now be administered by a government that had 'no
mandate from the Scottish people.' Dewar was adamant that 'in terms
of Scottish domestic affairs . . . those who control them, who initiate the
legislation, should be directly responsible to and directly reflect Scottish
political opinion.'[126]

Of course, and as Dewar recognised, such an argument might appear
to rest upon nationalist foundations. Certainly, Gordon Wilson, one of
just two SNP MPs to be returned at the May 1979 general election,

had been keen to underscore the new Conservative government's lack of legitimacy in Scotland, suggesting that repealing the Scotland Act would mean that the government was 'ignoring a popular majority when they themselves do not command the support of the majority of electors in Scotland.'[127] Despite the warnings issued by Conservative MPs, who, not unreasonably, cited Labour's lack of a majority in England in the preceding parliament in response, Dewar, and many of his colleagues within Labour's Scottish ranks, continued to pursue the question of the government's lack of a Scottish mandate. Nevertheless, it should be noted that this turn towards arguments based on conceptions of sovereignty was not an early or anticipatory response to Thatcherism. Instead, as Jack Geekie and Roger Levy recognised in an assessment critical of what they saw as Labour's embrace of nationalist arguments, the immediate 'precedent' for the idea that governments at Westminster had to give special consideration to the views of Scottish electors could be traced to the March 1979 devolution referendum, which, in their view, 'had reinforced, indeed legitimised, the idea of the sovereign Scottish mandate.'[128] But it remains necessary to amend the chronology still further. The 1979 referendum was not merely an ad hoc political device; rather, it was, in an important sense, the product of a debate over the relationship between politicians and the public that had unfolded over the previous decade. Engendered by a growing sense that traditional methods of political representation no longer functioned and reinforced by the adoption of direct democracy on the issues of Northern Ireland and the Common Market, by the late 1970s, there was, in Scotland, a growing conviction that, at least on constitutional questions, the people were sovereign. It was the arrival of appeals to the people as a central factor within Scottish politics, a product of the 1970s, that would serve to reshape the political landscape in the 1980s and 1990s.

NOTES

1. Bogdanor, *The People and the Party System*, pp. 11–35; Atkinson, Blick and Qvortrup, *The Referendum in Britain*, Chapter 1.
2. Biagini and Reid (eds), *Currents of Radicalism*; MacDonald, *The Radical Thread*.
3. Bogdanor, *The New British Constitution*, p. 173.
4. Quoted in: Atkinson, Blick and Qvortrup, *The Referendum in Britain*, p. 23.
5. On developments after 1979, see: Atkinson, Blick and Qvortrup, *The Referendum in Britain*, Chapter 3.
6. Qvortrup, *The Politics of Participation*, pp. 116 and 120.

7. *Hansard* HC Deb. vol. 893 col. 37, 9 Jun. 1975.
8. Qvortrup, *Government by the People*, pp. 111–22.
9. Kalyvas, 'Popular Sovereignty, Democracy and the Constituent Power'.
10. Tierney, 'Constitutional Referendums', pp. 361–3.
11. Tierney, *Constitutional Referendums*, p. 16.
12. Tierney, 'Constitutional Referendums', pp. 374–5.
13. Bogdanor, 'The 40 per cent rule'.
14. *Dundee Courier and Advertiser*, 10 Nov. 1948.
15. *Glasgow Herald*, 28 Jul. 1977.
16. *Hansard* HC Deb. vol. 940 cols. 1288–1332, 6 Dec. 1977.
17. On the Scottish Plebiscite Society, see: Mitchell, *Strategies for Self-Government*, pp. 149–57.
18. *The Scotsman*, 8 Mar. 1947.
19. On this perspective, see above, Chapter 1.
20. Kidd, *Union and Unionisms*, p. 260.
21. *Dundee Courier and Advertiser*, 19 Oct. 1946.
22. *Dundee Courier and Advertiser*, 10 Nov. 1948.
23. *Aberdeen Press and Journal*, 2 Feb. 1949.
24. *The Scotsman*, 31 Jul. 1947.
25. See, for example, the editorial in: *The Scotsman*, 2 Feb. 1949.
26. On the background to Scottish Convention's formation, see: MacCormick, *The Flag in the Wind*, pp. 102–13.
27. Levitt, 'Britain, the Scottish Covenant movement and Devolution', p. 37.
28. Mitchell, *Strategies for Self-Government*, pp. 88–9.
29. For further discussion of the context surrounding the Paisley by-election, see Chapter 1, and: MacCormick, *Flag in the Wind*, pp. 119–24; Dyer, 'A Nationalist in the Churchillian Sense'.
30. Mitchell, *Strategies for Self-Government*, pp. 123–5.
31. NLS Acc. 7295/9: Scottish National Assembly, *Blueprint for Scotland: Practical Proposals for Scottish Self-Government*; MacCormick, *Flag in the Wind*, p. 116.
32. *The Scotsman*, 22 Mar. 1948; *Aberdeen Press and Journal*, 9 Feb. 1949; *Dundee Courier and Advertiser*, 9 Feb. 1949.
33. *Hansard* HC Deb. vol. 463 col. 87, 28 Mar. 1949; *The Scotsman*, 29 Mar. 1949.
34. *The Scotsman*, 2 and 27 Jun. 1949.
35. MacCormick, *Flag in the Wind*, p. 128; Mitchell, *The Scottish Question*, p. 102.
36. Mitchell, *The Scottish Question*, p. 108; Petrie, 'John MacCormick'; *The Scotsman*, 14 Oct. 1961.
37. Cameron, *Impaled upon a Thistle*, pp. 277–8; Mitchell, *Strategies for Self-Government*, p. 146.
38. Quoted in: MacCormick, *Flag in the Wind*, pp. 137 and 139–40.

39. *The Scotsman*, 2 Jun. 1949.
40. *The Scotsman*, 31 Oct. 1949.
41. Mitchell, *The Scottish Question*, p. 102.
42. Jackson, *The Case for Scottish Independence*, pp. 129–35.
43. *Glasgow Herald*, 9 Jan. 1950.
44. *The Scotsman*, 24 Oct. 1949.
45. Kidd, *Union and Unionisms*, pp. 116–33, at 117.
46. Mitchell, *Strategies for Self-Government*, pp. 151–2.
47. NLS Acc. 13546/2: L. M. Thomson, *Letter to the Electorate of Peebles*, 15 May 1959.
48. *The Scotsman*, 2 and 15 Dec. 1961.
49. *The Times*, 12 Dec. 1945.
50. *The Guardian*, 3 Jun. 1948.
51. In the first referendum, there were 69,400 votes for 'responsible government', 64,066 for joining Canada, and 22,311 for the continuation of the Commission of Government. At the second referendum, which excluded the option of Commission of Government, the Canadian option triumphed over responsible government by 78,323 votes to 71,334. See: Neary, 'Newfoundland Referenda, 1948', in Hallowell (ed.), *The Oxford Companion to Canadian History*.
52. Mitchell, *Strategies for Self-Government*, p. 150.
53. *Hansard* HC Deb. vol. 463 col. 202–3, 22 Mar. 1949.
54. Bod. Lib. CPA SUMC 2/5: John MacCormick to James Stuart, 7 Aug. 1950.
55. *The Guardian*, 2 and 6 May 1964.
56. *Hansard* HC Deb. vol. 740 col. 270, 7 Feb. 1967.
57. *Hansard* HC Deb. vol. 748 col. 563–72, 14 Jun. 1967.
58. *The Times*, 11 Sept. 1967.
59. *Hansard* HC Deb. vol. 748 col. 570, 14 Jun. 1967.
60. *Hansard* HC Deb. vol. 762 col. 1581–2, 11 Apr. 1968.
61. Mitchell, *Strategies for Self-Government*, pp. 157–60.
62. *The Scotsman*, 15 Feb. 1969.
63. *Hansard* HC Deb. vol. 777 col. 1725–829, 14 Feb. 1969.
64. *Hansard* HC Deb. vol. 777 col. 1758–63, 14 Feb. 1969.
65. Bogdanor, *The People and the Party System*, pp. 29–31.
66. *Hansard* HC Deb. vol. 750 col. 1450–4, 17 Jul. 1967.
67. Benn's speech was delivered on 25 May 1968. A full transcript was published in: *The Guardian*, 27 May 1968.
68. *The Times*, 27 May 1968.
69. *Hansard* HC Deb. vol. 766 col. 29–30, 11 Jun. 1968. Capitalisation in original.
70. *Hansard* HC Deb. vol. 792 col. 199–200, 25 Nov. 1968.
71. *Hansard* HC Deb vol. 798 col. 197–8, 17 Mar. 1970.

72. *Hansard* HC Deb vol. 796 col. 1086–8, 24 Feb. 1970.
73. The parliamentary path was the one offered in evidence by the SNP to the Kilbrandon Commission in late 1970. See the report in: *Glasgow Herald*, 1 Oct. 1970.
74. *The Times*, 13 Dec. 1970.
75. Butler and Kitzinger, *The 1975 Referendum*, Chapter 1.
76. *Hansard* HC Deb vol. 852 col. 429–36, 7 Mar. 1973.
77. MPs voted against Baxter's proposals by 82 votes to 49.
78. *The Scotsman*, 8 Mar. 1973.
79. *The Scotsman*, 10 Mar. 1973.
80. *Glasgow Herald*, 10 Mar. 1973.
81. *The Observer*, 15 Sept. 1974.
82. *Referendum on United Kingdom Membership of the European Community* (Cmnd. 5925, 1975), p. 6.
83. National Archives, Cabinet Papers 129/181/6: *Practical Implications of Holding a Referendum on European Community Membership – Report by Official Working Party*, 17 Jan. 1975.
84. *The Guardian*, 24 Feb. 1975.
85. *Hansard* HC Deb vol. 888 col. 299, 11 Mar. 1975.
86. *Hansard* HC Deb vol. 888 col. 330, 11 Mar. 1975. Capitalisation in original.
87. *Hansard* HC Deb vol. 888 col. 374, 11 Mar. 1975.
88. The question was debated – inconclusively – at the SNP Conference in 1974. See: *The Guardian*, 1 Jun. 1974.
89. *Hansard* HC Deb vol. 888 col. 371–2, 11 Mar. 1975.
90. *Hansard* HC Deb vol. 888 col. 377, 372–3, 11 Mar. 1975.
91. Bod. Lib. CPA CCO 180/29/1/4: *Survey on Scottish attitudes to devolution, oil and the EEC* (Jun. 1975), p. 8. Capitalisation in original.
92. *Hansard* HC Deb vol. 889 col. 1465–8, 10 Apr. 1975.
93. Scottish MPs voted by a margin of 33 to 32 against the revised terms of membership. See: *The Scotsman*, 10 Apr. 1975.
94. *New Statesman*, 11 Apr. 1975, p. 465.
95. *The Scotsman*, 24 Apr. 1975; *The Times*, 24 Apr. 1975.
96. *The Scotsman*, 25 Apr. 1975.
97. Tierney, 'Constitutional Referendums', p. 363.
98. *Hansard* HC Deb vol. 888 col. 324, 11 Mar. 1975.
99. *The Guardian*, 22 May 1975.
100. *The Guardian*, 10 Jun. 1975.
101. *Glasgow Herald*, 9 Jun. 1975.
102. *Hansard* HC Deb vol. 888 col. 378, 11 Mar. 1975.
103. *The Times*, 27 Oct. 1975. For the proposals, see: *Our Changing Democracy* (Cmnd. 6348, 1975).
104. *The Times*, 3 Nov. 1975.
105. *The Times*, 4 Nov. 1975.

106. Kerr, 'The Failure of the Scotland and Wales Bill', pp. 113–19; Cameron, *Impaled upon a Thistle*, pp. 305–6.
107. *The Scotsman*, 17 Dec. 1976.
108. NLS Acc. 10754/16: Margo MacDonald, *Report on SNP Tactics and Prospects in a Referendum*, 10 Nov. 1976.
109. *The Scotsman*, 17 Dec. 1976.
110. *Hansard* HC Deb vol. 922 col. 1745–6, 16 Dec. 1976.
111. *Hansard* HC Deb vol. 922 col. 1825, 16 Dec. 1976.
112. *Hansard* HC Deb vol. 925 col. 1716–17, 10 Feb. 1977.
113. Tierney, *Constitutional Referendums*, p. 16.
114. Naughtie, 'The Scotland Bill in the House of Commons', pp. 16–35; Bogdanor, 'The 40 per cent rule'.
115. See, for example: Mackintosh, 'Commentary: The Killing of the Scotland Bill'.
116. *Hansard* HC Deb vol. 942 col. 1463–4, 25 Jan. 1978.
117. Naughtie, 'The Scotland Bill in the House of Commons', p. 30.
118. For a contemporary discussion of the campaign and results, see: Balsom and McAllister, 'The Scottish and Welsh Devolution Referenda of 1979', pp. 400–1.
119. *Hansard* HC Deb vol. 963 col. 1483–4, 8 Mar. 1979.
120. Naughtie, 'The Year at Westminster'.
121. *The Scotsman*, 3 Mar. 1979.
122. Figures taken from: *Glasgow Herald*, 3 Mar. 1979; Cameron, *Impaled upon a Thistle*, p. 311.
123. Naughtie, 'Year at Westminster', p. 50.
124. *Hansard* HC Deb vol. 968 col. 1332, 20 Jun. 1979.
125. *Hansard* HC Deb vol. 968 col. 1342, 20 Jun. 1979.
126. *Hansard* HC Deb vol. 968 col. 1376–7, 20 Jun. 1979.
127. *Hansard* HC Deb vol. 968 col. 1365, 20 Jun. 1979.
128. Geekie and Levy, 'Devolution and the Tartanisation of the Labour Party', p. 401.

Conclusion
1979 and After

IN THE WEEK PRIOR to the March 1979 devolution referendum, the novelist William McIlvanney, a convinced supporter of a devolved assembly, offered a gloomy prediction of the likely outcome of the poll. Sensing a prevailing mood of 'indifference' and 'virile apathy' among the Scottish electorate, McIlvanney wondered whether this attitude of 'hesitancy' towards the constitutional question masked a deeper crisis of confidence, whether Scots were, in fact, too 'feart' to vote for devolution. McIlvanney concluded by confessing his own 'wee fear': 'what', he speculated, 'if we get a bare majority in favour of the assembly but fall well short of the 40% limit'? He accepted that such a result, which he likened to a 'hung jury', might 'be a peculiarly Scottish response'; it was, all the same, one he hoped would be avoided. Of course, as we have seen in the previous chapter, McIlvanney's forecast of the dread scenario of an inconclusive outcome came to pass, and the Labour government's devolution proposals collapsed. Vindicated by subsequent events, McIlvanney's evocation of the atmosphere surrounding the devolution referendum has been of lasting influence, not least because of the cartoon that accompanied it, drawn by James Turnbull and frequently referenced thereafter, which depicted a timid, thumb sucking, indecisive Scottish lion, chained to a ball marked 'apathy' and announcing bluntly 'I'm feart'.[1] The 1979 devolution referendum, and the ambiguous verdict it produced, has, as a consequence, come to symbolise the uncertainty and doubts of a Scottish public yet to be fully convinced that constitutional reform was worth the associated risks.[2] It would, in this reading, require the experience of the lengthy period of Conservative government that followed the 1979 general election, and the unpopular economic policies imposed during Margaret Thatcher's premiership, to convince a decisive majority of Scottish voters of the merits of devolution.[3] By early 1994, it was possible for John Smith, by then the leader of the Labour Party but a veteran of the constitutional debates of the 1970s, to describe devolution as 'the settled will of the Scottish people'.[4] Smith's assessment was seemingly confirmed by the overwhelming support recorded in a referendum for the devolved Scottish Parliament legislated for by Labour after the party's return to office in 1997.

The 1997 referendum certainly revealed the extent to which devolution enjoyed a broader base of support across Scotland than had been the case in the 1970s. The fears that any devolved legislature would be dominated by the interests of Edinburgh and Glasgow appeared to have faded: in 1979 the Borders, Dumfries and Galloway, Tayside, Grampian, Orkney, and Shetland had all voted against devolution; in 1997, in contrast, every Scottish local authority area returned a majority in favour of devolution and only Dumfries and Galloway and Orkney voted against granting the new Parliament the authority to vary the basic rate of income tax.[5] There is, to be sure, little question that the severity of the economic downturn experienced in Scotland in the early 1980s, and the rising levels of unemployment that followed, provoked widespread anger and discredited the policies of the Conservative government, sentiments that would deepen later in the decade following the introduction of the 'poll tax'.[6] Nevertheless, care should be taken not to overemphasise the extent to which the 1979 general election signalled a critical moment in the divergence between Scottish and English politics, nor to place excessive explanatory weight on popular dislike of Margaret Thatcher among Scottish voters. Economic historians have underlined that deindustrialisation was a long-term process that unfolded from the 1950s onwards; it was the Thatcher administration's response to economic changes already underway that was significant.[7] Similarly, for all that the Thatcher governments have come to occupy a prominent, and largely negative, place in popular political memory, the electoral performance of the Conservative Party in Scotland during this period was not anomalous in comparison to the previous decade. Indeed, although the party's parliamentary representation in Scotland fell sharply at the 1987 general election, with the number of Scottish Conservative MPs decreasing from twenty-one to ten, this was almost wholly a result of the vagaries of the electoral system: the Conservative Party's share of the Scottish vote remained at just under a quarter, almost exactly where it had been in October 1974.

In a similar vein, the strengthening of popular support for devolution apparent in Scotland during the 1980s and 1990s, although it was clearly aided by anti-Conservative feeling, nonetheless relied heavily upon developments that had taken place in the previous decades. A central element in this process were the changes that occurred in the rhetoric used by political actors in Scotland. In the decades after 1945 there had been two principal languages available to those who wished to criticise either Scotland's constitutional position or the broader relationship between government and the people. The first was an anti-statist language unsympathetic towards the growth of centralised government bureaucracies, especially where these were located outside Scotland. This initially took the form of an extension of an anti-socialist appeal first exploited in the 1920s by the Unionists, and which was renewed after 1945 as a means of attacking the reforms introduced by the post-war Labour government. By the mid-1960s, however, the political right had begun to relinquish its monopoly on this rhetoric. If, in the 1940s and 1950s, anti-statism had been expressed in terms that focused on questions of economic policy and the perceived negative impact of Labour's policies in a Scottish context, then in the years that followed this rhetoric shed this firm ideological mooring amid a growing mood of disillusionment with Westminster in general. While the general frustration with the performance of the Labour government during the 1960s, and a wider sense of disappointment with the reality – and limits – of the welfare state, could at times strengthen a right-wing assessment of the weaknesses of socialism, there was also a parallel interpretation from the left that stressed individual freedom and a need for greater popular participation in decision-making. It was the rise of this latter trend, with its roots in the New Left of the late 1950s and early 1960s, that allowed the SNP, and advocates of constitutional reform more broadly, to modify the existing critique of central government, and direct it towards constitutional as opposed to economic questions.[8] In the early 1970s, the twin issues of UK membership of the Common Market and the proposed creation of a two-tier system of local government combined to give this revised iteration of an anti-statist appeal renewed political relevance. The immediate electoral beneficiary was the SNP, which found its appeal to both individual and national freedom especially well-suited to this new political landscape. Conversely, Scottish Conservatives suffered the most acute losses, as the party's support for both Common Market membership and the restructuring of local government proved unpopular with large parts of the party's traditional support.

The second language was concerned overtly with constitutional issues, and, in particular, with changing understandings of Scottish sovereignty. In the two decades after 1945 there was certainly a sense that Scotland was a distinct nation and even political community, not

merely a region of the United Kingdom. Nevertheless, Scottish sovereignty was widely held to reside in representatives and institutions rather
than the people; even for advocates of independence, Scotland's sovereignty had, since the Union of 1707, been located at Westminster, and
was embodied in the Scottish members of the Commons. Sovereignty
remained parliamentary, not popular, and any change in Scotland's constitutional status would require the support of a majority of Scottish
MPs. This was, as the debate triggered by the Covenant campaign of the
late 1940s demonstrated, a conclusion broadly shared by all political
parties in Scotland, including the SNP. If the argument that Scotland
enjoyed a more democratic political culture, one less trammelled by class
and privilege, was an established trope in nationalist rhetoric, the potential constitutional significance of this was not yet fully grasped. Again,
however, the crucial shift occurred during the second half of the 1960s.
It was in this period that the conviction that popular sovereignty prevailed in Scotland, and that this was incompatible with the supposedly
English tradition of parliamentary sovereignty, began to be popularised.
This change was in part the product of that same mood of frustration
and disillusionment with the established parties that had underlain the
steady growth in support for the SNP in the preceding decade. Here,
though, the influence of wider considerations over what role, if any,
direct democratic methods such as the referendum should have within
the UK constitution was vital. The sanctioning of referendums in Malta
and Gibraltar by successive UK governments in the mid-1960s did not
go unnoticed by those who wished to see constitutional reform in a
Scottish context; a further precedent was provided by the 'border poll'
arranged in Northern Ireland in 1973. By the time of the June 1975 referendum on UK membership of the EEC, it was problematic for Labour
and Conservative figures to maintain, as they had done a generation earlier, that the referendum was a device somehow alien to British constitutional traditions. These debates had two chief outcomes. First, the idea
that a popular Scottish sovereignty existed, and that this might in certain
contexts enjoy a greater legitimacy than the Westminster Parliament,
began to be voiced more widely, especially within the ranks of the SNP.
Second, it soon became an expectation that major constitutional reforms
would require public endorsement via a referendum: a clear manifesto
commitment would no longer be sufficient. Accordingly, it was maintained that popular support at a referendum would be necessary before
the Labour government's devolution proposals could be implemented.
While it is true that the referendum was adopted as a spoiling tactic by
those opposed to devolution, the impact of the implicit affirmation of

popular sovereignty that it represented in a Scottish context must still be recognised.

Together, the ways in which these languages evolved moved political debate in Scotland away from debates over political economy, and the relationship between the individual and the state, and towards constitutional issues. This is not, of course, to suggest that what emerged during the 1960s and 1970s was necessarily coherent. Indeed, one of the most arresting aspects of the campaign preceding the 1979 devolution referendum in Scotland was the extent to which it exposed the competing ways in which these languages could be deployed. For supporters of devolution, one of the main benefits of the proposed Assembly was that it would enhance political accountability in Scotland by reducing the distance between voters and their representatives and ensuring that the Scottish Office was subjected to a greater degree of democratic oversight. In a press release issued by the SNP in October 1978, Douglas Crawford, then still the MP for Perth and East Perthshire, argued that a devolved assembly would end the previous era of 'rule by red tape' and loosen 'the vice-like grip of the bureaucrats over Scotland'.[9] But, equally, those campaigning for a 'No' vote in the referendum were able to resuscitate that earlier anti-socialist appeal that viewed additional layers of government as inherently bureaucratic and therefore undesirable, aided, in no small part, by the legacy of unhappiness left by the local government reforms undertaken earlier in the decade. For example, a pamphlet produced by the 'Scotland Says No' campaign group accepted that a devolved assembly might 'bring government "closer to the people"', but maintained that the result would be 'suffocatingly so'. The constitutional reforms proposed by 'the Scotland Act' would, it was suggested, lead only to 'even more government, even more bureaucracy right on our backs, breathing closer down our necks than ever.'[10] As Tom Nairn, a prominent figure in the British New Left and a caustic observer of Scottish politics who nonetheless supported devolution, remarked in his review of the referendum campaign, 'the anti-devolution movement' had relied upon an assertion that, were devolution to become a reality, 'everything would be pretty much like now but worse, *a lot worse . . .* more jobs for the boys, extra bureaucrats boxing us in, fiddling politicians everywhere.' The 'No' campaign, Nairn concluded, had been driven by a 'crass . . . frustrated populism' resentful of government interference and 'ready to hit out against one farther burden or attack.'[11]

Nevertheless, the revival of these earlier forms of anti-statist language, which relied upon a suspicion of socialism formed in the first half of the twentieth century, was a rear-guard action, and would prove to be short-lived. After 1979 criticisms of central government began to blend with ever more blunt assertions of the sovereignty of the Scottish people; rejecting domineering rule from Westminster was now increasingly a question of national rather than individual freedom, with the potential resumption of efforts at constitutional reform the critical issue. The political possibilities of such a rhetoric had, of course, been intimated by the successes enjoyed by the SNP in the early 1970s. Certainly, the arguments adopted by leading SNP figures during the June 1975 Common Market referendum had indicated how condemnations of overbearing and distant bureaucracies could be framed in such a way as to aid the case for Scottish independence. Still, the 1979 referendum would represent the terminus for that particular strand of nationalist argumentation. Devolution not only provoked distrust from those within the SNP who viewed the planned Assembly as a device designed to deflect support for independence: it was also difficult to reconcile devolution with the party's long-held suspicion that Scots had, for much of the twentieth century, suffered as a result of too much government.

It was, in the aftermath of 1979, the Labour Party that would, ironically, prove to be most at ease with a rhetoric that merged the idea of a distinctive Scottish mandate, rooted in the belief that in Scotland sovereignty was popular and not parliamentary, with condemnations of Scotland's alleged neglect at the hands of Westminster. For much of the preceding decade this had, to be sure, been an overtly nationalist combination that held little attraction for Labour in Scotland, even after the party had moved to a position of supporting constitutional reform. But the twin defeats suffered in the spring of the 1979, first in the referendum and then in the general election, allowed devolution to be recast as an anti-Conservative measure, no longer just a concession forced by SNP electoral success. Central here were the results of the devolution referendum, which, although disappointing to those in favour of constitutional change, demonstrated that backing for devolution had been highest in those regions of Scotland where Labour support was strongest, most notably in the local authority areas of Central, Fife, and Strathclyde. For many within Labour it was, for the first time, possible to view devolution through the lens of class, as something relevant to the party's 'traditional' voters; further, stances on the constitution could, in a way not possible in the 1970s, begin to be aligned with party allegiances. For Tom Nairn, the class nature of the constitutional issue had been 'resoundingly confirmed by the vote', with 'Scotland's sociological and geographical heartland' delivering a relatively clear majority in favour of devolution.[12] In his post-referendum assessment for *The Scotsman*

Neal Ascherson, a close friend and flatmate of Nairn's, reckoned that two-thirds of working-class voters had voted in favour of a devolved assembly, 'while less than half the middle-class voters did so.' It was, Ascherson determined, 'among the working people of Scotland that the national movement, to use that good phrase . . . is most firmly lodged.' Looking to the future, Ascherson argued that if a decisive majority 'of ordinary Scots' were to be convinced to 'give their vote to a national party of self-government', it would 'have to be a force standing far more boldly for radical democracy and for the interests of the working class to win their trust.' This, he concluded, would need to be the Labour Party and not the SNP: despite 'the stunning blow of devolution's failure', the bond between the 'ideals' of the Labour Party and 'Scottish constitutional change' could not now 'be severed.'[13]

Neither Nairn nor Ascherson enjoyed much direct influence within the Labour movement at this time. Indeed, in 1979 both were still members of the short-lived Scottish Labour Party, founded in early 1976 by Jim Sillars, the former Labour MP for South Ayrshire, in order to make the left-wing case for more far-reaching constitutional change than had been offered by the Labour government.[14] Their shared contention that the referendum result had confirmed that it would be the Scottish working class that would deliver constitutional change, and that any campaign for self-government must appeal directly to the economic interests of that constituency, did find some adherents with the SNP, particularly among those involved in the ''79 Group', which included Margo MacDonald, Stephen Maxwell and Alex Salmond in its ranks.[15] Likewise, the decision by some members of the ''79 Group', guided by Jim Sillars, who had joined the SNP in 1980 following the collapse of the Scottish Labour Party, to encourage their party to pursue a campaign of civil disobedience, a stance endorsed – somewhat unenthusiastically – at the SNP's May 1981 conference, was informed by the new prominence of notions of a Scottish tradition of popular sovereignty.[16] When, in October 1981, Sillars, accompanied by five fellow ''79 Group' members, broke into the Royal High School in Edinburgh, which was to have been the site of the Scottish Assembly, the location of the act was obviously chosen with the intention of highlighting the continued importance of the constitutional question, as well as raising awareness of Scotland's economic plight.[17] But the underlying impetus for the break-in was the hope that the court case that would inevitably ensue would provide a forum in which, in Sillars' words, 'the supremacy of the Scottish people' could be asserted to rank above 'the supremacy of the UK Parliament'. Sillars and the other participants in the break-in were charged with vandalism under the provisions of the Criminal Justice (Scotland) Act 1980. At the initial trial and subsequent appeal, they presented an innovative, if still unsuccessful, defence. Citing both the result of the 1979 devolution referendum and the fact that 'a clear majority of [Scottish] electors had voted against the Conservative (or Unionist) party' at the subsequent general election, they contended that the decision to repeal the Scotland Act 1978 had been unlawful, since it was clearly 'not in accordance with the wishes of the Scottish people', who were, in this framing, sovereign. Since the 1978 Act would have placed criminal justice matters within the legislative competence of the proposed Assembly, this meant, so the argument went, that the 1980 legislation was invalid. Further, it was suggested that the 'introduction of referenda into the process of legislation' on the questions of Europe and devolution signified an admission that Parliament's authority was, on certain issues, subordinate to that of the people.[18] As Sillars would recollect, when in a similar position, his nationalist forerunners, such as Douglas Young and John MacCormick, had always elected to rely on alleged breaches of the Act of Union to justify their actions.[19] The turn to popular sovereignty was, then, a novel approach, one that reflected the influence of the debates of the 1970s.

For all Sillars' efforts, however, the SNP remained ill at ease with such arguments, not least because they were focused on devolution rather than independence. After 1979 devolution was a cause that Labour, from the shelter of opposition and with the SNP now a seemingly chastened political presence, was able to embrace more wholeheartedly. There was, no doubt, still some concern within the Labour Party in Scotland regarding the potential dangers of an over-enthusiastic focus on the constitution. Labour declined to formally participate in the Campaign for a Scottish Assembly (CSA), founded in 1980 on the first anniversary of the devolution referendum; rather, overt engagement with the CSA was limited to individual pro-devolution MPs such as Dennis Canavan.[20] And while some within the Labour Party, particularly George Foulkes, were willing to echo the demands for more confrontational and disruptive tactics heard within the SNP, such calls met with little broader support.[21] Yet the essential shift in Labour's stance during the early 1980s was not driven by debates over whether to participate in cross-party campaigns or the wisdom of direct action, but instead by the almost commonplace acceptance of the language of the Scottish mandate, and the accompanying assertion that Scotland was ill-served by an unresponsive, excessively centralised Westminster regime. Labour's continued commitment to Scottish devolution in this period depended upon the authority held to have been granted by the majority vote recorded in the 1979 referendum and the subsequent results of the 1979 and 1983 general elections, at which parties favouring devolution had received a majority of the Scottish vote. Despite the often-indifferent attitude of the wider party, support for an Assembly was reaffirmed at the 1983 Labour Party conference; a year later, a revised scheme for a Scottish Assembly was detailed in the party's 'green paper' on devolution.[22]

The decision of the Scottish Executive of the Labour Party to participate in the Scottish Constitutional Convention, established in 1988 by the CSA, must be understood in this broader context. The immediate stimulus was, no doubt, the outcome of the 1987 general election, which delivered a third successive Conservative victory at Westminster despite the collapse in the party's parliamentary representation in Scotland. The Labour Party, victorious in fifty of Scotland's seventy-two constituencies, was compelled to demonstrate that it could do something to address the perceived rise of a 'democratic deficit' now that Scotland's electoral preferences had been repeatedly overridden by the scale of the Conservative victories in England. Additional pressure was provided by the emergence of the internal pro-devolution pressure group, Scottish Labour Action, and by the subsequent revival in the fortunes of the SNP amid popular opposition to the 'poll tax', which was made clear by the victory secured by Jim Sillars at the November 1988 Govan by-election, a result that, perversely, persuaded the SNP leadership they did not need to join the Convention.[23] Yet the growing credence accorded to the idea of a Scottish mandate within the Labour Party since 1979 was a vital precondition, as was the willingness of the party to accept a denunciation of Westminster that was not limited to attacking the social and economic measures pursued by a specific government but was instead concerned with underlying constitutional and political structures. The *Claim of Right*, published in 1988 by the Constitutional Steering Committee of the CSA, detailed the proposed remit and structure of the Scottish Constitutional Convention. Overseen by the former Scottish Office civil servant Jim Ross, a onetime Labour member, the *Claim of Right* made the general case for devolution while also bemoaning the growing 'centralisation and standardisation' imposed upon Scotland by the UK government and the 'diminishing autonomy' enjoyed by Scots in areas nominally protected under the terms of the Union of 1707.[24] In the 'Epilogue' to the *Claim*, it was emphasised that the case for constitutional reform did not rest upon 'the merits or demerits of particular policies at particular times'; rather, 'the crucial questions' were ones of 'power and consent', of 'making power accountable', and of addressing 'the fraudulence and the fragility' of the existing constitutional settlement.[25]

The following year every Labour MP in Scotland, with the exception of the long-time critic of devolution Tam Dalyell, subscribed to a revised version of the *Claim of Right*, which now incorporated a seemingly unambiguous articulation of Scottish popular sovereignty that recognised 'the sovereign right of the Scottish people to determine the form of government best suited to their needs'.[26] If it can be questioned whether this collective endorsement should be taken as signalling a straightforward acceptance of every statement within the *Claim of Right*, it remains true that these positions were a consequence of the arguments generated by the referendums of the 1970s, which had granted notions of the people a privileged place in Scottish political debate.

There were, then, certain ironies visible in the course of Scottish politics after 1979. Although devolution remained hypothetical so long as a Conservative government hostile to constitutional reform continued in office, support for a devolved assembly became more firmly rooted in the Labour Party, while the party's participation in the Constitutional Convention provided the broader movement with much-needed political credibility. More than this, the case for constitutional reform, as it came to be made during the 1980s, resembled in certain key regards the arguments made by Unionists, Liberals and Nationalists in the preceding decades. When, in November 1988, John Home Robertson, since 1978 the Labour MP for East Lothian, warned his colleagues in the House of Commons that the Conservative government's intransigence on the question of devolution risked increasing support for Scottish independence, he spoke in terms that would, in an earlier period, easily have found favour among Labour's post-war opponents. Referring explicitly to the 'mandate' that he argued Labour had 'been given by the people of Scotland', Home Robertson advised the government, in language that echoed that used by the Unionists four decades earlier, that the UK was 'a union of nations' and that there had to 'be respect between the nations in the union if the union is to survive'. Equally, he criticised the unaccountable and undemocratic bureaucracy that governed Scotland without majority support.[27] The following year, David Martin, the Labour Member of the European Parliament for the Lothians, criticised the Conservative government's 'centralising, anti-democratic' tendencies, which, he maintained, were 'greatly accentuated in Scotland'.[28] Kenyon Wright, the Episcopal priest who chaired the Constitutional Convention's executive committee, echoed this criticism, describing the 1980s as a period 'of gathering gloom as the growing centralisation of government' and 'the cancerous spread of unelected quangos' contributed to a sense that Scotland was suffering under 'the imposition of something like an alien ideology.'[29]

The economic policies pursued by the Thatcher governments of the 1980s, and the social costs they carried, were undoubtedly deeply unpopular with large parts of Scottish society. Yet the most serious political weakness of Thatcherism in Scotland was its unashamed willingness to use the powers of central government to impose change in spheres long considered to be the preserve of local actors, whether in the public or private sectors.[30] After 1979, Scottish Conservatism came to resemble precisely that domineering, unresponsive and remote style of government that Unionists had once attributed to the Labour Party's inherent flaws. A rhetoric that had been used by Unionists to articulate their opposition to socialism, and then by the SNP to condemn Scotland's treatment by both Labour and Conservative administrations, became a way of expressing support for the creation of a devolved parliament that would be able to protect Scotland from the overbearing power exercised by the Westminster government. It is this process that reveals the essential argument of this study. Accounts of the evolution of the debate surrounding devolution that emphasise the importance of a growing sense of cultural nationalism have rightly been challenged on the basis that they underestimate the centrality of political alliances and negotiations after 1979.[31] Nevertheless, it is possible to also observe that, in certain respects, 1979 signalled an exchanging of roles rather than a more fundamental reordering of Scottish politics. The focus on Scotland's relationship with Westminster, the perception that Scottish opinion was being disregarded by remote bureaucracies, the rhetoric of distance and neglect: these all remained but were, after 1979, firmly in the hands of the political left, rather than the right. This was, then, a language that could be adapted to suit changing political contexts. Moreover, when combined with the belief in a distinctive Scottish tradition of popular sovereignty that came to the fore during the 1970s, this language could be used to argue that constitutional reform was required to preserve Scotland's position within the United Kingdom. There was, however, no guarantee that this framing would remain stable, or that other political actors who saw the mandate in more explicitly nationalist terms would not, in the future, prove able to guide such rhetoric back towards the question of Scottish independence.

NOTES

1. *Glasgow Herald*, 24 Feb. 1979.
2. See for example: Devine, 'The Challenge of Nationalism', p. 156.
3. Finlay, 'Thatcherism, Unionism and Nationalism', pp. 171–5.

4. Smith replaced Neil Kinnock as Labour Party leader after the 1992 general election. He died of a heart attack, aged 55, in May 1994. See: Mitchell, *The Scottish Question*, p. 240.
5. Cameron, *Impaled upon a Thistle*, pp. 349–55.
6. Barker, 'Legitimacy in the United Kingdom'; Gibbs, 'Civic Scotland' and 'Historical Tradition and Community Mobilisation'.
7. Tomlinson, 'Deindustrialization not Decline'; Gibbs, *Coal Country*.
8. Gibbs and Scothorne, '"Origins of the Present Crisis": The Emergence of "Left-Wing" Scottish Nationalism'.
9. NLS Acc. 10754/15: SNP Press Release, 3 Oct. 1978.
10. NLS Acc. 11368/81: Scotland Says No, *The Assembly: Know Your Mythology* (Glasgow, 1979).
11. Nairn, 'After the Referendum', pp. 59–61.
12. Nairn, 'After the Referendum', p. 65.
13. *The Scotsman*, 3 Mar. 1979.
14. On the Scottish Labour Party, see: Drucker, *Breakaway*; Sillars, *Case for Optimism*, pp. 55–63. For Ascherson and Nairn's involvement, see the records of the Edinburgh branch of the Scottish Labour Party in: NLS Acc. 7472.
15. The ''79 Group' would be proscribed in 1982. Torrance, 'The Journey from the 79 Group to the Modern SNP', pp. 162–5 and 169–71.
16. Torrance, 'The Journey from the 79 Group to the Modern SNP', pp. 168–9; Hames, *The Literary Politics of Scottish Devolution*, pp. 128–32. For coverage of the conference decision, see: *The Times*, 29 May 1981.
17. *Glasgow Herald*, 17 Oct. 1981.
18. 'Sillars v Smith', *Scots Law Times* (26 Nov. 1982), pp. 539–41, at 540.
19. Sillars, *A Difference of Opinion*, pp. 144–5.
20. Canavan, *Let the People Decide*, pp. 203–5.
21. Naughtie, 'Labour, 1979–1988', pp. 162–3.
22. Geekie and Levy, 'Devolution and the Tartanisation of the Labour Party', p. 401; McLean, *Getting it Together*, pp. 75-6 and 83; Torrance, *Standing up for Scotland*, pp. 136–7.
23. Naughtie, 'Labour, 1979–1988', pp. 166–70; McLean, *Getting it Together*, pp. 111–13; Torrance, *Standing up for Scotland*, pp. 139–44.
24. Campaign for a Scottish Assembly, *A Claim of Right for Scotland*, p. 2. The title of the document was intended to evoke the previous 'Claims of Right' of 1689 and 1842. On the composition and work of the Steering Committee, see: McLean, *Getting it Together*, pp. 104–8.
25. Campaign for a Scottish Assembly, *A Claim of Right for Scotland*, p. 23.
26. Scottish Constitutional Convention, *Towards Scotland's Parliament*, p. 1. For further discussion of the context surrounding the *Claim of Right*, see: Hames, *The Literary Politics of Devolution*, pp. 164–70 and 176–83; Jackson, *The Case for Scottish Independence*, pp. 137–44.
27. *Hansard* HC Deb vol. 142 col. 195, 23 Nov. 1988.

28. Martin, 'The Democratic Deficit', p. 80.
29. Wright, *The People Say Yes*, p. 22. Prior to taking up his role as in the Convention, Wright had been a member of the Labour Party. See: McLean, *Getting it Together*, pp. 118–19.
30. See, for example, Stewart, *Path to Devolution and Change*, Chapter 5.
31. For a recent statement of the case for the significance of culture, see Craig, *The Wealth of the Nation*, pp. 274–81. For the critique, see: Hames, *The Literary Politics of Devolution*.

Bibliography

MANUSCRIPT SOURCES

Aberdeen City Council Archives
DD312, Aberdeen Labour Party Records

Conservative Party Archive, Bodleian Library, University of Oxford
CCO 1, Constituency Correspondence
CCO 2, Area Files
CCO 4, Subject Files
CCO 20/11, Chairman's Office (Scottish Correspondence)
CCO 180/29, Public Opinion Research Department
CCO 500, Organisation Department
CRD, Research Department
PUB, Published and Printed Material: Election Addresses
SUMC, Records of the Scottish Unionist Members' Committee, 1932–69

Dundee City Council Archives
GD/DLA, Dundee Liberal Association

Falkirk Council Archives
A398, Falkirk Labour Party Records
A1660, Airth Labour Party Records
A1703/F.1, Stirling, Falkirk and Grangemouth Burghs Conservative and
    Unionist Association Records
A1703, Falkirk Unionist Association Records
A1703/1030, Falkirk West Conservative Association Records

Glasgow City Archives, Mitchell Library
TD1384, Scottish Council of the Labour Party Records

Labour History Archive and Study Centre, People's History Museum, Manchester
Labour Party NEC and SEC Papers
Judith Hart Papers

National Library of Scotland
Dep. 363, Jo Grimond Papers
Acc. 5542, George Dott Papers
Acc. 6038, Arthur Donaldson Papers
Acc. 6058, Tom Gibson Papers
Acc. 6419, Douglas Young Papers
Acc. 6679, Scottish National Party Records
Acc. 6721, Walter Elliot Papers
Acc. 7295, Scottish National Party Records
Acc. 7472, Scottish Labour Party Records
Acc. 7505, James Porteous Papers
Acc. 7656, Arthur Woodburn Papers
Acc. 7915, David Murray Papers
Acc. 9188, Andrew Dewar Gibb Papers
Acc. 10090, Robert McIntyre Papers
Acc. 10424, Scottish Conservative and Unionist Party Records
Acc. 10754, Scottish National Party Records
Acc. 11368, Scottish Conservative and Unionist Party Records
Acc. 11565, Gavin Kennedy Papers
Acc. 11682, Russell Johnston Papers
Acc. 11765, Scottish Liberal Party Records
Acc. 11884, Lady Tweedsmuir Papers
Acc. 11987, Scottish National Party Records
Acc. 12509, Robert McIntyre Papers
Acc. 12769, Donald Stewart Papers
Acc. 12944, Frank Cameron Yeaman Papers
Acc. 12917, Robert McIntyre Papers
Acc. 13099, Gordon Wilson Papers
Acc. 13101, William K. Archibald Papers
Acc. 13116, George Younger Papers
Acc. 13417, James Halliday Papers
Acc. 13476, John P. Mackintosh Papers
Acc. 13477, David Steel Papers
Acc. 13491, Rosemary Hall Papers
Acc. 13546, Scottish Plebiscite Society Records
Acc. 13569, Scottish Plebiscite Society Records
Acc. 13687, Gordon Wilson Papers

Perth and Kinross Council Archives
MS 152, Perth and East Perthshire Conservative and Unionist Association Records

MS 152, Kinross and West Perthshire Conservative and Unionist Association Records

University of Aberdeen Archives
MS 2663, Aberdeen City Labour Party Records
MS 2891, Banffshire Labour Party Records
MS 2892, Keith Labour Party Records
MS 3037, Liberal Party Records, 1957–66
MS 3179, Mary Esslemont Papers
MS 3889, Michael Dyer Papers

University of Dundee Archives
MS 193, Malcolm Slesser Papers
MS 270, Dundee Conservative and Unionist Association Records
MS 309, North Tayside Conservative and Unionist Association Records
MS 312, South Angus Constituency Labour Party Records
MS 315, Gordon Wilson Papers
MS 325, Dundee City Labour Party Records
UR-SF-45, Election Materials (Masterson Papers)

University of Stirling, Scottish Political Archive
SPA/DC/SN/ASSEM, Dennis Canavan Collection
SPA/GA/STIR/DD, Douglas Drysdale Collection
SPA/GF, George Foulkes Collection
SPA/GW, Gordon Wilson Collection
SPA/OH, Devolution Referendums Oral History Collection
SPA/RR, Robert Robertson Collection

PRINTED PRIMARY SOURCES

Autobiographies, diaries and memoirs
Bannerman, John, *Memoirs* (Aberdeen: Impulse Books, 1972).
Benn, Tony, *Office without Power: Diaries, 1968–1972* (London: Hutchison, 1989).
Canavan, Dennis, *Let the People Decide: The Autobiography of Dennis Canavan* (Edinburgh: Birlinn, 2009).
Crossman, Richard, *The Crossman Diaries: Selections from the Diary of a Cabinet Minister, 1964–1970* (London: Methuen, 1979).
Dalyell, Tam, *The Importance of Being Earnest: The Autobiography of Tam Dalyell* (Edinburgh: Birlinn, 2011).
Douglas-Home, Alec, *The Way the Wind Blows: An Autobiography* (London: Collins, 1976).

Ewing, Winnie, *Stop the World: The Autobiography of Winnie Ewing* (Edinburgh: Birlinn, 2004).

Grimond, Jo, *Memoirs* (London: Heinemann, 1979).

Halliday, James, *Yours for Scotland: A Memoir* (Stirling: Scots Independent Newspapers, 2011).

Herdman, John, *Another Country: An Era of Scottish Politics and Letters* (Edinburgh: Argyll Publishing, 2013).

Johnston, Thomas, *Memories* (London: Collins, 1952).

Junor, John, *Listening for a Midnight Tram: Memoirs* (London: Chapman, 1990).

MacCormick, John, *The Flag in the Wind: The Story of the National Movement in Scotland* (London: Gollancz, 1955).

Maxwell, Stephen, *The Case for Left Wing Nationalism* (Edinburgh: Luath, 2013).

Reid, Jimmy, *Reflections of a Clyde-built Man* (London: Souvenir Press, 1976).

Sillars, Jim, *The Case for Optimism* (Edinburgh: Polygon, 1986).

Stewart, Donald, *A Scot at Westminster* (Sydney, NS: Catalone Press, 1994).

Stuart, James, *Within the Fringe* (London: Bodley Head, 1967).

Thornton-Kemsley, Colin, *Through Winds and Tides* (Montrose: Standard Press, 1974).

Wilson, Gordon, *SNP: The Turbulent Years, 1960–1990* (Stirling: Scots Independent Newspapers, 2009).

——. *Pirates of the Air: The Story of Radio Free Scotland* (Stirling: Scots Independent Newspapers, 2013).

Wolfe, William, *Scotland Lives* (Edinburgh: Reprographia, 1973).

Wood, Wendy, *Yours sincerely for Scotland* (London: Barker, 1970).

Wright, Kenyon, *The People Say Yes: The Making of Scotland's Parliament* (Glendaruel: Argyll Publishing, 1997).

Contemporary political manifestoes, pamphlets and reports

Campaign for a Scottish Assembly: Constitutional Steering Committee, *A Claim of Right for Scotland* (Edinburgh: Campaign for a Scottish Assembly, 1988).

Conservative and Unionist Central Office, *The Industrial Charter: A Statement of Conservative Industrial Policy* (London: Conservative and Unionist Party, 1947).

Grimond, Jo, *The New Liberal Democracy* (London: Liberal Publication Department, 1958).

——. *The Liberal Future* (London: Faber and Faber, 1959).

Jay, Douglas, *After the Common Market: A Better Alternative for Britain* (Harmondsworth: Penguin, 1968).

Lamont, Archie, *Small Nations* (Glasgow: W. Maclellan, 1944).

Liberal Party, *Liberalism Leads: Liberal Policy* (London: Liberal Publication Department, 1959).

Scott, Christopher, *The Liberals, the Common Market and the SNP* (Galashiels: Vanguard, 1970).

Scottish Constitutional Convention, *Towards Scotland's Parliament* (Edinburgh: Scottish Constitutional Convention).

Scottish Council of the Labour Party, *The Government of Scotland: Evidence of the Labour Party in Scotland to the Commission on the Constitution* (Glasgow: Labour Party, 1970).

Scottish National Party, *Aims and Policy of the SNP* (Glasgow: Scottish National Party, 1947).

——. *SNP and You: Aims and Policy of the Scottish National Party* (Glasgow: Scottish National Party, 1966).

——. *The Scotland We Seek* (Glasgow: Scottish National Party, 1967).

——. *The New Scotland* (Glasgow: Scottish National Party, 1970).

——. *Scotland's Future: SNP Manifesto* (Edinburgh: Scottish National Party, 1974).

——. *SNP and You: Aims and Policy of the Scottish National Party* 4th ed. (Edinburgh: Scottish National Party, 1974).

Scottish Trades Union Congress, *72nd Annual Report* (Glasgow: Scottish Trades Union Congress, 1969).

Scottish Unionist Association, *Scotland and the United Kingdom* (Edinburgh: Scottish Unionist Association, 1948).

——. *Scottish Control of Scottish Affairs* (Edinburgh: Scottish Unionist Association, 1949).

——. *Scotland with the Unionists* (Edinburgh: Scottish Unionist Association, 1964).

Sillars, Jim, *Independence in Europe* (Glasgow: the author, 1989).

Government and parliamentary papers and reports
Hansard
Scottish Affairs (Cmnd. 7308, 1948).

The Modernisation of Local Government in Scotland (Cmnd. 2067, 1963).

Development and Growth in Central Scotland (Cmnd 2188, 1963).

Royal Commission on Local Government in Scotland, 1966–1969 (Cmnd. 4150, 1969).

Scotland: Local Government Reform (Short Version of the Report of the Royal Commission on Local Government in Scotland) (Cmnd. 4150-I, 1969).

Royal Commission on the Constitution, *Minutes of Evidence IV: Scotland* (London: HMSO, 1971).

Reform of Local Government in Scotland (Cmnd. 4583, 1971).

Referendum on United Kingdom Membership of the European Community (Cmnd. 5925, 1975).

Our Changing Democracy: Devolution to Scotland and Wales (Cmnd. 6348, 1975).

National Archives, Cabinet Papers 129/181/6: *Practical Implications of Holding a Referendum on European Community Membership – Report by Official Working Party*, 17 Jan. 1975.

Newspapers and periodicals
Aberdeen Press and Journal
Argyllshire Advertiser
Daily Express
Daily Telegraph
Dundee Courier and Advertiser
Falkirk Herald
Glasgow Herald
Grangemouth Advertiser
Grangemouth Advertiser and Eastern District Chronicle
Holyrood
New Left Review
New Statesman
Perthshire Advertiser
Political Quarterly
Scots Independent
Scots Law Times
Socialist Commentary
Stirling Journal
Stirling Observer
Stirling Sentinel
Sunday Mail
The Economist
The Guardian
The Northern Scot
The Observer
The Scotsman
The Sunday Times
The Times
Weekly Scotsman

SECONDARY SOURCES

Books
Addison, Paul, *The Road to 1945: British Politics and the Second World War* (London: Cape, 1975).
Aitken, Keith, *The Bairns o' Adam: The Story of the STUC* (Edinburgh: Polygon, 1997).
Ascherson, Neal, *Games with Shadows* (London: Radius, 1988).
——. *Stone Voices: The Search for Scotland* (London: Granta, 2002).
Atkinson, Lucy, Andrew Blick and Matt Qvortrup, *The Referendum in Britain: A History* (Oxford: Oxford University Press, 2020).
Bale, Tim, *The Conservatives since 1945: The Drivers of Party Change* (Oxford: Oxford University Press, 2012).

Ball, Stuart, and Anthony Seldon (eds), *The Heath Government, 1970–1974: A Reappraisal* (London: Longman, 1996).

Beers, Laura, *Your Britain: Media and the Making of the Labour Party* (Cambridge MA: Harvard University Press, 2010).

Benewick, Robert, R. N. Berki and Bhikhu Parekh (eds), *Knowledge and Belief in Politics: The Problem of Ideology* (London: Allen and Unwin, 1973).

Black, Lawrence, Hugh Pemberton and Pat Thane (eds), *Reassessing 1970s Britain* (Manchester: Manchester University Press, 2013).

Black, Lawrence, *The Political Culture of the Left in Affluent Britain, 1951–64: Old Labour, New Britain?* (Basingstoke: Palgrave, 2003).

——. *Redefining British Politics: Culture, Consumerism and Participation, 1954–70* (Basingstoke: Palgrave, 2010).

Bochel, John, David Denver and Allan Macartney (eds), *The Referendum Experience: Scotland, 1979* (Aberdeen: Aberdeen University Press, 1981).

Bogdanor, Vernon, (ed.), *The British Constitution in the Twentieth Century* (Oxford: Oxford University Press, 2003).

Bogdanor, Vernon, *The People and the Party System: The Referendum and Electoral Reform in British Politics* (Cambridge: Cambridge University Press, 1981).

——. *Devolution in the United Kingdom* (Oxford: Oxford University Press, 1999).

——. *The New British Constitution* (Oxford: Oxford University Press, 2009).

Brand, Jack, *The National Movement in Scotland* (London: Routledge and Kegan Paul, 1978).

Brown, Gordon (ed.), *The Red Paper on Scotland* (Edinburgh: Edinburgh University Student Publications Board, 1975).

Burness, Catriona, *'Strange Associations': The Irish Question and the Making of Scottish Unionism, 1886–1918* (East Linton: Tuckwell, 2003).

Butler, David, and Michael Pinto-Duschinsky, *The British General Election of 1970* (London: Macmillan, 1971).

Butler, David, and Uwe Kitzinger, *The 1975 Referendum* (London: Macmillan, 1976).

Cairncross, Alec, *Years of Recovery: British Economic Policy, 1945–1951* (London: Methuen, 1985).

Calder, Angus, *The People's War: Britain, 1939–1945* (London: Cape, 1969).

Cameron, Ewen A., *Impaled upon a Thistle: Scotland since 1880* (Edinburgh: Edinburgh University Press, 2010).

Campbell, John, *Edward Heath: A Biography* (London: Cape, 1993).

Cockett, Richard, *Thinking the Unthinkable: Think-Tanks and the Economic Counter-Revolution, 1931–1983* (London: HarperCollins, 1994).

Cowling, Maurice, *The Impact of Labour, 1920–1924* (Cambridge: Cambridge University Press, 1971).

Craig, Cairns, *The Wealth of the Nation: Scotland, Culture and Independence* (Edinburgh: Edinburgh University Press, 2018).

Craig, F. W. S., *British Parliamentary Election Results, 1918–1949* (Glasgow: Political Reference Publications, 1969).

——. *British Parliamentary Election Results, 1950–1973* (Chichester: Parliamentary Research Services, 1983).

——. *British Parliamentary Election Results, 1974–1983* (Chichester: Parliamentary Research Services, 1984).

Devine, T. M., and R. J. Finlay (eds), *Scotland in the Twentieth Century* (Edinburgh: Edinburgh University Press, 1996).

Devine, T. M. (ed.), *Scotland and the Union, 1707–2007* (Edinburgh: Edinburgh University Press, 2007).

Devine, T. M., *The Scottish Nation, 1700–2000* (London: Allen Lane, 1999).

Dickinson, H. T., and Michael Lynch (eds), *The Challenge to Westminster: Sovereignty, Devolution and Independence* (East Linton: Tuckwell, 2000).

Donnachie, Ian, Christopher Harvie and Ian S. Wood (eds), *Forward! Labour Politics in Scotland, 1888–1988* (Edinburgh: Polygon, 1989).

Douglas, Dick, *At the Helm: The Life and Times of Dr Robert D McIntyre* (Buckie: NPFI Publications, 1996).

Drucker, H. M., *Breakaway: the Scottish Labour Party* (Edinburgh: Edinburgh University Student Publications Board, 1978).

Dutton, David, *Liberals in Schism: A History of the National Liberal Party* (London: I. B. Tauris, 2008).

Edgerton, David, *The Rise and Fall of the British Nation: A Twentieth-Century History* (London: Allen Lane, 2018).

Edwards, Owen Dudley (ed.), *A Claim of Right for Scotland* (Edinburgh: Polygon, 1989).

Finlay, Richard J., *A Partnership for Good: Scottish Politics and the Union since 1880* (Edinburgh: John Donald, 1997).

Gibbs, Ewan, *Coal Country: The Meaning and Memory of Deindustrialization in Postwar Scotland* (London: University of London Press, 2021).

Green, E. H. H., *The Ideologies of Conservatism: Conservative Political Ideas in the Twentieth Century* (Oxford: Oxford University Press, 2002).

Greenleaf, W. H. *The British Political Tradition, II: The Ideological Heritage* (London: Methuen, 1983).

Hallowell, Gerald (ed.), *The Oxford Companion to Canadian History* (Toronto: Oxford University Press, 2004).

Hames, Scott, *The Literary Politics of Scottish Devolution: Voice, Class, Nation* (Edinburgh: Edinburgh University Press, 2020).

Hanham, H. J., *Scottish Nationalism* (London: Faber, 1969).

Harvie, Christopher, *Scotland and Nationalism: Scottish Society and Politics, 1707–1977* (London: Allen and Unwin, 1977).

——. *No Gods and Precious Few Heroes: Scotland, 1914–1980* (London: Arnold, 1981).

Hassan, Gerry (ed.), *The Modern SNP: From Protest to Power* (Edinburgh: Edinburgh University Press, 2009).

Hassan, Gerry, and Eric Shaw, *The Strange Death of Labour Scotland* (Edinburgh: Edinburgh University Press, 2012).

Heffer, Simon, *Like the Roman: The Life of Enoch Powell* (London: Phoenix, 1999).

Hutchison, I. G. C., *Scottish Politics in the Twentieth Century* (Basingstoke: Macmillan, 2001).

Jackson, Alvin, *The Two Unions: Ireland, Scotland, and the Survival of the United Kingdom, 1707–2007* (Oxford: Oxford University Press, 2012).

Jackson, Ben, and Robert Saunders (eds), *Making Thatcher's Britain* (Cambridge: Cambridge University Press, 2012).

Jackson, Ben, *The Case for Scottish Independence: A History of Nationalist Political Thought in Modern Scotland* (Cambridge: Cambridge University Press, 2020).

Jones, Harriet, and Michael Kandiah (eds), *The Myth of Consensus: New Views on British History, 1945–64* (Basingstoke: Macmillan, 1996).

Keating, Michael, and David Bleiman, *Labour and Scottish Nationalism* (London: Macmillan, 1979).

Kellas, James, *The Scottish Political System* (Cambridge: Cambridge University Press, 1973).

Kemp, Arnold, *The Hollow Drum: Scotland since the War* (Edinburgh: Mainstream, 1993).

Kenny, Michael, *The First New Left: British Intellectuals after Stalin* (London: Lawrence and Wishart, 1995).

Kidd, Colin, *Union and Unionisms: Political Thought in Scotland, 1500–2000* (Cambridge: Cambridge University Press, 2008).

Knox, W. W. J, *Industrial Nation: Work, Culture and Society in Scotland, 1800–present* (Edinburgh: Edinburgh University Press, 1999).

Knox, W. W. J., and Alan McKinlay, *Jimmy Reid: A Clyde-Built Man* (Liverpool: Liverpool University Press, 2019).

Lawrence, Jon, and Miles Taylor (eds), *Party, State and Society: Electoral Behaviour in Britain since 1820* (Aldershot: Scolar, 1997).

Lawrence, Jon, *Electing our Masters: The Hustings in British Politics from Hogarth to Blair* (Oxford: Oxford University Press, 2009).

Lee, C. H., *Scotland and the United Kingdom: The Economy and the Union in the Twentieth Century* (Manchester: Manchester University Press, 1995).

Levy, Roger, *Scottish Nationalism at the Crossroads* (Edinburgh: Scottish Academic Press, 1990).

Lynch, Peter, *SNP: The History of the Scottish National Party* (Cardiff: Welsh Academic Press, 2002).

McCrone, David, *Understanding Scotland: The Sociology of a Stateless Nation* (London: Routledge, 1992).

MacDonald, C. M. M. (ed.), *Unionist Scotland, 1800–1997* (Edinburgh: John Donald, 1998).

MacDonald, C. M. M., *Whaur Extremes Meet: Scotland's Twentieth Century* (Edinburgh: John Donald, 2009).

McKibbin, Ross, *The Ideologies of Class: Social Relations in Britain, 1880–1950* (Oxford: Clarendon, 1994).

——. *Parties and People: England, 1914–1951* (Oxford: Oxford University Press, 2010).

McLean, Bob, *Getting it Together: The History of the Campaign for a Scottish Assembly/Parliament, 1980–1999* (Edinburgh: Luath, 2005).

Marr, Andrew, *The Battle for Scotland* (Harmondsworth: Penguin, 1992).

Miller, W. L., Jack Brand and Maggie Jordan, *Oil and the Scottish Voter, 1974–1979* (London: Social Science Research Council, 1980).

Miller, W. L., *The End of British Politics? Scots and English Political Behaviour in the Seventies* (Oxford: Clarendon Press, 1981).

Mitchell, James, and Gerry Hassan (eds), *Scottish National Party Leaders* (London: Biteback, 2016).

Mitchell, James, *Conservatives and the Union: A Study of Conservative Party attitudes to Scotland* (Edinburgh: Edinburgh University Press, 1990).

——. *Strategies for Self-Government: The Campaigns for a Scottish Parliament* (Edinburgh: Polygon, 1996)

——. *Devolution in the United Kingdom* (Manchester: Manchester University Press, 2009).

——. *The Scottish Question* (Oxford: Oxford University Press, 2014).

——. *Hamilton 1967: The by-election that transformed Scotland* (Edinburgh: Luath, 2017).

Morgan, Kenneth O., *Labour in Power, 1945–1951* (Oxford: Oxford University Press, 1984).

——. *Britain since 1945: The People's Peace* (Oxford: Oxford University Press, 2001).

Morton, Graeme, *Unionist-Nationalism: Governing Urban Scotland, 1830–1860* (East Linton: Tuckwell, 1999).

Murdoch, Alexander (ed.), *The Scottish Nation: Identity and History, Essays in Honour of William Ferguson* (Edinburgh: John Donald, 2008).

Nairn, Tom, *The Break-up of Britain: Crisis and Neo-Nationalism* (London: New Left Books, 1977).

——. *After Britain: New Labour and the Return of Scotland* (London: Granta, 2000).

Panitch, Leo, and Colin Leys, *Searching for Socialism: The Project of the Labour New Left from Benn to Corbyn* (London: Verso, 2020).

Petrie, Malcolm R., *Popular Politics and Political Culture: Urban Scotland, 1918–1939* (Edinburgh: Edinburgh University Press, 2018).

Phillips, Jim, *The Industrial Politics of Devolution: Scotland in the 1960s and 1970s* (Manchester: Manchester University Press, 2008).

Pimlott, Ben, *Harold Wilson* (London: HarperCollins, 1993).

Pittock, Murray, *The Road to Independence? Scotland since the Sixties* (London: Reaktion, 2008).

Qvortrup, Mads (ed.), *Nationalism, Referendums and Democracy: Voting on Ethnic Issues and Independence* (London: Routledge, 2014).

Qvortrup, Mads (ed.), *Referendums around the World: The Continued Growth of Direct Democracy* (Basingstoke: Palgrave, 2014).

Qvortrup, Mads, *Government by the People: A Comparative Study of Referendums* (Manchester: Manchester University Press, 2002).

——. *The Politics of Participation: From Athens to E-Democracy* (Manchester: Manchester University Press, 2007).

Ramsden, John, *The Age of Churchill and Eden, 1940–1957* (London: Longman, 1995).

——. *The Winds of Change: From Macmillan to Heath* (London: Longman, 1996).

Saunders, Robert, *Yes to Europe! The 1975 Referendum and Seventies Britain* (Cambridge: Cambridge University Press, 2018).

Schofield, Camilla, *Enoch Powell and the Making of Postcolonial Britain* (Cambridge: Cambridge University Press, 2013).

Schwarz, Bill, *The White Man's World: Memories of Empire, Volume 1* (Oxford: Oxford University Press, 2011).

Seawright, David, *An Important Matter of Principle: The Decline of the Scottish Conservative and Unionist Party* (Aldershot: Ashgate, 1999).

Seldon, Anthony, and Stuart Ball (eds), *Conservative Century: The Conservative Party since 1900* (Oxford: Oxford University Press, 1994).

Seldon, Anthony, *Churchill's Indian Summer: The Conservative Government, 1951–55* (London: Hodder and Stoughton, 1981).

Sloman, Peter, *The Liberal Party and the Economy, 1929–1964* (Oxford: Oxford University Press, 2014).

Smith, Evan, and Matthew Worley (eds), *Waiting for the Revolution: The British Far Left from 1956* (Manchester: Manchester University Press, 2017).

Somerville, Paula, *Through the Maelstrom: A History of the Scottish National Party, 1945–1967* (Stirling: Scots Independent Newspapers, 2013).

Stewart, David, *The Path to Devolution and Change: A Political History of Scotland under Margaret Thatcher* (London: I. B. Tauris, 2009).

Supple, Barry, Peter Clarke and Clive Trebilcock (eds), *Understanding Decline: Perceptions and Realities of British Economic Performance* (Cambridge: Cambridge University Press, 1997).

Thorpe, Andrew, *Parties at War: Political Organization in Second World War Britain* (Oxford: Oxford University Press, 2009).

——. *A History of the British Labour Party* 4th ed. (Basingstoke: Palgrave Macmillan, 2015).

Tierney, Stephen, *Constitutional Referendums: The Theory and Practice of Republican Deliberation* (Oxford: Oxford University Press, 2012).

Tomlinson, Jim, *Employment Policy: The Crucial Years, 1939–1955* (Oxford: Clarendon, 1987).

——. *Democratic Socialism and Economic Policy: The Attlee Years, 1945–1951* (Cambridge: Cambridge University Press, 1996).

Torrance, David (ed.), *Whatever Happened to Tory Scotland?* (Edinburgh: Edinburgh University Press, 2012).

Torrance, David, *The Scottish Secretaries* (Edinburgh: Birlinn, 2006).

——. *Standing up for Scotland: Nationalist Unionism and Scottish Party Politics, 1884–2014* (Edinburgh: Edinburgh University Press, 2020).

Toye, Richard, *The Labour Party and the Planned Economy, 1931–1951* (Woodbridge: Boydell and Brewer, 2003).

Ward, Paul, *Unionism in the United Kingdom, 1918–1974* (Basingstoke: Palgrave Macmillan, 2005).

Webb, Keith, *The Growth of Nationalism in Scotland* (Glasgow: Molendinar Press, 1977).

Williamson, Philip, *Stanley Baldwin: Conservative Leadership and National Values* (Cambridge: Cambridge University Press, 1999).

Zweiniger-Bargielowska, Ina, *Austerity in Britain: Rationing, Controls and Consumption, 1939–1955* (Oxford: Oxford University Press, 2000).

Chapters in edited collections

Cannadine, David, 'Apocalypse When? British Politicians and British "Decline" in the Twentieth Century', in Supple, Clarke and Trebilcock (eds), *Understanding Decline: Perceptions and Realities of British Economic Performance* (Cambridge: Cambridge University Press, 1997), pp. 261–84.

Craigen, James, 'The Scottish TUC: Scotland's Assembly of Labour', in Donnachie, Harvie, and Wood (eds), *Forward! Labour Politics in Scotland, 1888–1988* (Edinburgh: Polygon, 1989), pp. 130–55.

Devine, T. M., 'The Challenge of Nationalism', in Devine (ed.), *Scotland and the Union, 1707–2007* (Edinburgh: Edinburgh University Press, 2007), pp. 143–56.

Finlay, Richard J., 'Unionism and the Dependency Culture: Politics and State Intervention in Scotland, 1918–1997', in MacDonald (ed.) *Unionist Scotland, 1800–1997* (Edinburgh: John Donald, 1998), pp. 100–16.

——. 'Thatcherism and the Union', in Devine (ed.), *Scotland and the Union, 1707–2007* (Edinburgh: Edinburgh University Press, 2008), pp. 157–74.

——. 'Early Years: From the inter-war period to the mid-1960s', in Hassan (ed.), *The Modern SNP: From Protest to Power* (Edinburgh: Edinburgh University Press, 2009), pp. 19–30.

——. 'Patriotism, Paternalism and Pragmatism: Scottish Toryism, Union and Empire, 1912–65', in Torrance (ed.), *Whatever Happened to Tory Scotland?* (Edinburgh: Edinburgh University Press, 2012), pp. 29–42.

——. 'Thatcherism, Unionism and Nationalism: A Comparative Study of Scotland and Wales', in Jackson and Saunders (eds), *Making Thatcher's Britain* (Cambridge: Cambridge University Press, 2012), pp. 165–79.

Gibbs, Ewan, and Rory Scothorne, '"Origins of the Present Crisis": The Emergence of "Left-Wing" Scottish Nationalism, 1956–1979', in Smith and Worley (eds), *Waiting for the Revolution: The British Far Left from 1956* (Manchester: Manchester University Press, 2017), pp. 163–81.

Green, E. H. H., 'The Conservative Party, the State and the Electorate, 1945–1964', in Lawrence and Taylor (eds), *Party, State and Society: Electoral Behaviour in Britain since 1820* (Aldershot: Scolar, 1997), pp. 176–200.

Greenleaf, W. H., 'Modern British Conservatism', in Benewick, Berki and Parekh (eds), *Knowledge and Belief in Politics: The Problem of Ideology* (London: Allen and Unwin, 1973), pp. 177–212.

Hutchison, I. G. C., 'Scottish Unionism between the two world wars', in MacDonald (ed.), *Unionist Scotland, 1800–1997* (Edinburgh: John Donald, 1998), pp. 73–99.

——. 'The Scottish Young Conservatives: A Local Case Study – Central Ayrshire Constituency c.1950–1979', in Murdoch (ed.), *The Scottish Nation: Identity and History, Essays in Honour of William Ferguson* (Edinburgh: John Donald, 2008), pp. 120–35.

Jarvis, David, 'The Shaping of Conservative Electoral Hegemony, 1918–39' in Lawrence and Taylor (eds), *Party, State and Society: Electoral Behaviour in Britain since 1820* (Aldershot: Scolar, 1997), pp. 131–52.

Jones, Harriet, 'A Bloodless Counter-Revolution: The Conservative Party and the Defence of Inequality, 1945–51', in Jones and Kandiah (eds), *The Myth of Consensus: New Views on British History, 1945–64* (Basingstoke: Macmillan, 1996), pp. 1–16.

Kellas, James, 'Scottish Nationalism', in Butler and Pinto-Duschinsky, *The British General Election of 1970* (London: Macmillan, 1971), pp. 446–62.

——. 'The Party in Scotland', in Seldon and Ball (eds), *Conservative Century: The Conservative Party since 1900* (Oxford: Oxford University Press, 1994), pp. 671–93.

McKibbin, Ross, 'Class and Conventional Wisdom: The Conservative Party and the Public in inter-war Britain', in McKibbin, *The Ideologies of Class: Social Relations in Britain, 1880–1950* (Oxford: Clarendon, 1994), pp. 259–93.

Martin, David, 'The Democratic Deficit', in Edwards (ed.), *A Claim of Right for Scotland* (Edinburgh: Polygon, 1989), pp. 79–85.

Mitchell, James, 'From Breakthrough to Mainstream: The Politics of Potential and Blackmail', in Hassan (ed.), *The Modern SNP: From Protest to Power* (Edinburgh: Edinburgh University Press, 2009), pp. 32–41.

Naughtie, James, 'Labour, 1979–1988', in Donnachie, Harvie and Wood (eds), *Forward! Labour Politics in Scotland, 1888–1988* (Edinburgh: Polygon, 1989), pp. 156–70.

Neary, Peter, 'Newfoundland Referenda, 1948', in Hallowell (ed.), *The Oxford Companion to Canadian History* (Toronto: Oxford University Press, 2004).

Pentland, Gordon, 'Douglas Young', in Mitchell and Hassan (eds), *Scottish National Party Leaders* (London: Biteback, 2016), pp. 145–64.

Petrie, Malcolm R., 'John MacCormick', in Mitchell and Hassan (eds), *Scottish National Party Leaders* (London: Biteback, 2016), pp. 43–63.

Saville, John, 'The Ideology of Labourism', in Benewick, Berki, and Parekh (eds), *Knowledge and Belief in Politics: The Problem of Ideology* (London: Allen and Unwin, 1973), pp. 213–26.

Torrance, David, 'The Journey from the 79 Group to the Modern SNP', in Hassan (ed.), *The Modern SNP: From Protest to Power* (Edinburgh: Edinburgh University Press, 2009), pp. 162–76.

Journal articles

Ascherson, Neal, 'After Devolution', *Bulletin of Scottish Politics* 1 (1980), pp. 1–6.

Baines, Malcolm, 'A United anti-socialist party? Liberal/Conservative relations 1945–55', *Contemporary Record* 4(3) (1991), pp. 13–15.

Balsom, Denis, and Ian McAllister, 'The Scottish and Welsh devolution referenda of 1979: constitutional change and popular choice', *Parliamentary Affairs* 32 (1979), pp. 394–409.

Barker, Rodney, 'Legitimacy in the United Kingdom: Scotland and the poll tax', *British Journal of Political Science* 22 (1992), pp. 521–33.

Beers, Laura, 'Whose Opinion? Changing Attitudes Towards Opinion Polling in British Politics, 1937–1964', *Twentieth Century British History* 17(2) (2006), pp. 177–205.

Bochel, J. M., and David T. Denver, 'The Decline of the SNP – an alternative view', *Political Studies* 20 (1972), pp. 311–16.

Bogdanor, Vernon, 'The 40 Per Cent Rule', *Parliamentary Affairs* 33(1) (1980), pp. 49–63.

——. 'Referendums in British Politics', *Contemporary Record* 2(4) (1988), pp. 12–14.

Cameron, Ewen A., 'The Political Histories of Modern Scotland', *Scottish Affairs* 85(1) (2013), pp. 1–28.

Cragoe, Matthew, '"We like local patriotism": The Conservative Party and the Discourse of Decentralisation, 1947–51', *English Historical Review* 122 (2007), pp. 965–85.

Devenney, Andrew D., 'Regional Resistance to European Integration: The Case of the Scottish National Party', *Historical Social Research* 33(3) (2008), pp. 319–45.

——. 'Joining Europe: Ireland, Scotland and the Celtic response to European integration, 1961–75', *Journal of British Studies* 49(1) (2010), pp. 97–116.

Devine, T. M., 'The Break-Up of Britain? Scotland and the End of Empire', *Transactions of the Royal Historical Society* 16 (2006), pp. 163–80.

Dutton, David, '"A Stepping-Stone for Wavering Radicals": Conservatives, National Liberals and Denbighshire Politics, 1947–64', *Contemporary British History* 22(1) (2008), pp. 111–25.

Dyer, Michael, 'The Evolution of the Centre-Right and the State of Scottish Conservatism', *Political Studies* 49(1) (2001), pp. 30–50.

——. '"A Nationalist in the Churchillian Sense": John MacCormick, the Paisley By-Election of 18 February 1948, Home Rule, and the Crisis in Scottish Liberalism', *Parliamentary History* 22(3) (2003), pp. 285–307.

Fielding, Steven, 'Activists against "Affluence": Labour Party culture during the "Golden Age", c.1950–1970', *Journal of British Studies* 40(2) (2001), pp. 241–67.

Findley, Richard, 'The Conservative Party and Defeat: The Significance of Resale Price Maintenance for the General Election of 1964', *Twentieth Century British History* 12(3) (2001), pp. 327–53.

Finlayson, Alan, and James Martin, '"It Ain't What You Say . . .": British Political Studies and the Analysis of Speech and Rhetoric', *British Politics* 3 (2008), pp. 445–64.

Foster, John, 'Upper Clyde Shipbuilders 1971–2 and Edward Heath's U-Turn: How a United Workforce Defeated a Divided Government', *Mariner's Mirror* 102 (2016), pp. 34–48.

Flores, Alejandro Quiroz, and Paul Whitely, 'The "Beeching Axe" and Electoral Support in Britain', *European Review of Economic History* 22 (2018), pp. 361–79.

Freeman, James, 'Reconsidering "Set the People Free": Neoliberalism and Freedom Rhetoric in Churchill's Conservative Party', *Twentieth Century British History* 29(4) (2018), pp. 522–46.

Geekie, Jack, and Roger Levy, 'Devolution and the Tartanisation of the Labour Party', *Parliamentary Affairs* 42(3) (1989), pp. 399–411.

Gibbs, Ewan and Rory Scothorne, 'Accusers of Capitalism: Masculinity and Populism on the Scottish radical left in the late Twentieth Century', *Social History* 45(2) (2020), pp. 218–45.

Gibbs, Ewan, '"Civic Scotland" versus Communities on Clydeside: Poll Tax Non-Payment, c.1987–1990', *Scottish Labour History* 49 (2014), pp. 86–106.

——. 'Historical Tradition and Community Mobilisation: Narratives of Red Clydeside in Memories of the anti-Poll Tax Movement in Scotland', *Labor History* 57(4) (2016), pp. 439–62.

——. 'The Moral Economy of the Scottish Coalfields: Managing Deindustrialization under Nationalization c.1947–1983', *Enterprise and Society* 19(1) (2018), pp. 124–52.

Green, E. H. H., 'The Treasury Resignations of 1958: A Reconsideration', *Twentieth Century British History* 11(4) (2000), pp. 409–30.

Harrison, Brian, 'The Rise, Fall and Rise of Political Consensus in Britain since 1940', *History* 84 (1999), pp. 301–24.

Harvie, Christopher, 'Labour and Scottish government: the age of Tom Johnston', *Bulletin of Scottish Politics* 2 (1981), pp. 1–20.

——. 'Labour in Scotland during the Second World War', *Historical Journal* 26(4) (1983), pp. 921–44.

Hill, Christopher R., 'Nations of Peace: Nuclear Disarmament and the Making of National Identity in Scotland and Wales', *Twentieth Century British History* 27(1) (2016), pp. 26–50.

Hinton, James, 'Militant Housewives: The British Housewives' League and the Attlee Government', *History Workshop* 28 (1994), pp. 128–56.

Jackson, Ben, 'At the Origins of Neo-Liberalism: The Free Economy and the Strong State, 1930–1947', *Historical Journal* 53(1) (2010), pp. 129–51.

——. 'The Political Thought of Scottish Nationalism', *Political Quarterly* 85(1) (2014), pp. 50–6.

——. 'Currents of Neo-Liberalism: British Political Ideologies and the New Right, c.1955–1979', *English Historical Review* 131 (2016), pp. 823–50.

Jaensch, Dean, 'The Scottish vote 1974: a realigning party system?', *Political Studies* 24 (1976), pp. 306–19.

Jarvis, David, 'British Conservatism and Class Politics in the 1920s', *English Historical Review* 111 (1996), pp. 59–84.

Kalyvas, Andreas, 'Popular Sovereignty, Democracy and the Constituent Power', *Constellations* 12(2) (2005), pp. 223–44.

Kavanagh, Dennis, 'The Post-War Consensus', *Twentieth Century British History* 3(2) (1992), pp. 175–90.

Keating, Michael, 'The Strange Death of Unionist Scotland', *Government and Opposition* 45(3) (2010), pp. 365–85.

Kendrick, Stephen, and David McCrone, 'Politics in a Cold Climate: the Conservative decline in Scotland', *Political Studies* 37(4) (1989), pp. 589–603.

Kerr, John, 'The Failure of the Scotland and Wales Bill', *Scottish Government Yearbook* (1978), pp. 113–19

Knox, W. W. and Alan McKinlay, 'The Remaking of Labour: Scotland in the 1930s', *Twentieth Century British History* 6(2) (1995), pp. 174–93.

Levitt, Ian, 'The Origins of the Scottish Development Department, 1943–62', *Scottish Affairs* 14 (1996), pp. 42–63.

——. 'Britain, the Scottish Covenant movement and Devolution, 1946–50', *Scottish Affairs* 22 (1998), pp. 33–57.

Levy, Roger, 'The Search for a Rational Strategy: The Scottish National Party and Devolution, 1974–79', *Political Studies* 34 (1986), pp. 236–48.

——. 'The Scottish Constitutional Convention: Nationalism and the Union', *Government and Opposition* 27 (1992), pp. 222–34.

Lowe, Rodney, 'The Second World War, Consensus and the Foundation of the Welfare State', *Twentieth Century British History* 1(2) (1990), pp. 152–82.

McLean, Iain, 'The Rise and Fall of the SNP', *Political Studies* 18(3) (1970), pp. 357–72.

Mackintosh, John P., 'Scottish Nationalism', *Political Quarterly* 38(4) (1967), pp. 389–402.

——. 'A Bed of Thistles', *Socialist Commentary* (Dec. 1967), pp. 11–12.

——. 'Commentary: The Killing of the Scotland Bill', *Political Quarterly* 49(2) (1978), pp. 127–32.

Nairn, Tom, 'After the Referendum', *New Edinburgh Review* (Jun. 1979), pp. 53–70.

——. 'A Nation in Revolt', *Marxism Today* (Jul. 1987), pp. 3–5.

Naughtie, James, 'The Scotland Bill in the House of Commons', *Scottish Government Yearbook* (1979), pp. 16–35.

——. 'The Year at Westminster', *Scottish Government Yearbook* (1980), pp. 42–52.

Nielsen, Jimmi O., and Stuart Ward, '"Cramped and Restricted at Home"? Scottish Separatism at Empire's End', *Transactions of the Royal Historical Society* 16 (2015), pp. 159–85.

O'Hara, Glen, 'A Journey without Maps: The Regional Policies of the 1964–70 British Labour government', *Regional Studies* 39 (2005), pp. 1183–95.

Pentland, Gordon, 'Edward Heath, the Declaration of Perth and the Scottish Conservative and Unionist Party, 1966–70', *Twentieth Century British History* 26(2) (2015), pp. 249–73.

Petrie, Malcolm R., '"Contests of Vital Importance": By-elections, the Labour Party and the Reshaping of British Radicalism', *Historical Journal* 60(1) (2017), pp. 121–48.

——. 'Anti-Socialism, Liberalism and Individualism: Rethinking the Realignment of Scottish Politics, 1945–1970', *Transactions of the Royal Historical Society* 28 (2018), pp. 197–217.

Phillips, Jim, 'Oceanspan: Deindustrialisation and Devolution in Scotland, c.1960–1974', *Scottish Historical Review* 84(1) (2005), pp. 63–84.

——. 'The 1972 Miners' Strike: Popular Agency and Industrial Politics in Britain', *Contemporary British History* 20(2) (2006), pp. 187–207.

——. 'Deindustrialization and the Moral Economy of the Scottish Coalfields, 1947 to 1991', *International Labor and Working-Class History* 84 (2013), pp. 99–115.

——. 'The Closure of Michael Colliery in 1967 and the Politics of Deindustrialization in Scotland', *Twentieth Century British History* 26(4) (2015), pp. 551–72.

Phillips, Jim, Valerie Wright and Jim Tomlinson, 'Deindustrialization, the Linwood Car Plant and Scotland's Political Divergence from England in the 1960s and 1970s', *Twentieth Century British History* 30(3) (2019), pp. 399–423.

Ramsden, John, '"A Party for Owners or a Party for Earners?": How far did the Conservative Party really change after 1945?', *Transactions of the Royal Historical Society* 37 (1987), pp. 49–63.

——. 'The Conservative Party since 1945', *Contemporary Record* 2(1) (1988), pp. 17–22.

——. '1961–64: Did the Conservatives lose direction?', *Contemporary Record* 2(5) (1989), pp. 26–31.

Ringe, Astrid, 'Background to Neddy: Economic Planning in the 1960s', *Contemporary British History* 12(1) (1998), pp. 82–98.

Robinson, Emily, Camilla Schofield, Florence Sutcliffe-Braithwaite and Natalie Thomlinson, 'Telling Stories about Post-war Britain: Popular Individualism and the "Crisis" of the 1970s', *Twentieth Century British History* 28(2) (2017), pp. 268–304.

Saleh, Taym, 'The Decline of the Scottish Conservatives in North-East Scotland, 1965–79: A Regional Perspective', *Parliamentary History* 36(2) (2017), pp. 218–42.

Schwarz, Bill, '"The only white man in there": the re-racialisation of England, 1956–1968', *Race and Class* 38 (1996), pp. 65–78.

Seawright, David, and John Curtice, 'The Decline of the Scottish Conservative and Unionist Party: Religion, Ideology or Economics?', *Contemporary Record* 9(2) (1995), pp. 319–42.

Seawright, David, 'Scottish Unionist Party: What's in a Name?', *Scottish Affairs* 14 (1996), pp. 90–102.

——. 'Scottish Unionism: An East-West Divide?', *Scottish Affairs* (1998), pp. 54–72.

Sloman, Peter, 'Rethinking a progressive moment: The Liberal and Labour parties in the 1945 general election', *Historical Research* 84 (2011), pp. 722–44.

Smith, Jeremy, '"Ever reliable friends?": the Conservative Party and Ulster in the twentieth century', *English Historical Review* 121 (2006), pp. 70–103.

Smyth, J. J., 'Resisting Labour: Unionists, Liberals, and Moderates in Glasgow between the Wars', *Historical Journal* 46(2) (2003), pp. 375–401.

Stewart, T. A. W., 'By-Elections and Political Change in a Local Context: The Case of the 1973 Dundee East By-Election and the SNP', *Parliamentary History* 38(2) (2019), pp. 262–77.

——. '"A Disguised Liberal Vote?" Third-Party Voting and the SNP under Gordon Wilson in Dundee during the 1970s and 1980s', *Contemporary British History* 33(3) (2019), pp. 357–82.

Tanner, Duncan, 'Richard Crossman, Harold Wilson and devolution, 1966–70: the making of government policy', *Twentieth Century British History* 17(4) (2006), pp. 545–78.

Taylor, Andrew, '"The Record of the 1950s is irrelevant": The Conservative Party, Electoral Strategy and Opinion Research, 1945-64', *Contemporary British History* 17(1) (2003), pp. 81–110.

Tierney, Stephen, 'Constitutional Referendums: A Theoretical Enquiry', *Modern Law Review* 72(3) (2009), pp. 360–83.

Tomlinson, Jim, 'Inventing "Decline": The Falling Behind of the British Economy in the Postwar Years', *Economic History Review* 49(4) (1996), pp. 731–57.

——. 'Conservative modernisation, 1960–64: Too little, too late?', *Contemporary British History* 11(3) (1997), pp. 18–38.

——. 'The Decline of the Empire and the Economic "Decline" of Britain', *Twentieth Century British History* 14(3) (2003), pp. 201–21.

——. 'Thrice Denied: "Declinism" as a Recurrent Theme in British History in the Long Twentieth Century', *Twentieth Century British History* 20(2) (2009), pp. 227–51.

——. 'Re-inventing the "Moral Economy" in Post-War Britain', *Historical Research* 84 (2011), pp. 356–73.

——. 'Deindustrialization not Decline: A New Meta-Narrative for Post-war British History', *Twentieth Century British History* 27(1) (2016), pp. 76–99.

Torrance, David, '"Standing up for Scotland": The Scottish Unionist Party and "Nationalist Unionism", 1912–1968', *Scottish Affairs* 27(2) (2018), pp. 169–88.

Toye, Richard, 'Winston Churchill's "Crazy Broadcast": Party, Nation, and the 1945 Gestapo Broadcast', *Journal of British Studies* 49(3) (2010), pp. 655–80.

Urwin, D. W., 'The Development of the Conservative Party Organisation in Scotland until 1912', *Scottish Historical Review* 44(2) (1965), pp. 89–111.

——. 'Scottish Conservatism: A Party Organisation in Transition', *Political Studies* 44 (1966), pp. 145–62.

Walker, Graham, 'The Scotland is British campaign, 1976–8', *Scottish Affairs* 61 (2007), pp. 74–100.

——. 'Scotland, Northern Ireland and Devolution, 1945–1979', *Journal of British Studies* 49(1) (2010), pp. 117–42.

——. 'Scotland, Northern Ireland and Devolution: Past and Present', *Contemporary British History* 24(2) (2010), pp. 235–56.

——. 'John P. Mackintosh, Devolution and the Union', *Parliamentary Affairs* 66 (2013), pp. 557–78.

Whipple, Amy, 'Revisiting the "Rivers of Blood" Controversy: Letters to Enoch Powell', *Journal of British Studies* 48(3) (2009), pp. 717–35.

Williamson, Adrian, 'The Trade Disputes and Trade Unions Act 1927 Reconsidered', *Historical Studies in Industrial Relations* 37 (2016), pp. 33–82.

Zweiniger-Bargielowska, Ina, 'Bread rationing in Britain, July 1946–July 1948', *Twentieth Century British History* 4(1) (1993), pp. 57–85.

——. 'Rationing, Austerity and the Conservative Recovery after 1945', *Historical Journal* 37(1) (1994), pp. 173–97.

Unpublished theses

Crawford, Robert 'The Scottish National Party, 1960–1974: An Investigation into its Organisation and Power Structure' (Unpublished PhD Thesis, University of Glasgow, 1982).

Dyer, Michael, 'The Politics of Kincardineshire' (Unpublished PhD Thesis, University of Aberdeen, 1974).

Jones, Harriet, 'The Conservative Party and the Welfare State' (Unpublished PhD Thesis, University of London, 1992).

Ritscherle, Alice, 'Opting out of utopia: race and working-class political culture in Britain during the age of decolonization, 1948–1968' (Unpublished PhD thesis: University of Michigan, 2005).

Index

EU Authorised Representative:

Easy Access System Europe Mustamäe tee 50, 10621 Tallinn, Estonia

gpsr.requests@easproject.com

Printed and bound by CPI Group (UK) Ltd, Croydon, CR0 4YY

13/10/2025

01975091-0009